Applied Sociolinguistics

Applied Language Studies

Edited by David Crystal

Applied Sociolinguistics

Edited by

Peter Trudgill

Department of Linguistic Science
University of Reading

1984

Academic Press

(Harcourt Brace Jovanovich, Publishers)

London · Orlando · San Diego · San Francisco · New York
Toronto · Montreal · Sydney · Tokyo · São Paulo

ACADEMIC PRESS INC. (LONDON) LTD.
24/28 Oval Road
London NW1

United States Edition published by
ACADEMIC PRESS INC.
(Harcourt Brace Jovanovich, Inc)
Orlando, Florida 32887

British Library Cataloguing in Publication Data
Applied sociolinguistics. – (Applied language
  studies)
  1. Sociolinguistics
  I. Trudgill, Peter   II. Series
  401'.9   P40

  ISBN 0-12-701220-6

  LCCCN 83-71853

Phototypeset by Oxford Verbatim Limited
Printed in Great Britain by
Whitstable Litho Ltd
Whitstable, Kent

Contributors

Allan Bell
4/6 Parau Street, Mt. Roskill, Auckland 4, New Zealand

Jenny Cheshire
Department of Applied Linguistics, Birkbeck College, University of London, Malet Street, London WC1, UK

John Edwards
Department of Psychology, St. Francis Xavier University, Antigonish, Nova Scotia, Canada

Ralph Fasold
Department of Linguistics, Georgetown University, Washington D.C. 20057, USA

Howard Giles
Department of Psychology, Bristol University, Berkeley Square, Bristol BS8 1HH, UK

James Milroy
Department of Linguistics, Sheffield University, UK

Lesley Milroy
Department of Speech, The University, Newcastle-upon-Tyne, UK

Michael Stubbs
Department of Linguistics, Nottingham University, University Park, Nottingham, NG7 2RD, UK

Peter Trudgill
Department of Linguistic Science, Faculty of Letters and Social Sciences, University of Reading, Whiteknights, Reading, RG6 2AA, UK

Alastair Walker
Nordfriesische Wörterbuchstelle, Neue Universität Kiel, Olsenhousenstrasse 40-60, 2300 Kiel, West Germany

Foreword

Sociolinguistics, more than any other branch of linguistics, has in recent years been simultaneously pulled in several different directions. Most of its practitioners are primarily concerned with the theoretical question of how to explain the linguistic variation which society manifests, and with the methodological question of how to explore it. But, because their field encounters the social implications and repercussions of language use much more immediately than other branches of linguistics, sociolinguists have regularly found themselves called upon to participate in language decision-making: evaluating or planning linguistic proposals related to a wide range of local or international issues. Some sociolinguists have avoided the publicity which often ensues from such encounters, preferring that their research be directed towards the publication of statements along conventional academic lines. Others have willingly become involved in social encounter, feeling that the application of their skills in the public domain is a responsible and desirable step. Yet others have taken this step with reluctance, believing that the application of sociolinguistic knowledge in this domain is premature, given the limited theoretical and empirical development of the subject to date.

I believe that there have now been sufficient moves in these various directions to permit a clearer analysis of the subject-matter of sociolinguistics than has hitherto been possible or desirable; and that the distinction between "general" and "applied", which has proved so useful in other fields, might prove to be a realistic and fruitful model in the present case also. The general field is well-represented by the several textbooks and monographs; but there has been no corresponding attempt to bring togther the various topics that could be construed as applications: in effect, to address the question, "What problems can sociolinguistics help to solve?". It might be that there are parallels in the way sociolinguists have approached these topics, such that the problems enountered in one area might be illuminated by the findings of another. It might be that a systematic consideration of what is involved in "applying" sociolinguistics might bring to light neglected topics which could usefully be studied along such lines. At the very least, I would hope that the juxtaposition of topics will lead to the discovery of correspondences in approach which are theoretically or methodologically interesting. And if the existence of a field of applied sociolinguistics can be usefully demonstrated, it may thereby provide a perspective within which the concerns of the general field can be more coherently defined. The present book is a pioneering work, in its intention and scope, and one whose appearance in a series on applied language studies I warmly welcome.

Reading   *David Crystal*
October 1983

Preface

Sociolinguistics is the science which deals with the relationship between language and society. It is therefore a very broad topic, encompassing the study of social dialects, language attitudes, stylistic variation, conversational interaction, multilingualism, language change, and much more. This book is a reflection of the fact that a great deal of work in this field is of direct or indirect practical relevance in a number of different spheres of life, including education and politics.

The book brings together for the first time work by experts in particular branches of sociolinguistics and is intended to demonstrate the range of real-world activities in which the findings of sociolinguistic studies can be of some assistance and interest. Sociolinguistics is an area of study that concerns itself with the ways in which human beings actually use language in social interaction in their everyday lives. It is therefore no surprise that it turns out to be of concern for workers in a wide range of fields. *Applied Sociolinguistics* should be of interest to sociolinguists, language teachers, social psychologists, educationists, media specialists, lawyers, and just about anybody else who speaks a language.

Reading   *Peter Trudgill*
October 1983

Contents

1
Introduction

Peter Trudgill

As is well-known, the term "Applied Linguistics" has acquired, in the literature, both a narrow and a broad interpretation. In its narrow interpretation, the term has come to refer to the application of the results of theoretical linguistic research to the teaching and learning of foreign and second languages. In its broad interpretation, on the other hand, "Applied Linguistics" refers to the application of linguistic research to the solution of practical, educational and social problems of all types. In the title of this book, *Applied Sociolinguistics*, (used here, we believe, for the first time), the term "applied" is employed in the second, wider sense. This book is an attempt to present information on the ways in which sociolinguistic findings and sociolinguistic insights can be and have been of assistance in the tackling of real-world problems.

As a field of study involving the interaction of language and society, sociolinguistics has naturally been a form of linguistics which has typically been more "applied" than most. We believe, nevertheless, that it is perfectly legitimate to point to a distinction between "pure" or "theoretical" sociolinguistics, on the one hand, and its applications, on the other. Sociolinguistics is a science which has among its objectives (some would say its only objective) the achievement of a greater understanding of the nature of language, as well as (others would say), and at least in some of its manifestations, a greater understanding of the nature of society. At its most linguistic, sociolinguistics is a way of doing linguistics, a methodology referred to by William Labov as "secular linguistics". And even at its most social and least linguistic, sociolinguistics is a subject which has some linguistic objectives.

"Applied sociolinguistics", however, is clearly to be interpreted as re-

APPLIED SOCIOLINGUISTICS
ISBN: 0-12-701220-6

ferring to activities in which the research of sociolinguists is employed (very often by sociolinguists themselves) in other fields where it can be of some value. In some cases sociolinguistic research (unlike, say, research in theoretical syntax) has been carried out with an avowedly practical purpose. In other cases, sociolinguists have found themselves involved in "applying" their findings, if not exactly against their will, at least without initially intending that they should be used in this way. One area of sociolinguistic work of which this has undoubtedly been true is "secular linguistics". Following Labov's lead in this field, large amounts of often very exciting work have been carried out in the form of empirical studies of language as it is spoken in its social context. Research of this type has been aimed principally at improving linguistic theory, and acquiring a better understanding of the nature of language variation and the sources of linguistic change. However, the results of Labov's work, and that of his followers, were very rapidly, from the 1960s onwards, applied in a highly significant way to two different but related educational problems: the debates concerning non-standard (especially American Black English) dialects in education; and so-called "verbal deprivation" or "language deficit". In the first of these debates, it was the sociolinguists' increased understanding of linguistic variation and their phonological and grammatical descriptions of non-standard dialects that became important. In the second, on "verbal deprivation", one crucial factor proved to be the large amounts of spontaneous, relatively unmonitored, casual speech recorded by sociolinguists concerned to overcome the "observer's paradox".

In the present volume, the chapter by J. Milroy, on "Sociolinguistic methodology and the identification of speakers' voices in legal proceedings" exemplifies a new use for quantitative studies of the Labovian type: the employment of sociolinguistic findings in a field we can perhaps call "forensic sociolinguistics". And in another examination of the uses of work of this type, Fasold, in his chapter on language learning, looks at the application of *variation theory*, a relatively recent theoretical development out of Labov-style secular linguistics. His chapter "Variation theory and language learning" starts from attempts to incorporate sociolinguistic findings concerning the structure and probabilistic nature of linguistic variation into theoretical models, and links these to foreign language acquisition processes.

This book, however, is not only concerned with the applications of secular linguistics. We are concerned also with the less than purely linguistic forms of sociolinguistics, such as the social psychology of language; the ethnography of speaking; the sociology of language; and discourse analysis. The *social psychology of language* is an area of study which deals with attitudes to varieties of language, and with the way in which speakers interact with each other through conversation. Clearly, its range of potential applications is enormous, and it already has a very respectable applied history, notably for example in the study of teachers' attitudes to their children's language. In this volume, Edwards and Giles examine the applications of the social psychology of language to the sphere of education in general.

The *ethnography of speaking* is that area of sociolinguistics which looks at norms for using language in different cultures. It is therefore of obvious importance in foreign language teaching, and also clearly crucial in the increasingly important field of cross-cultural communication. The chapter by L. Milroy on "Comprehension and Context" deals, in part, with this topic.

The applications of *the sociology of language* to the solution of social and other problems is already a very well-known field with an established label of its own: language planning. "Language planning" has come to refer to governmental or quasi-governmental activities, particularly in multilingual situations, designed to influence or solve linguistic problems. Walker's chapter in this book, "Applied Sociology of Language", deals with language planning, but with particular reference to the issue of vernacular languages in education.

Discourse analysis looks analytically, in various ways, at texts and conversational interaction with a view to achieving a greater understanding of textual cohesion and coherence, and rules for carrying out and interpreting conversation. It, too, is increasingly coming to be recognized as an area which has important applications as in, for example, the study of doctor–patient communication. In this volume, Stubb's chapter "Applied discourse analysis and educational linguistics" deals with mother-tongue and foreign-language teaching, while Bell actually applies the techniques of textual analysis to an examination of what happens to the language of news reporting in his chapter "Good Copy – Bad News".

Finally, we may note that one of the most important and best publicized areas of sociolinguistic research in recent years has been the study of *language and sex*. Work in this area has a number of components and involves work in a number of different aspects of sociolinguistics. Researchers in this field have variously dealt with sex differences in the usage of particular linguistic features, sex differences in the use of conversational strategies, attitudes to language use by men and women, and sexism in language. In her chapter on the "Applications of research on language and sex", Cheshire discusses some of the implications of this type of research.

The extent to which work in the area of sociolinguistics can be of practical value has been discussed by Labov in his article "Objectivity and commitment in linguistic science: the case of the Black English trial in Ann Arbor" (*Language in Society*, 1982). In this paper, Labov brings two principles to the attention of researchers in sociolinguistics. They are:

The principle of error correction
A scientist who becomes aware of a widespread idea or social practice
with important consequences that is invalidated by his own data is
obligated to bring this error to the attention of the widest possible
audience.

The principle of the debt incurred
An investigator who has linguistic data from members of a speech
community has an obligation to make knowledge of that data available
to the community, when it has need of it.

The chapters contained in this book are all, to varying degrees, motivated
by these principles, and are concerned with putting them into practice. It is
our hope that the book will help to bring to the attention of those concerned
the practical value of sociolinguistic research in all the disciplines dealt with
here. We hope, too, that it will stimulate further research, and further
applications.

Social Issues

2

Comprehension and context: successful communication and communicative breakdown

Lesley Milroy

Introduction

The major theoretical issue to which this paper addresses itself is the manner in which hearers use a combination of linguistic knowledge, knowledge of a heterogeneous range of factors which broadly might be called "contextual", and various perceptual strategies when they interpret utterances in context. This issue is approached using methods familiar in sociolinguistics; that is, the data base is real utterances as they are spoken in their social context rather than constructed data intuitively interpreted. It seems likely that *both* intuitive *and* empirical approaches are necessary (and a combination of the two) if we wish to advance our knowledge of how speakers comprehend what they hear in everyday situations. The problem is tackled initially by looking at a number of communications which have gone wrong; as Gumperz and Tannen (1979) point out: "by studying what has gone wrong when communication breaks down, we seek to understand a process that goes unnoticed when it is successful" (p. 308). A similar approach to speech production may be found in Fromkin (1973 and 1981).

Most of the miscommunications examined here are between people from different dialect backgrounds: that is people whose internal grammars are different in some specifiable way. This limitation is important methodo-

APPLIED SOCIOLINGUISTICS
ISBN: 0-12-701220-6

logically as it helps us to assess the role of specifically *linguistic* knowledge in comprehension, and it seems likely that conclusions on this wider matter can be extended to communications between people with the *same* dialect background.

Although it may be seen as a contribution to a major theoretical issue, this chapter is primarily intended as an exercise in applied sociolinguistics; the insights of sociolinguistics are used to analyse the manner in which *communicative breakdown* occurs between speakers in everyday situations and the consequences of this breakdown are considered. These two issues, the theoretical and the applied, will be considered in parallel throughout the discussion.

A miscommunication may be said to take place when there is a mismatch between the speaker's intention and the hearer's interpretation. When two persons *do* communicate successfully, it is clear that much more is involved than the mapping of internal structures (or linguistic rules) on to external sequences, or conversely (from the listener's point of view), mapping external sequences on to internal structures (Bever, 1970, p. 286). A number of perceptual strategies or "short-cuts" appear to be implemented by a listener in decoding utterances, and it is probably most sensible to adopt for the moment Aitchison's notion of a person's grammar as a "linguistic archive", available and ready for consultation in interpreting utterances, but not necessarily consulted. Thus, a sentence like the following is difficult to comprehend, although it is perfectly grammatical:

The pig pushed in front of the piglets ate all the food.

This is because the perceptual strategies adopted by the listener are to

assume that the first noun will go with the first verb in an NP–VP (actor-action) sequence as part of the main clause . . . So he understandably makes the wrong guess when he hears the words *the pig pushed* . . ., especially as his knowledge of the world tells him that pigs are not usually pushed they generally do the pushing. (Aitchison, 1976, p. 203).

Thus, the relation between internal grammars and comprehension is indirect, especially since comprehension in natural settings (as opposed to the experimental settings from which much of the psycholinguistic work discussed by Aitchison derives) is often assisted by such factors as the following:

I. Natural language contains a great deal of redundancy (see Lyons, 1977, p. 44 for a discussion of this).

II. "Context" and "shared background knowledge" assist interlocutors in interpreting utterances (Smith and Wilson, 1979). I refer to both linguistic and extra-linguistic context here, and will return to a discussion of it shortly.

III. Interlocutors in unplanned discourse have a range of strategies for monitoring comprehension, for clarifying and for repairing mistakes and misunderstandings as they follow the facial, gestural and interjectional cues which accompany interactions. Constant repetition and repair are important components of communication in context and are themselves highly systematic (Schegloff *et al.*, 1977; Givón, 1979, p. 230).

IV. It appears that out of consideration for each other's and their own "face", speakers often make remarks whose ambiguity has a clear social motivation (Brown and Levinson, 1978, p. 74). Speakers also appear to be willing to allow a great deal of vagueness and ambiguity to pass, on the assumption that meanings will become clear as the talk proceeds (Cicourel, 1973, p. 54).

Thus, when miscommunication *does* take place, a whole range of factors may be responsible. It is probably the indirectness of the relationship between "linguistic knowledge" (in Chomsky's sense) and language use which accounts for the fact that speakers with partly different grammars understand each other much of the time in natural settings; they rely on a wide and varied range of comprehension strategies. However, when comprehension between such speakers is tested experimentally (i.e. when factors I to IV above are controlled), they appear to be unable to associate sentences not generated by their own grammar with an appropriate semantic structure (see Labov, 1972a; Trudgill, 1981). Generally speaking, arguments for a "polylectal grammar" as a reflection of a speaker's pan-dialectal competence have not been supported by experiments such as Labov's or Trudgill's which require subjects either to select a paraphrase for sentences generated by other dialect grammars, or to judge whether such sentences are "possible" English sentences (see also Ross, 1979 for a different, but related, approach). The gap between these experimental results and results of the observational research reported in this paper is sometimes quite large, and will be discussed below. Meantime, it is perhaps worth noting Plutchik's comments on the value of observational (as opposed to experimental) research in a field where knowledge is limited (Plutchik, 1976, p. 23).

While then it is certainly true that speakers with markedly different grammars are frequently able to understand each other in context, it does not seem quite justifiable to adopt uncritically the common view cited by (for example) Smith and Wilson that differences between the grammars of dialects are essentially trivial, and that potential misunderstandings can be resolved by the implementation of perceptual strategies, or by context (Smith and Wilson, 1979, p. 197). One purpose of this chapter will be to try and isolate the conditions under which differences in speakers' grammars may produce misunderstandings in natural settings; that is when the various comprehension strategies available to a speaker have failed to work and he is forced to consult his "linguistic archive" to assist him in interpreting utterances.

Since Labov's initial demonstration of the "limits" of individual grammars, it has been generally accepted (at least by sociolinguists) that pan-dialectal competence, active or passive, is extremely sharply constrained. However, there is an implicit tendency to assume that it is competence in non-standard grammars which is limited. It is significant, for example, and quite characteristic of work in this area, that all the sentences discussed in Trudgill's 1981 paper are designed to test knowledge of *non-standard* grammars. In an earlier publication, Trudgill expressed the view more explicitly that non-standard speakers had at least a passive competence in standard English (Trudgill, 1979) and Trudgill's view does not seem at all uncommon.

In relation to this issue, it is worth noting Lyons' observation (made generally, rather than with reference to cross-dialectal communication) that misunderstandings are probably rather frequent during communicative acts, and that this likelihood should be allowed for in any theoretical model of communication (Lyons, 1977, p. 33). It is only rarely that speakers are provided with feedback in any consistent way, and when this does happen (as when students write down in examinations what they think has been said to them) the level of misunderstanding is frequently revealed to be quite horrifying (Aitchison, 1976, p. 197). If we take comments such as those of Lyons and Aitchison into account, as well as the complex of knowledge and strategies underlying comprehension, I think we have to treat the idea that non-standard speakers "understand" standard English as a not very clearly defined and quite unsupported assumption, rather than a self-evident truth (in fact, some data will be discussed below which suggests that the assumption requires some modification). A more interesting question may well be concerned with the extent to which miscommunications are associated with cross-dialectal communication.

The approach taken in this chapter will be to examine and analyse instances of miscommunication against the extremely complicated but still by no means comprehensive background which has been outlined so far; an attempt will be make to bring together material from a number of relevant academic perspectives. The main focus of interest will be in identifying as precisely as possible the linguistic and contextual factors contributing to miscommunication, but there will also be some brief discussion of the consequences of miscommunication. This will be both in terms of speakers' responses, and in more general social terms. However, preliminary to analysis of data two of the issues already raised are looked at in a little more detail. These are, first, the relationship between standard and non-standard English (this will be a brief section), and next the generalized notion of "context" to which linguists frequently appeal when they are attempting an explanation of how speakers comprehend utterances in real situations.

Standard and non-standard English

It is important to remember in a study like this one, which looks primarily at cross-dialectical communication, that any account of a language-system like English is extremely idealized and abstract and inevitably based on the standard form of the language (a form routinely used, it should be noted, by only a small minority of speakers). Although the notion of a standard is notoriously complicated and hard to pin down, it is useful here to ignore the social dimensions of standardization and adopt Lyons' view of it as one kind of idealization of the data in which the linguist ignores differences within a system and "discounts all but the major systematic variations in the language behaviour of the community" (Lyons, 1977, p. 587). Standard English then is the form of the language from which most linguists cite their examples, and it is usually believed that structural differences between standard and non-standard varieties are relatively superficial and can be accounted for in terms of rule addition or rule loss. Some examples of syntactic differences within British English are cited by Hughes and Trudgill (1979) which include differences in tense and aspectual systems, and in the formal distribution of individual verbs such as *have* and *do*.

The question of genuine communication problems arising from structural differences of this kind is not often seriously discussed, the assumption generally being that non-standard speakers can "understand" standard English presumably in the sense that in some hypothetical context-free situation they are able to assign the same semantic structure as a standard speaker to a given phonetic string. The reason for this assumption (which is noted here mainly to encourage readers to consider whether they themselves hold it) is probably the constant dissemination of spoken and written standard English through the news media and the educational system. The possibility that some speakers do not "understand" standard English appears for the most part to be mooted only when their systems are so divergent that they may, like West Indian creole-speakers in England, or Black English-speakers in the United States, be thought of in some unsatisfactorily specified way as not being English speakers at all (Edwards,

1979; Nelson and McRoskey, 1978). However, in a recent extensive study of the Hiberno-English perfect (associated with a larger study of non-standard English) John Harris refers to frequent misinterpretations by Hiberno-English speakers of such standard English utterances as

How long are you staying here?

This type of structure is often interpreted as being equivalent to standard English

How long have you been staying here?

Harris goes on to argue convincingly that there is no semantic isomorphism between any given set of Hiberno-English and standard-English sentences which exemplify the range of perfect constructions. For example, the three sentences

(a) Joe has sold the boat
(b) Joe has just sold the boat
(c) Has Joe sold the boat?

exemplify the simple perfect tense-aspect form in Standard English. However, they are all quite anomalous in even educated Hiberno-English and would be "translated" as follows:

(a) Joe has the boat sold
(b) Joe is just after selling the boat
(c) Did Joe sell the boat?

The non-isomorphism is semantic as well as formal, since, for example Hiberno-English (c) is not only a translation of Standard-English (c) but is also equivalent to the same standard English string. Thus, Hiberno-English cannot distinguish between "Has Joe sold the boat?" and "Did Joe sell the boat?" However, an action completed in the *recent* past is expressed by a construction of the (b) type. Cross-dialectal miscommunications are very commonly reported which seem to be located in the disparity between the two versions of sentence (b) and these may be seen as symptomatic of a deep structure disparity between the grammars of the two dialects. The two dialects cannot be related satisfactorily simply by applying slightly different transformational rules to derive them from the same deep structure (Harris, 1982). This suggests that dialect grammars may sometimes be more different than is commonly supposed, and justifies a somewhat closer examination of how far the communicative competence of a non-standard speaker includes the capacity to assign the same semantic structure as standard speaker to a given phonetic string.

The notion of context

We have already noted that comprehension involves very much more than knowledge of phonological, syntactic and semantic rules. So much redundant information is introduced into communicative situations by a combination of linguistic and real world knowledge that it is often possible to produce an appropriate response to an utterance without any knowledge at all of the structural rules underlying its production. For example, during a recent visit to a rural area of Austria, I was able to comprehend a request (from a shopkeeper) to shut the door even though I was quite unable (despite my knowledge of standard German) to recognize in the utterance any familiar syntactic patterns or even a single lexical item. A combination of cold weather, gestural cues, and limitations on the kind of message likely to be transmitted in a service encounter of that kind facilitated successful communication; that is, an appropriate response was produced to the utterance. It is of course a truism to assert that actual utterances are always interpreted in context, and instances like this one seem to have encouraged linguists to exaggerate the capacity of context to resolve ambiguity, while at the same time not defining particularly closely what is meant by context. It is still commonplace to find the term used freely without any more careful examination of its scope. Yet, context-boundedness is an important inherent characteristic of all natural languages and arguably should be accounted for explicitly in any comprehensive linguistic theory, rather than being used as a "terminological immunization" (Klein and Dittmar, 1979, p. 4) to cover up problems of fitting data to theory.

That linguists are in general aware of this problem is evidenced by the major and long-running controversy within generative semantics as to whether the illocutionary potential of an utterance should in some way be incorporated into a formal grammar (Ross, 1975) or whether the interpretation of utterances in context should be accounted for by separate sets of conversational rules (Sperber and Wilson, forthcoming; Smith and Wilson, 1979; Gordon and Lakoff, 1971). More recently, attempts have been made to resolve empirically the issue of how far the social and situational context affects understanding and judgement (Ervin-Tripp, n.d.). Preliminary findings suggest that some, but not all, listeners rely heavily on routine non-linguistic knowledge, and on what might be described as "pragmatic intelligence". Stimulus utterances are decoded by applying linguistic rules only if something unusual or discordant occurs (cf. the notion of the "linguistic archive", discussed above).

It is useful here to note Lyons' distinction between the layman's intuitive, pre-theoretical concept of context to which speakers frequently make appeal when they discuss interpretations of utterances, and on the other hand context as a theoretical construct which has been analysed from various points of view by different traditions of scholarship. Lyons' working definition of context (in the second sense) is as follows:

> a theoretical construct in the postulation of which the linguist abstracts from the actual situation and establishes as contextual all the factors which, by virtue of their influence upon the participants in a language event, *systematically* deter-mine[my italics] the form, the appropriacy and the meaning of utterances. (Lyons, 1977, p. 572)

We look now at two different approaches to the systematization of context, both of which are relevant to the discussion here.

Hymes's discussion of the nature of "communicative competence" attempts to provide a theoretical framework for describing components of context which have just the kind of systematic effect referred to by Lyons on the production and comprehension of particular phonological, syntactic and lexical options within the language system (Hymes, 1972). They are mani-fold and complex, and the reader is referred to Hymes' own paper for a comprehensive account and to Coulthard (1977, p. 30) for a brief but useful discussion. Examples of the kind of knowledge which forms part of com-municative competence in any real society are knowledge of status systems and social roles, and of the language appropriate to various settings and topics. Many linguists regard communicative competence as part of a speaker's linguistic knowledge in just the same way as his knowledge of syntactic and semantic rules. For example, Lyons suggests that a French speaker's knowledge of when to select the intimate or the polite second person pronoun is as much part of his linguistic competence as his knowl-edge of the French language-system (Lyons, 1980, p. 248); others would argue that this is an example of encyclopaedic, rather than strictly linguistic, knowledge.

A different approach to the systematization of context follows the tradi-tions of Searle (1975) and Grice (1975). Scholars working along these lines are generally concerned with specifying those contextual cues, logical pro-cesses and other conditions which enable interlocutors to interpret utter-ances in context appropriately. Particularly interesting attempts to apply analyses of this kind to real speech events have been made by Labov and Fanshel (1977) and Gumperz and Tannen (1979). But on the whole, the most sophisticated analyses of utterances in context are applied to isolated pieces of constructed data, and have not yet been challenged by being tested in real conversations. In the sections which follow, an attempt will be made to assess the relative importance of these various systematic components of context, of perceptual strategies, and of internal grammars in enabling successful communication. Particular attention will be paid to those instances where a miscommunication seems to be located in a mismatch between the grammars of the speaker and the hearer.

Some miscommunications: an analysis

First, a brief note of some terminological and methodological points. For reasons which will become clear, it is important to try and maintain a distinction between two different kinds of miscommunication. What will be described as *misunderstandings* involve simple disparity between the speaker's and the hearer's semantic analysis of a given utterance. However, misunderstandings are not perceived as interrupting communicative efficiency, and it is probable that many more misunderstandings take place than are ever discovered. *Communicative breakdown* on the other hand occurs when one or more participants perceive that something has gone wrong. This "something" may or may not be analysed as linguistic; if it is, the breakdown may or may not be repaired.

All the data discussed below are taken from real conversations. Only (1) is tape-recorded, having cropped up by a happy chance during a long conversation between myself and an inner-city informant in Belfast. The rest of the data were recorded in notebooks by myself and colleagues, and the researchers were usually able to report their own reaction to a miscommunication. By its nature, material on miscommunications is hard to collect in any systematic way, since unlike some of the classic linguistic variables described in the quantitative literature they occur unpredictably and sometimes infrequently. I tackled this problem simply by searching out, over a period of time, analysable examples of miscommunication which seemed to be located in disparate individual grammars. These were transcribed on the spot, and where necessary contextual factors were noted in as much detail as seemed appropriate. An analysis was then carried out to try and locate the source of the miscommunication.

This *post hoc* type of procedure is very similar to that of Gumperz (see especially Gumperz and Tannen, 1979) who deals with those miscommunications which result from disparities in the inferences drawn by conversational participants from utterances in context. Both pieces of research follow the principles of careful observation in the tradition of social anthropology pioneered by Evans-Pritchard, and more recently in linguistic research recommended by Ferguson (1977) for dealing with phenomena about which little is known. Careful observation of this kind is of course an essential preliminary to the development of a predictive and testable theory.

Youse wash the dishes

This heading is part of a narrative told to me during a fieldwork session by a Belfast working-class woman. The rest of it, which may serve as an illustration of vernacular second person pronoun usage, is as follows:

   (1) /So I says to our Trish and our Sandra/youse wash the dishes/and I might as well have said you wash the dishes/for our Trish just got up/and put her coat on and walked out/

In much of Scotland and Ireland the second person pronoun can be marked for number as illustrated here, giving the plural form *youse*. This extract is quoted here because it shows clearly that the speaker considers *you* an inappropriate choice for a plural referent. This fact is relevant to analysis of subsequent miscommunications between myself and some Belfast vernacular speakers.

An examination of the sociolinguistic distribution of *youse* in Belfast reveals rather more complexity than might at first be assumed. First of all, as we might expect, many relatively standardized speakers have categorical *you* for both singular and plural pronouns. For these speakers, the *youse* form is highly stigmatized (despite the obvious usefulness of the distinction), and is often singled out for overt criticism. As a consequence of this stigma many speakers who do have the *you/youse* distinction in their grammars alternate between the marked and the unmarked form of the plural pronoun according to various contextual (and possibly syntactic) constraints. For example, one local post-graduate student was observed to address the class as *you* while giving a seminar paper, but to revert to *youse* as the class broke up and the topic changed. Thus the pronoun appears to be a classic social and stylistic variable rather similar to, for example, the double negative. It has of course quite a different sociolinguistic distribution from the T and V pronouns studied by Brown and Gilman.

The really surprising fact to emerge during a lengthy and systematic study of the language of several very low-status social groups in Belfast was that many speakers *categorically* distinguished *you* (singular) and *youse* (plural); that is, evidence began to build up which suggested that they never alternated between the marked and the unmarked form of the pronoun.

This sociolinguistic distribution might be diagrammed as in Table I, with three different groups of speakers distinguished, which are likely to correspond to hierarchical social stratifications. What is of interest here is the communicative consequence when a Group I speaker and a Group III speaker interact. Do categorical differences in this portion of their grammars result in communicative difficulties? Or do Group III speakers have the kind

Table I. The sociolinguistic distribution of "youse".

	singular	plural
Group I	you	you
Group II	you	you/youse
Group III	you	youse

of passive competence in standard English which is often assumed to exist? In fact, the speaker of (1) was almost certainly a Group III speaker and the addressee (myself, as the listener to the narrative) a Group I speaker. It is perhaps worth emphasizing that the social contexts in which speakers from these two socially distant groups interact are likely to be quite limited, and to be in situations where Group I speakers have a measure of control over the proceedings and may be interacting on a one-to-one or one-to-many basis. Examples are classroom, legal, medical and bureaucratic situations. In other words, as a consequence of the social norms governing cross-group communications, occasions on which the categorical nature of the mismatch between the two grammars might emerge are likely to be quite limited.

It has been suggested by James Miller (personal communication), correctly I think, that as speakers grow older and become more firmly established in educationally and occupationally determined statuses, they interact less and less on a symmetrical basis with socially distant persons. This constitutes a social problem which vitiates systematic knowledge of non-standard dialects and gives rise to unsupported claims which tend to exaggerate not only the similarities between the grammars of these dialects and of Standard English but also the knowledge which non-standard speakers have of Standard English. Thus, evidence of how efficiently people from socially distant groups decode each others' utterances is extremely difficult to collect. The fieldwork situation which involved a Group I speaker in prolonged and relatively relaxed conversation with Group III speakers is rare, and so is a valuable source of data. The evidence and conclusions which emerged are as follows.

First, it is fairly clear from (1) that the speaker takes the *you/youse* distinction for granted to the extent that she comments on its communicative importance to a socially distant addressee without any apparent awareness of the stigma attached to it, or that the addressee might not use such a distinction. Secondly, one consequence of this categorical distinction was that during the field-work period I consistently encountered problems when I used the unmarked form of the plural. For example a conventional greeting such as "How are you?", addressed to two or more persons usually elicited a zero response (silence) and an exchange of puzzled glances. Since I found it hard to believe that the *youse* rule was responsible for these breakdowns, they initially went unrepaired. However, the sequence "How are youse doing?" always elicited an appropriate response such as "Not too bad, what about yourself?" Further examples can be cited to illustrate the categorical nature of the distinction for some speakers, the most spectacular of which is a letter to two researchers who are consistently addressed as *youse*. Other examples of *youse* in formal written communication have been reported. It seems that the communicative competence of these speakers is limited to a knowledge of the choice appropriate within their own social group. The same can probably be said of more standardized speakers.

It is also clear that the usage exemplified in (1) bears strongly on the issue discussed above, that is the kind of linguistic knowledge which non-standard speakers may be said to have of standard English. At the very least we may conclude that there is a great deal which we simply do not know about this matter. Although the assumption (made usually by Group I speakers) that all speakers have at least a passive competence in standard English seems on the face of it perfectly reasonable, the *youse* evidence suggests that this may be correct for Group II speakers but not for the more socially distant Group III speakers. In a similar vein, Miller shows that Scottish speakers who do not use the *will/shall* distinction have it in their passive competence only in the limited sense that they recognize it as belonging to some variety of English. When pressed to state the basis of the distinction, they either confess to bafflement or manufacture "rules" which bear little relation to linguistic reality such as "Shall is more polite than will" (Miller, 1981, p. 87). All in all, Labov's argument that linguists derive many of their facts about low-status vernaculars from upwardly mobile and relatively standardized speakers with whom they have a measure of social affinity seems to be depressingly near the mark (Labov, 1972, p. 287).

In view of our general ignorance both of non-standard grammars and of the limits of communicative competence, I do not think that we can afford to dismiss the breakdowns located in the *you/youse* disjunction as isolated and unrepresentative of cross-dialectal interactions; the extent to which breakdown located in other sociolinguistically distributed grammatical elements might occur is at the moment simply a matter of speculation.

Whenever he came in he hit me

The set of data discussed in this section has a sociolinguistic distribution quite different from that of the *youse* variable. The temporal conjunctions *whenever* and *when* do not contrast even in educated varieties of Hiberno-English. Thus, Hiberno-English *whenever* has a meaning quite different from the *whenever* of standard British English, and need not be interpreted as indefinite or as referring to more than one occasion in the past (Milroy, 1978). [1] The following utterances are taken from four separate conversations:

(2) Whenever I saw her I fell for her.
(3) Whenever he came in he hit me.
(4) My husband died whenever I was living on the New Lodge Road.
(5) Whenever Chomsky wrote *Syntactic Structures* there was a revolution in linguistics.

It is clear that Irish and English listeners are likely to map these utterances on to different grammars, and so produce different interpretations. However, (2) and (3) differ from (4) and (5) in that (2) and (3) are semantically acceptable for both sets of speakers. But, for the standard English speaker, (4) and (5) simply do not make sense, because the interpretation suggested by his grammar conflicts with real world knowledge. What appears to happen then in real situations (but not under experimental conditions, as we shall see shortly) is that he concludes correctly that Hiberno-English *whenever* is equivalent to standard English *when* probably because this is the easiest way of extracting relevance from the utterance. This feature of Hiberno-English grammar is in fact quite frequently the subject of overt comment by standard English speakers, and *where an interpretation is impossible for them in accordance with their own grammars* does not appear to be a source of miscommunication.

The same cannot be said of utterances like (2) and (3). While the temporal clause in (2) was misinterpreted by a standard English speaker as referring to several different occasions, the misunderstanding did not have the effect of producing communication problems and was not noticed by either of the interlocutors. Only direct questioning after the exchange revealed the disparate interpretations, and it is very likely that a great many unimportant misunderstandings of this kind go both unresolved and unnoticed. A similar case is documented by Berdan (1977, p. 15), where in cross-dialectal communication speakers may communicate successfully with each other despite the fact that both are mapping quite different grammars on to utterances containing *got* as a verb of possession. In the terms which we have adopted here, the ambiguity of (2) resulted in misunderstanding but not in communicative breakdown.

The misunderstanding resulting from (3), which passed unnoticed at the time, was potentially more serious simply because of the propositional content of the utterance. The addressee was myself, and the topic of conversation was the unreasonable behaviour of the speaker's husband. Being at that time unfamiliar with this part of the Hiberno-English system, I interpreted the reference of the utterance as a large number of assaults upon the speaker. Only many weeks later did it become apparent, on reflection,

that I had drawn an entirely wrong series of inferences from the miscommunication.

If these observations on examples (2) to (5) are taken together, we can
begin to isolate some structural and pragmatic conditions which appear to be
necessary before syntactically located cross-dialectal miscommunications
take place. First, the utterance must be semantically acceptable to both
speakers; otherwise it is simply odd, like (4) and (5) rather than ambiguous
(but see further below). Second (and this is a matter of social norms) the
reference must be of some "real world" importance. Otherwise, as with (2),
the interaction will proceed without the interlocutors necessarily being
aware of the misunderstanding. In contrast, the misunderstanding following
utterance (3), although not noticed at the time, was identified retrospectively
because in our society a man who repeatedly beats his wife attracts more
notice than one who repeatedly falls in love with the same woman. Thus, it
appears that successful cross-dialectal communication in context depends
on a fairly complicated combination of structural and pragmatic factors.

It is worth drawing attention here to an experimental study by Trudgill
where subjects are asked to select an interpretation of a range of sentences
generated by non-standard English dialect grammars (Trudgill, 1981). The
whenever sentence selected (*whenever it was born I felt ill*) is semantically
acceptable only if *whenever* is interpreted as equivalent to *when*, and so is of
the same type as utterances (4) and (5) above. Contrary to what appears to
happen in real contexts, where such utterances do not seem to result in
communication problems, Trudgill found that "the grammatical constraints
of their own dialects forced a majority of subjects to select [an] anti-
commonsense interpretation". Subjects often regarded the sentence as
complete nonsense or, in some cases, attempted a contextualization of their
semantically odd interpretation. This disparity between experimental and
observational results is instructive, and is probably best viewed as showing
the unwillingness of speakers in real social situations to regard any utterance
as complete nonsense. Relevance will always be assumed (in Grice's sense)
and a likely interpretation will be sought, while a subject in an experiment (a
constructed situation) will not be under the same social pressures to locate
the speaker's intention. Additionally, he may not assume that the stimulus
sentence is relevant.

An interesting parallel to this mismatch between experimental results and
the results of naturalistic observation may be found in recent psycholinguistic
work on the basis of linguistic intuitions (Carroll *et al.*, 1981). Here, the
authors describe the manner in which judgments of "borderline" sentences
as acceptable vary in quite a systematic way, as the judges' mental states are

manipulated towards either "objective self-awareness" or "subjective self-awareness". These states may well be parallel to states in experimental as opposed to real life situations.

How long are youse here?

This utterance is the opening sequence of (6). A is a native of South West Donegal; B and C are both standard English speakers (and linguists).

(6) A: (i) How long are youse here?
    B: Till after Easter
             (A looks puzzled; a pause of two seconds follows)
    C: We came on Sunday
    A: (ii) Ah, Youse're here a while then.

The miscommunication here is located in an extremely complicated difference between the aspect the systems of Standard English and Hiberno-English, which may for the present purposes be outlined as follows (but see also p. 12 above).

A standard English speaker will usually interpret an utterance like A (i) as equivalent to *How long will you be here for?* Hiberno-English generally avoids the use of the *have* auxiliary as a marker of the perfect, and has a range of structures, including the A (i) type, which appear to be equivalent to the standard English perfect (see Harris, 1982 for further discussion). Utterance B was therefore an inappropriate response to A (i), and speaker A was quite unable to interpret it. For him, A (i) and B simply constituted an ill-formed exchange. The breakdown was, after a time lag, noticed and repaired. It is by no means certain that a linguistically unsophisticated speaker such as A (both B and C were linguists) could have located the breakdown and effected the repair.

This is an extremely clear example of a cross-dialectal breakdown which can be located specifically in a disparity between the grammars of speaker and hearer. The difference between the two semantic structures associated with A (i) involves the existence of a state in time *either* up to a certain point, *or* from a certain point. The somewhat intangible nature of this difference, together with the absence of further relevant contextual cues, appear to rule out comprehension strategies which involve contextual factors or real world knowledge. The claim made by, for example, Smith and Wilson (1979, p. 197) that perceptual strategies of various kinds facilitate cross-dialectal communication, to the extent that differences in internal grammars are communicatively unimportant, seems to be contradicted by this example. Moreover, the fact that speakers B and C knew (in the encyclopedic rather than the linguistic sense) of the disparity between this portion of the two grammars was not enough to prevent the breakdown in the first place, although it was eventually noticed. It may be concluded then that there are specifiable situations where grammars (as opposed to strategies) are crucial to effective communication between speakers of different dialects.

Finally, it is worth noting the reaction of the participants to the breakdown. During the two-second pause, B and C at least had an extremely unpleasant sense of simply not knowing what was going on and being quite unable to analyse it; this is very reminiscent of the reactions of puzzlement and frustration reported by Gumperz (1976) when breakdown involving differences in the kind of conversational inferences drawn by speaker and hearer takes place. Thus, the possibility that breakdowns of this kind may not be analysed as linguistic at all is another reason for caution in assuming that they are rare.

The communicative breakdown exemplified in (6) may be compared with (7), a successful communication between an Ulsterman and an Englishman working as a temporary lecturer in Northern Ireland.

(7) A: How long are you here?
     B: Just this term.

Here the misunderstanding was not noticed (although the same Englishman had experienced problems in understanding similar constructions) apparently because the response can be construed as "length of time during which", i.e. unlike 6B it does not contain a temporal item referring to either future or past. Alternatively we may assume ellipsis, and restructure 7B as either 8 or 9:

(8) Just (until the end of) this term.
(9) Just (since the beginning of) this term.

Since neither past nor future time were overtly marked in the response by a temporal conjunction, each speaker was able to associate the response with a different underlying semantic structure. A comparison with (6) and (7) suggests that *ellipsis* may play a part in masking miscommunications.

A somewhat surprising insight into the role of *linguistic* context in successful cross-dialectal communication is provided in an important experimental study by Berdan (1977). (In view of the facts reported above, we should be cautious however of drawing over-general conclusions about comprehension-in-context from experimental studies.) Berdan presented to two groups of American students (one black and one white) a number of potentially ambiguous sentences and, as a means of determining their interpretation of these sentences, asked them to construct tag questions for them. The rule of copula deletion in Black English was the locus of the ambiguity.

Where contracted *is* appears on the surface, it is often phonetically indistinguishable from the plural morpheme. Thus, the sequence [frɛnz] in (10), with contracted *is*, is indistinguishable from plural *friends* in (11), although each is derived from a different underlying sentence:

(10) Her best friend is playing jump rope.
(11) Her best friends are playing jump rope.

On hearing the resulting identical phonetic sequence, speakers of a dialect which does not allow copula deletion would allow, Berdan considered, only the interpretation shown in (10) while speakers of a dialect which *does* allow copula deletion would find both (10) and (11) possible interpretations.

In fact, for the sequence *Her best* [frɛnz] *playing jump rope*, all of the white and all but two of the black students provided a singular tag, showing that they understood the sentence as (10). However, Berdan noted that it appeared to be possible to change semantic and other contextual cues in an ambiguous sentence to make one reading at first sight more plausible than another without making either reading ungrammatical. He suggested, for example, that a superlative like *best* seemed to facilitate a singular interpretation, although plurals with *best*, such as (12) clearly do occur:

(12) They are my best friends.

He also suggested that a singular possessive pronoun like *her* might facilitate a singular reading, while a plural pronoun like *their* might increase the possibility of a plural reading. To explore the effects of these contextual cues, the sequences (13) to (16) were included among the test items:

(13) Her best [frɛnz] playing jump rope.
(14) Her [frɛnz] playing jump rope.
(15) Their best [frɛnz] playing jump rope.
(16) Their [frɛnz] playing jump rope.

As predicted, singular interpretation frequencies decreased progressively from (13) through to (16), most spectacularly among black students. However, one unexpected finding was a significant number of plural readings of (15) and (16) even among the white students whose grammars were thought not to allow the deletion rule.

Berdan's results confirm the extremely indirect relationship between comprehension and grammatical rules. They add to our knowledge of comprehension strategies in that they show that for some white informants, logically irrelevant linguistic cues are sufficient to override interpretations suggested by the application of grammatical rules. However, the magnitude

of the contextual conditioning was smaller for the white than for the black
students; therefore it seems that the capacity of contextual cues to encourage
persons to employ particular perceptual strategies is greater when the cues
do not conflict with linguistic rules, than when they do conflict with them.

Although Berdan's findings confirm the importance of perceptual strategies in skewing the interpretation of ambiguous sentences, it appears that
quite simple lexical changes such as those which he manipulates may
influence comprehension one way or another. However, these cues do not
operate independently of a speaker's internal grammar or, as has sometimes
been suggested, take precedence over it. Rather, grammatical rules and
perceptual strategies operate in conjunction with each other (and, as we
have seen, with extra-linguistic contextual factors) in an orderly way in
influencing the interpretation of utterances.

Conversational inferences

Since much reference has been made in this chapter to contextual and
pragmatic cues, it is appropriate to note that the locus of a miscommunication may be specifically "pragmatic" rather than "structural". By this I mean
that it is located in a disparity between the *inferences* which conversational
participants draw from a given utterance, rather than in a disparity of the
kind discussed here so far between the *semantic structures* from which they
derive that utterance. This section relies heavily on the work of Gumperz
and his associates on cross-cultural communicative breakdowns (Gumperz,
1976, 1977(a), 1977(b); Gumperz *et al.*, 1979; Gumperz and Tannen, 1979).

Fundamentally, Gumperz argues that difficulties in inter-ethnic communication arise not only as a result of generalized prejudice, but through
differences in various kinds of shared knowledge and in culture-specific
communicative preferences. These differences affect the kind of inferences
drawn in conversation to interpret a given utterance. For example, ethnic
groups differ in the uses which they make of a given prosodic pattern: the
tune appropriate for polite questions in one culture may signal an emphatic
statement in another. Many miscommunications are documented which
may be located specifically in disparate interpretations of prosodic cues
(Gumperz, 1977(b); Gumperz and Tannen, 1979, Gumperz *et al.*, 1979).
The culture-specific nature of different levels of loudness and different
proxemic behaviours in a given situation has been shown elsewhere to be the
source of miscommunication (Watson and Graves, 1966; Hall, 1963; see also
Brown and Levinson, 1978, p. 258). Similarly, culture-specific differences in
"the distribution of required and preferred silence" (Hymes, 1972) have
been documented as a source of miscommunication (Philips, 1976; Milroy,

1980). In Milroy (1980) the differences were between norms appropriate to different status groups rather than different ethnic groups in the usual sense.

A source of miscommunication which may be labelled as more specifically *pragmatic* may be located in disparate interpretations of the illocutionary force of indirect speech acts. For example, an utterance such as (17) can in some situations be interpreted as a directive, and in others as a simple comment with no particular illocutionary force, while (18) might be interpreted either as a request for information, or a request for action:

(17) It's dinner time and I'm hungry.
(18) Can you play the *Moonlight Sonata*?

In the absence of clear prosodic cues, the speaker's communicative intent is interpreted in relation to certain presuppositions which are influenced by aspects of the (extra-linguistic) context such as setting, topic, the speakers' knowledge of each other and of their mutual rights and obligations. Currently there is a great deal of interest in the presuppositions and logical processes which underlie the interpretation of such indirect speech acts; but as Gumperz points out, what is meant by context and the manner in which it enters into the interpretation process has been discussed only in general terms (Gumperz, 1976; but see Labov and Fanshel, 1977 for an attempt at a more precise formulation). More seriously, it seems to be commonly assumed, though not explicitly stated, that conversational participants generally share a kind of pragmatic competence which enables them to interpret contextual factors in much the same way (Gumperz, 1976, p. 281). This assumption is particularly clear in an early article by Lakoff (1971), and more recently Smith and Wilson (1979) refer to utterances-in-context as containing "items of non-linguistic knowledge shared by speaker and hearer, and a set of shared inference rules" (p. 174). Leaving aside for a moment the question of how much relevant non-linguistic knowledge persons with different cultural norms might be said to share, it is clear that the "shared inference rules" are often insufficient to prevent misinterpretation of the illocutionary force of indirect speech acts even between persons who know each other well; sometimes these misinterpretations are repaired. Many examples of exchanges such as the following could no doubt be provided by the reader:

(19) Wife: Will you be home early today?
       Husband: When do you need the car?
       Wife: I don't, I just wondered if you'd be home early.

It may in fact be more accurate to talk of "inferential preferences" of a probabilistic nature, rather than "inference rules", so as to allow for the fact that such misinterpretations are quite frequent (cf. the comments of Lyons and Aitchison above, and see Klein and Dittmar, 1979 for a good discussion of probabilistic models). Tannen (1981) has recently made a very similar suggestion, viz. that in explaining how persons interpret indirect speech acts, the notion of *patterns of interpretation* is more appropriate than that of *rules of discourse*. These patterns of interpretation depend, in a complex way, on "context, individual and social differences and interpersonal dynamics" (p. 484).

While taking the non-categorical nature of the inference process into account, Gumperz suggests tentatively, on the basis of a number of documented conversations and direct questions put to judges, that a predisposition to interpret contextual cues in a given manner may vary *systematically* between speech communities. For example, he considers that American speakers are more likely than British speakers to interpret interrogatives of a pragmatically ambiguous kind (such as (18)) as requests for information. Interestingly, the miscommunication between himself and an American salesman reported by Trudgill (1981) seems to support this view. More recently, Gumperz and Tannen have examined in some detail a number of miscommunications, some but not all of which may be located in the systematically different types of inference likely to be drawn by a number of American ethnic groups. Further, Tannen reports that in a study of cross-cultural differences in inferential preferences, more Greeks than Americans, when presented with a sample of conversation, interpreted *why* utterances (such as *Why are you here?*) as indirect speech acts (Tannen, 1981).

One point made by Gumperz repeatedly is that communicative breakdowns are seldom analysed as *linguistic*. Speakers typically react with a sense of frustration and hostility; frequently each participant accuses the other of perverse and wilfully difficult behaviour, and if confronted with a re-run of the conversation, claims that his own interpretation of a given prosodic pattern, or a given utterance, is the only reasonable one. In the case of cross-ethnic communication, this kind of breakdown appears to contribute to hostile stereotyping, and one concern of Gumperz has been to devise training programmes for those whose work involves them in communicating with other ethnic groups. This would appear to be an important application of any theory of communication which could account elegantly and systematically for the frequent miscommunications which do undoubtedly take place. It seems likely, moreover, that the kind of culturally distributed problems and reactions to these problems which Gumperz describes are not limited to inter-ethnic communication. They almost certainly occur in a similarly systematic manner in conversations between, for example, Englishmen who, like the Group I and Group III speakers discussed in relation to *youse wash the dishes*, are socially distant from each other.

Summary and conclusion

By focussing on miscommunications, the purpose of this chapter has been to explore the manner in which people communicate successfully. Comprehension is a complicated matter, requiring a multidisciplinary approach; it seems that the perspective offered by sociolinguistics, concerned as it is with the analysis of speech events in their social context, might be a helpful one. Analysis of a number of miscommunication has shown that, despite the complex range of strategies involved in comprehension, it is possible to locate some problems specifically in the mismatch between the dialect grammars of speaker and hearer.

The first of the miscommunications examined (altogether three relevant areas of Hiberno-English grammar were isolated) was located in a syntactic disparity which also had a clear sociolinguistic distribution; that is, the *you/youse* contrast. Analysis suggested that the non-standard speaker's general communicative competence, as well as his passive competence in standard English, might be more limited than is commonly supposed.

The analysis focussing on Hiberno-English *whenever* suggested that structurally located miscommunications were likely to occur and be noticed under specifiable conditions: the ambiguous utterance had to be semantically acceptable to both speaker and hearer; and the ambiguity had to be located in a message which was of "real world" importance to the hearer. However, it was noted that under experimental conditions, subjects appeared to misinterpret even semantically *unacceptable* sentences. This may be because experimental subjects do not search out relevance in "odd" sentences whereas conversationalists do. In other words, Grice's maxim of relevance may not apply in test conditions. A further analysis which focussed on the Hiberno-English perfect suggested that, probably because of the abstract nature of the reference, non-linguistic context was often of little use in helping conversationalists avoid breakdowns. However, ellipted responses sometimes concealed misunderstandings. The question of how specifically *linguistic* context influenced comprehension was pursued further, and some experimental results were discussed which suggested that in cross-dialectal communication perceptual strategies worked together with linguistic rules in an orderly manner when persons interpreted ambiguous sentences.

Since consideration of all the data suggests that it is possible to specify conditions under which syntactic mismatches are likely to produce miscommunications, we may consider these observations as a modest contribution towards a more explicit and testable theory of communication.

Finally, some breakdowns located in disparate *inferential strategies* were briefly discussed, and it was suggested that the notion of *inferential preferences* of a probabilistic kind might be easier to work with than that of *inference rules*, so as to allow theoretically for frequently occuring miscommunications.

One particularly interesting (if negative) conclusion is that there is much about cross-dialectal communication which we simply do not know, although the general assumption in standard linguistics textbooks is that there is very little worth knowing. I do not think that we can afford to dismiss the instances discussed here as "marginal" in the sense that Hiberno-English has an unusally exotic grammar. There are many subtle differences between even Anglo-English dialects and standard English (such as those associated with the temporal conjunction *while* in Northern England) which might, if investigated, be found to be the locus of communicative problems.

Linguists who consider themselves to be socially responsible may also feel that the possibilities of applying work of this kind to situations where cross-dialectal communicative problems have unpleasant social consequences are considerable. Preliminary attention has already been given to the analysis of problems which are known to arise in language-testing situations (see for example, Labov, 1972(a); Taylor, 1977; Milroy and Milroy, forthcoming). It is hoped that this chapter will stimulate readers to consider further specific applications of a detailed, dispassionate and accountable analysis of cross-dialectal communication problems. These are problems which are of practical concern to many, but only a linguist is capable of carrying out such an analysis; if linguists do not do the job, it will be done, but less well, by others.

Note

Much of the work reported in this chapter was carried out in the course of research projects HR 3771 and HR 5777, funded by the Social Science Research Council. This support is gratefully acknowledged here.

I also acknowledge the contribution of my co-workers, James Milroy, John Harris and Linda Policansky, all of whom have been struggling to cope with the vagaries of non-standard syntax which sometimes seems to defy analysis. Thanks are due particularly to James Milroy for his initial insights into the very great differences between Hiberno-English and Standard English syntax. The following have been of great help in providing data or commenting on earlier drafts, and I thank them: Greg Brooks, Alison Davis, Michael McTear, John Harris, James Milroy, James Miller and Michael Stubbs and Margaret Deuchar.

References

Aitchison, J. (1976). "The articulate mammal: an introduction to psycholinguistics", Hutchinson, London.

Berdan, R. (1977). "Polylectal comprehension and the polylectal grammar", *In* (Fasold and Shuy, eds), pp. 12–29.

Bever, T. G. (1970). The cognitive basis for linguistic structures. *In* "Cognition and the development of language", (J. R. Hayes, ed.), Wiley, New York.

Brown, P. and Levinson, S. C. (1978). Universals in language usage: politeness phenomena. *In* Goody, (ed.), pp. 56–289.

Carroll, J. M., Bever, T. G. and Pollack, C. R. (1981). The non-uniqueness of linguistic intuitions. *Language*, **57.2**, 368–381.

Cicourel, A. (1973). "Cognitive Sociology", Penguin, Harmondsworth.

Coulthard, M. (1977). "An introduction to discourse analysis", Longmans, London.

Edwards, V. K. (1979). "The West-Indian language issue in British schools: challenges and responses", Routledge, London.

Ervin-Tripp, S. (n.d). "Structures of control", (mimeo, Department of Psychology, Berkeley).

Fasold, R. W. and Shuy, R. W. (1977). "Studies in language variation", Georgetown University Press, Georgetown.

Ferguson, C. A. (1977). Linguistics as anthropology. *In* Saville-Troike (ed.), pp. 1–12.

Fillmore, J., Kempler, D. and Wang, S. Y. (1979). "Individual differences in language ability and language behaviour", Academic Press, London and New York.

Fromkin, V. (ed.) (1973). "Speech errors as linguistic evidence", Mouton, The Hague.

Fromkin, V. (ed.) (1981). "Errors in linguistic performance", Academic Press, London and New York.

Givón, T. (1979). "On understanding grammar", Academic Press, London and New York.

Goody, E. N. (ed.) (1978). "Questions and politeness", C.U.P., Cambridge.

Gordon, D. and Lakoff, G. (1971). Conversational postulates. *In* "Papers from the seventh regional meeting of the Chicago Linguistic Society", CLS, Chicago.

Grice, H. P. (1975). Logic and conversation. *In* "Syntax and Semantics: speech acts", (P. Cole and J. Morgan, eds), Academic Press, London and New York.

Gumperz, J. J. (1976). Language, communication and public negotiation. *In* "Anthropology and the public interest: fieldwork and theory", (P. Sanday, ed.), Academic Press, New York and London.

Gumperz, J. J. (1977a). "The conversational analysis of interethnic communication", Mimeo: University of Berkeley.

Gumperz, J. J. (1977b). Sociocultural knowledge in conversational inferences. *In* Saville-Troike (ed.), pp. 191–211.

Gumperz, J. J., Tupp, T. C. and Roberts, C. (1979). "Crosstalk: a study of cross-cultural communication", National Centre for Industrial Language Training, Southall.

Gumperz, J. J. and Tannen, D. (1979). Individual and social differences in language use. *In* Fillmore *et al.* (eds), pp. 305–326.

Gumperz, J. J. and Hymes, D. (1972). "Directions in Sociolinguistics", Holt, Reinehart & Winston, New York.

Hall, E. T. (1963). A system for the notation of proxemic behaviour. *American Anthropologist*, **65**, 1003–26.

Harris, J. (1982). The Hiberno-English verb phrase: variation, change and dialect maintenance. In *Belfast Working Papers in Language and Linguistics*, **6**.

Hughes, A. and Trudgill, P. (1979). "English Accents and Dialects", Arnold, London.

Hymes, D. (1972). Models of the interaction of language and social life. *In* Gumperz and Hymes (eds), pp. 35–71.

Klein, W. and Dittmar, N. (1979). "Developing grammars", Springer, Berlin.

Labov, W. (1972a). Where do grammars stop? *In* "Sociolinguistics: current trends and prospects", (R. W. Shuy ed.), Georgetown University Press, Washington D.C.

Labov, W. (1972b). "Language in the inner city", Pennsylvania University Press, Philadelphia.

Labov, W. and Fanshel, D. (1977). "Therapeutic discourse", Academic Press, New York and London.

Lakoff, G. (1971). Presupposition and relative well-formedness. *In* "Semantics", (D. Steinberg and D. Jacobovits, eds), Cambridge University Press, London.

Lyons, J. (1977). "Semantics" (2 vols), Cambridge University Press, Cambridge.

Lyons, J. (1980). Pronouns of address in Anna Karenina: the stylistics of bilingualism and the impossibility of translation. *In* "Studies in English Linguistics", (S. Greenbaum, G. Leech and J. Svartvik, eds), Longmans, London.

Miller, J. (1981). "Spoken language, written language and competence", (Mimeo, Department of Linguistics, University of Edinburgh).

Milroy, J. (1978). Stability and change in non-standard English in Belfast. *Journal of the Northern Ireland Speech and Language Forum*, 72–82.

Milroy, L. (1980). "Language and Social Networks", Blackwell, Oxford.

Milroy, L. and Milroy J. (forthcoming). "Authority in language: a sociolinguistic study of prescriptivism", Routledge and Kegan Paul, London.

Nelson, N. W. and McRoskey, R. L. (1978). Comprehension of standard English at varied speaking rates by children whose major dialect is black English. *Journal of communication disorders*, **11**, 37–50.

Philips, S. (1976). Some sources of cultural variability in the regulation of talk. *Lang. Soc.* **5**, 81–95.

Plutchik, R. (1976). (2nd ed.). "Foundations of experimental research", Harper & Row, New York.

Ross, J. R. (1975). Where to do things with words. *In* "Syntax and Semantics 3: speech acts", (P. Cole and J. L. Morgan, eds), Academic Press, New York and London.

Ross, J. R. (1979). Where's English? *In* Fillmore *et al.* (eds), pp. 127–164.

Saville-Troike, M. (ed.) (1977). "Linguistics and Anthropology", Georgetown University Press, Washington D.C.

Schegloff, E. A., Jefferson, G. and Sacks, H. (1977). The preference for self-correction in the organisation of repair in conversation. *Language*, **53**, 361–382.

Searle, J. (1975). Indirect speech acts. *In* "Syntax and semantics 3: speech acts", (P. Cole and J. L. Morgan, eds), Academic Press, New York and London.

Smith, N. and Wilson, D. (1979). "Modern Linguistics", Penguin, Harmondsworth.

Sperber, D. and Wilson, D. (forthcoming). "Language and relevance; foundations of pragmatic theory", Oxford, Blackwell.

Tannen, D. (1981). Review of *Therapeutic Discourse* by W. Labov and D. Fanshel, *Language*, **57**, 2, 481–486.

Taylor, O. (1977). The sociolinguistic dimension in standardized testing. *In* Saville-Troike (ed.), pp. 257–266.

Trudgill, P. J. (1979). Standard and non-standard dialects of English in the United Kingdom: problems and policies. *International Journal of the Sociology of Language*, **21**, 9–24.

Trudgill, P. J. (1981). On the limits of passive "competence": sociolinguistics and the polylectal grammar controversy. *In* "Linguistic controversies: Festschrift for F. R. Palmer", (D. Crystal, ed.), Arnold, London.

Watson, O. M. and Graves, T. D. (1966). Quantitative research in proxemic behaviour. *American Anthropologist*, **68**, 971–985.

[1] It is also distinct, semantically, from Scottish *whenever*, which is equivalent to "as soon as".

3

The relationship between language and sex in English

Jenny Cheshire

Many sociolinguistic studies have shown how social divisions between speakers, such as age, socio-economic class or sex, are reflected in their language. In some tribal societies where men and women lead relatively separate lives, there are often clear phonological, lexical or syntactic differences in their speech: this was true, for example, of many AmerIndian and Australasian languages. Where the sexes are less segregated, as in modern Western societies, language differences are more subtle (for examples, see Trudgill, 1974a; Chapter 4). More recently, research on language and sex has gone beyond the analysis of sex-differentiated varieties of language, to investigate the way that language reflects and helps to maintain social attitudes towards women and men.

In Britain and the USA, for example, it has been shown that our conventional use of English treats men and women unequally, rather than simply differently. This paper will briefly collate some of the more important research findings in this area, and will discuss their implications. It will also document some examples of changes in the use of English, which reflect an increased social awareness of the way in which English discriminates against women. These changes result in part from the dissemination of research findings (Miller and Swift, 1977 and 1981, for example, are written for the general reader rather than for a purely academic audience), but they can also be seen as a natural result of the changing position of women in British

APPLIED SOCIOLINGUISTICS
ISBN: 0-12-701220-6

and American society, and of growing interest and support for some of the issues raised by the feminist movement.

The first two sections of this paper discuss research into sexism in English, and the way in which our use of language maintains stereotyped images of the sexes. They also discuss some of the implications of the research findings, and describe some efforts that have been made, by both individuals and group organizations, to avoid discriminatory language themselves and to encourage others to avoid it also. The following two sections point out some potential applications of research into two other aspects of language and sex: the analysis of sex differences in language use, and the evaluation of men's and women's speech.

Sexism in English

A great deal of research into sexism in English has focussed on the third person singular pronoun forms, which force speakers to specify the sex of the person to whom the pronoun refers. As Conklin (1974) points out, this means, among other things, that it is possible to write a recommendation for a job that avoids discrimination on the grounds of race, nationality, or religion; but it is not possible to avoid discrimination on the grounds of sex, since it is difficult to avoid using pronouns.

Several attempts have been made to introduce a neutral third person singular pronoun into English, one (*thon*) dating from as far back as 1859. This early proposal is, in fact, the one that has had the greatest impact; it was listed in Funk and Wagnell's New Standard Dictionary in 1913, and it was still sufficiently recognized in 1959 to be included in the second edition of Webster's International Dictionary. Other proposals have had more limited success. *Co* is used in some communes in the USA, particularly in Virginia and Missouri, and it is routinely used in the magazine "Communities". It has also been used in a book on radical therapy, published by Harper and Row in 1973 (see Miller and Swift, 1977, p. 130). Some recent novels have used *na* (Arnold, 1973) and *person* or *per* (Piercy, 1979) and a supervisors' guide issued by a division of American Management Associations uses *hir* (Killian, 1979). Other suggestions include *e, tey, hesh, po, re, xe* and *jhe*, but none of these has been widely accepted, perhaps, as Lakoff (1973) suggests, because of the difficulty of artificially introducing a new item into a closed linguistic system. A solution that might meet with more success is to extend the function of an item that is already in the system. The plural pronoun *they*, in fact, has been used in spoken English for centuries in phrases such as "everyone must do their best" (see Bodine, 1975). Prescriptive grammarians argue against this on the grounds that *they* is inaccurate in terms of number, and recommend *he* instead as a "sex-indefinite" pronoun. This, of course, is equally inaccurate, in terms of sex, but their insistence has meant that *he* is the form that is now generally used as a "neutral" pronoun in formal written English.

One important application of work on language and sex has been the experimental demonstration that "neutral" *he* is interpreted as referring not to both males and females, but to males only (see, for example, Martyna, 1978; Moulton *et al.*, 1978). Mackay (1979) found that this form occurs so often in university textbooks that educated Americans must be exposed to more than ten million occurrences during their lifetimes, which means that this cannot be dismissed as a trivial phenomenon. Furthermore, it is not only the intended "neutral" pronoun that is misinterpreted: generic *man*, in phrases such as *stone-age man* or *no man is an island*, is also interpreted as a masculine noun, by both children and adults (see Nilsen, 1973; Harrison, 1975; Schneider and Hacker, 1973). The main implication of these findings is that the use of these terms excludes women from our thinking and our culture. Most school and university textbooks, in fact, do exclude women and women's achievements, as Hoffmann (1981) points out. Another important implication is that the use of "false generics" in surveys, and of male-orientated thinking generally, may lead to inaccurate results in many areas of research. Goot and Reid (1975) suggest that most of the received wisdom about the political attitudes of women is inaccurate, because it stems from ambiguous questionnaires that ask about "the ordinary man", or "the man with high ideals". And Delamont (1980) points out that political scientists often talk of "democracies" that deny the vote to women and that cannot, therefore, be democracies. It seems probable that culturally conditioned sexist thinking has affected our "knowledge" in other areas of enquiry also (for some attempts to remedy this, see Roberts, 1981; Spender, forthcoming).

"Thinking male" is not confined to academic research, however. The following quotations, from everyday life, show that it is not only nouns of masculine gender that are assumed to have male reference. (They also, incidentally, provide examples of the way in which women are often considered to be the possessions of men.)

> My ambition is to have a show in London with the same sort of reputation that the Crazy Gang had. It would be glamorous, spicy, but above all a family show. People would bring their wives, mothers, and children. (Ken Dodd, in *Woman* magazine)

> What causes most distress to the residents is the kerbcrawlers, molesting their womenfolk. (James Hill, MP, on *This Week in Westminster*, Radio 4).

Lack of a neutral singular pronoun and the use of "generic" nouns of masculine gender are the most obvious examples of sexism in English; there are many other linguistic features, however, that reflect the social status of women (for examples, see Lakoff, 1973; Miller and Swift, 1971; 1981).

Recognition of the existence and of the implications of these features has led to conscious attempts to eliminate them from the language. These moves originated in the USA, but awareness of the issues is now spreading to Britain. Several American publishing companies issue guidelines for their authors and editors that suggest ways of avoiding sexist language. Scott, Foresman and Co., for example, issued "Guidelines for improving the image of women in textbooks" in 1972, and McGraw-Hill's "Guidelines for equal treatment of the sexes in McGraw-Hill book Publications" has been widely distributed since 1974 to individual writers as well as to government agencies, schools and universities, and the media. In Britain, the Women in the Publishing Industry Group drew up the "Non-sexist code of practice for book publishing" in 1976, and the British Edition of "The handbook of non-sexist writing" (Miller and Swift, 1981) contains examples of writing that is unintentionally sexist, from *The Sunday Times* and *The Observer*, and suggests ways of avoiding offending forms.

Some writers make a conscious effort to avoid sexism: Aitchison (1981), for example, uses both *she* and *he* as "sex-indefinite" pronouns in order, as she writes in the Preface, "to help conquer the all-pervading sexism which exists in the English language". Use of the written form *s/he* is becoming quite widespread, and the order of the nouns and pronouns in phrases like "he and she", "men and women", "mother and father" is sometimes purposely reversed. The reference book "Baby and Child" (Leach, 1977) uses *she* as a "neutral" pronoun throughout.[1] This is an important step, for the book is widely used, and although it is ultimately, of course, as sexist as using only *he*, it should attract the attention of readers who might otherwise not have been aware of the issue. Books on childcare appear to be leading the attack on the use of "neutral" *he*. Dr Spock has promised to alternate *she* and *he* in the next edition of his popular "Baby and Child Care", and Salk has already done so in his standard reference book for parents (Salk, 1974).

Professional organizations are also taking steps to encourage change in the language. The American Anthropological Association, for example, passed a resolution in 1973 urging its members to "become aware in their writing and teaching that their wide use of the term 'man' as generic for the species is conceptually confusing" (reported in Miller and Swift, 1977, p. 129). The American Library Association resolved in 1975 to avoid using sexist language in all future publications and official documents, and to change existing publications when they were revised. And in 1976, library cataloguers in the USA initiated a campaign to revise the use of sexist language in subject headings and in catalogue descriptions.

Several religious bodies are also changing the language used in their publications. In the USA, the General Synod of the United Church of Christ announced in 1973 that it would eliminate sex and race discrimination in all areas of its teaching, and it has, since then, been revising all its printed materials, including hymn books, service procedures and journals, to ensure that the language used is deliberately inclusive. The Jewish prayerbook "Gates of Prayer", was also revised in 1975, and it acknowledges in the Introduction to the Revised Edition a similar commitment to equality of the sexes. The revisions include substitutions such as "God of all generations" for "God of our fathers", and additions such as "God of our mothers, God of Sarah, Rebekah, Leah . . ." as a parallel to "God of our fathers, God of Abraham, Isaac and Jacob . . ." And the influential inter-denominational *Journal of Ecumenical Studies* devoted an editorial to "linguistic sexism" in 1974 (Volume XI, no. 2, Spring edition).

Although religious bodies in Britain are not renowned for equality in the treatment of the sexes (witness, for example, the refusal until last year to admit women into the Ministry, and the persistence of all-male choirs in the Anglican church), an initiative has come from the Methodist movement. The revised version of the Methodist Hymn Book, which is due to be published in 1983, omits some hymns that are considered to be blatantly sexist ("Rise up, O men of God", for example, has been excluded), and contains adapted versions of others. In many cases the adapted hymns are historically more accurate than the original versions: "O God our help in ages past", for example, contained the lines

Time, like an ever-rolling stream
Bears all its sons away

but the revised version, which substitutes "Bears mortal flesh away" for the second line, above, bears more resemblance to the wording of the psalm on which the hymn is based. The Methodist Hymn Book also makes some attempt to avoid male personification of God, by addressing the Deity directly as *Thou*, rather than indirectly as *He*. It continues, however, to use masculine imagery, referring to God as a father, king, shepherd and lord. Research into the language of religion has shown how the predominance of masculine imagery in religion results from the orientation of Western culture. Female imagery that was present in the Hebrew scriptures, for example, was often changed to masculine imagery during the process of translation (see Miller and Swift, 1977, Chapter 5; Spender, 1980, pp. 165–171). And until about AD200, Christian writers portrayed God as androgynous or feminine more often than as masculine (see Pagels, 1976). The use of masculine pronouns to refer to God must have some effect on the way that our culture conceptualizes a deity; and the effect will inevitably be greater for children, as the following "letter to God" from "Sylvia" suggests:

> Dear God, Are boys better than girls? I know you are one but try to be fair (from Marshall and Hample, 1966)

Children are particularly susceptible, of course, to discriminatory language. Although the majority of the school books used in Britain still contain sexist language, some teachers and educators are now pointing out the social implications to their colleagues and their pupils. The 1980 Special Issue of the journal *Women in Education*, for example, provides a checklist designed to be used by teachers for assessing the language used in school books. It warns that few books will be free of sexism, but gives suggestions for overcoming its effects, such as through class discussions or projects involving writing to publishers. There are also books designed for use in the classroom that point out the way in which the position of women in society is reflected in language. Though most of these are primarily concerned with sexual stereotyping, some also deal with sexism in English (see, for example, Adams and Laurikietis, 1976, 3, Unit 1: 3).

The changes in the use of English that have been discussed in this section are relatively minor when seen in isolation, but together they reflect an increasing awareness of the way in which language often discriminates against women, and of the need to change the way that we use language, if we are to change the way that society views women.

The linguistic maintenance of sexual stereotypes

It is sometimes difficult to separate linguistic features that are sexist from linguistic features that help to maintain sexual stereotypes. For example, the choice of *he* as the sex-indefinite pronoun is sexist because it excludes women, but it also perpetuates the idea that women are of secondary importance.

Sometimes language is used to make sexual divisions, but simply as one aspect of a more general sexual discrimination. Several schools, for example, use gender differences between pupils as a convenient way of dividing the class. Teachers list girls and boys separately in their registers; they may also play one gender off against the other, hoping to encourage the class to finish their work quickly (see Delamont, 1980). Language is involved here, but it is not the only way that a sexual division is enforced: girls and boys may be made to sit separately in assembly, and even to enter school by separate doors (again, see Delamont, 1980). This is not sexual stereotyping, but it prepares the way for it by encouraging children to strongly identify with their own sex and to view the opposite sex as completely distinct from themselves. Although language plays a part in this, it is not the language that needs to be changed, but the divisive practices of the schools.

Sometimes, however, language is more directly involved in making unnecessary gender distinctions. Some universities list male students with their surname and initials (as in *J. A. Smith*) but list female students with their full name and marital status (*Mrs Jane A. Smith*) (see Acker, 1980); and most make the same distinction in their lists of academic staff.

There are several cases, though, where language clearly reflects stereotyped sex-roles. Research in this area has been able to point to those features of language that need to be changed. For example, some "pairs" of words like *to mother* and *to father* are parallel in form (both are verbs derived from nouns) but not in meaning. As Lakoff (1973) points out, the phrase "she mothered the child" implies a psychological as well as a biological relationship, reflecting the fact that traditionally it is the mother who is responsible for the upbringing of children, whereas "he fathered the child" implies only a limited biological act. Some writers have made conscious efforts to dispel the stereotypes implied by pairs of this kind; Dodson (1975a) and Parke (1981) use *to father* as a semantic parallel to the verb *to mother* in their books "How to Father" and "Fathering", and Dodson introduces a neutral term in a second book entitled "How to Parent" (Dodson, 1975b).

Dictionary definitions often reveal the existence of sexual stereotypes and, of course, perpetuate them. The Concise Oxford Dictionary (1976), for example, defines *manly* in terms of virtues said to be possessed by men: "having a man's virtues, courage, frankness, etc." But if *manly* is used to describe a woman, qualities rather than virtues are involved: "(of woman) having a man's qualities". *Womanly*, in contrast, is defined not in terms of inherent virtues but in terms of unspecified qualities that are considered suitable for women (one wonders by whom!): "(of woman or her feelings, conduct, etc.) having or showing the qualities befitting a woman". The Shorter Oxford English Dictionary (1973), which gives fuller definitions, adds independence and uprightness to the list of manly virtues, and gives gentleness and devotion as examples of qualities of women.

One application of the analysis of language and sexual stereotyping has been to avoid these kinds of definitions in the compilation of the *American Heritage School Dictionary*. This uses examples that assign to women virtues that traditionally have been attributed to men (for example, "she has *brains* and courage"). Similarly, characteristics that are usually considered to be feminine are attributed to men, in sentences such as "tears *welled* up in his eyes" or "striving to attain *mastery* over his emotions". Job stereotyping is also corrected, by using sentences like "he *teaches* kindergarten" and "he *studies* typing at night" (see Graham, 1975). The dictionary is designed to be used by schoolchildren, which means that it will play an important role in educating the next generation towards a less sexually divisive society. Another result of work in this area has been the publication of *The Feminist English Dictionary* (Todasco *et al.*, 1973), which takes material from established dictionaries to show how their definitions embody sexual stereotypes.

Work on sexual stereotyping in children's books has led to attempts to correct it. Research has shown that the vast majority of children's books portray stereotyped sex roles; what is more, they do not merely fail to prepare children for a more egalitarian society, but they even fail to depict life as it is at present (see Hoffman, 1981). The reading schemes that are used most commonly in British schools have twice as many male characters as female characters, and show the male characters taking part in a wider variety of roles and activities than the female characters (see Lobban, 1974; 1975). Furthermore, the books that are read most widely by children are frequently the ones that are the most guilty of stereotyping: *Little Women*, for example, is among the five books most often read by children over ten (see Whitehead *et al.*, 1977); and some of the worst offenders have been specifically recommended by the Schools Council and by literary critics (see Hoffmann, 1981). School textbooks also perpetuate outdated stereotypes: junior science books, for example, show experiments conducted by boys, while girls look on (see Austerfield and Turner, 1972), and textbooks on other subjects usually portray stereotyped sex roles, or else omit women entirely (again, see Hoffmann, 1981).

In Britain the Equal Opportunities Commission (1979, 1980) and the National Council for Civil Liberties (1978) have published practical suggestions for avoiding inadvertent sex discrimination in schools, that include a discussion of stereotyping in children's books. Some writers of children's fiction have purposely made girls the central figures of their books (for example, Lindgren, 1971; Garner, 1979; Sutcliff, 1967); others portray girls as tough and daring, as well as compassionate (Bawden, 1967; Kemp, 1977), and boys as sensitive and caring, but still tough (Southall, 1971; Byars, 1976). Other writers attempt to dispel outdated stereotypes by using as characters a working mother (Gripe, 1973), a politically active mother (Avery, 1978), a mother active in the Women's Movement (Perl, 1978), and even a mother who is a pirate (Mahy, 1972). A useful list of children's books which are free of sex bias (and also of class and race bias) can be found in Dixon (1977). Collections of fairy stories that avoid sexual stereotyping have also been published, some in their original form (Phelps, 1981), others specially written (Williams, 1979) or rewritten (Merseyside Women's Liberation Movement, n.d.). Lists of books that are free of sexual stereotyping are provided by a number of publishers and organizations (for details, see Hoffmann, 1981; and *Women in Education, Special Issue, 1980*), and checklists and guidelines for assessing the sexist content of children's books are produced by the Centre for Urban Educational Studies, the Equal Opportunities Commission, the National Union of Teachers and several other organizations. Discussion material for use in schools is also available, on fiction (see, for example, Cadogan and Craig, 1976; Whyatt, 1980), on women's issues (for example, Fyson and Greenhill, 1979), and also on ways of avoiding sexism and sexual stereotyping in teaching history, science and other school subjects (for example, O'Faolain and Martines, 1979; Snail *et al.*, 1981). Excellent annotated bibliographies and resource lists can be found, again, in the Special Issue of *Women in Education* (1980) and also in Spender and Sarah (1980).

In the USA the problem of sexual stereotyping in education has been taken seriously for a very long time. Not only have writers and professional organizations taken steps to correct stereotyping, but government funds have been set aside for intervention programmes for teachers, both as in-service and pre-service training courses (for details, see Ekstrom, 1979).

Language also maintains (and exaggerates) sexual stereotypes in advertising. The advertisement below, used in the early 70s in the USA by Parker Pens, is a good example:

> You might as well give her a gorgeous pen to keep her checkbook unbalanced with. A sleek and shining pen will make her feel prettier. Which is more important to any girl than solving mathematical mysteries. (quoted in Komisar, 1971).

Nowadays stereotyping tends to be more subtle, and often results from the pictures rather than the wording of the advertisements (for examples, see Goffmann, 1979). Language is still sometimes involved, though, as in the current advertisements for TWA airlines, which have the words "Fly me" accompanying photographs of pretty air hostesses. In both the USA and Britain, stickers can be obtained with the messages "This ad insults women" or "This exploits women", and these have been used on advertisements in public places. In Britain the Women's Monitoring Network studies the representation of women in advertising and in the press generally, and relays its findings to offending companies.

Advertisements portray male stereotypes as well as female stereotypes, of course. In the USA some advertising companies are beginning to reverse traditional stereotypes in an attempt to correct them (for examples, see Komisar, 1971). In Britain a few advertisers appear to be aware of the issue: a recent television commercial for Sony, for example, plays on stereotyping by saying that since women may have been offended by their commercials, this one will deal only with the technical details that women are interested in.

And a current television commercial for British Rail makes a half-hearted attempt to avoid stereotyping by addressing "Business men and business ladies" – half-hearted because the choice of the word "ladies" rather than "women" gives the phrase an ironic air (for discussion of the different connotations of *lady* and *woman*, see Lakoff, 1973). These advertisements, of course, reinforce traditional stereotypes by making fun of the issue, but they may nevertheless attract the attention of people who had not thought about stereotyping before. And, as Komisar (1971) suggests, the images of men and women that appear in advertisements are so exaggerated and ludicrous that they may influence people to stop acting out sexual stereotypes.

Sex-role stereotyping also exists in job descriptions. Job titles have been officially revised, first in the USA, and then in Britain to comply with the Sex Discrimination Act of 1975: air hostesses, to give one example, are now officially referred to as flight attendants. Changing the titles of jobs will help to avoid sex-role stereotyping, but the language that is used in job descriptions needs to be changed also. The third person singular pronoun often indicates which sex employers have in mind: a recent advertisement in *The Guardian* (18th December, 1981), for instance, read "Our clients . . . are looking for a Secretary who can use her initiative". Careers Guides often perpetuate stereotyping in the same way: the "Daily Telegraph Careers A–Z" guide, which is aimed at school leavers, writes under "Accountant": "he may work in public practice" (p. 7).

Some books designed to counteract sexual stereotyping in schools contain examples of this, and suggestions for discussion. Adams and Laurikietis (1976, 1) for example, has a useful chapter on "Your choice of career". At least one Careers guide makes a conscious effort to dispel sexual stereotyping in career possibilities: "Equal Opportunities: a careers guide" (Miller, 1978) uses the feminine third person singular pronoun throughout, and explains in the introduction that its aim is to "chivvy girls off the tramlines" and "encourage girls to widen their career choice and speed their progress towards equality in the job market".

Language, as a social phenomenon, inevitably reflects social attitudes towards women and men. But it also influences and to some extent moulds the views of its speakers, as Kress and Hodge (1979) point out. This means that the changes in language use that have been outlined in this section should lead to changes in the way that society treats men and women, which, in turn, will lead to further changes in language. Language change and social change, in other words, are mutually reinforcing.

The formal analysis of linguistic differences
in male and female speech

Sociolinguistic surveys of American and British English usually include the sex of speakers as a sociological variable. Where linguistic features can occur in both a standard English and a non-standard form, the surveys have found that female speakers tend to use more of the standard English forms than male speakers. This is true for both phonological and morphosyntactic features (see, for example, Labov, 1966; Trudgill, 1974b). One reason may be that women are more conscious of the social significance of different linguistic features, so that they use more of the socially prestigious speech forms; another reason is, perhaps, that non-standard working-class speech has masculine connotations of "roughness" and "toughness" in Western society, so that men choose to use more non-standard forms (see Trudgill, 1974a). Conklin (1974) suggests that women are simply more sensitive to the constraints of different social contexts, so that they are less likely than men to use their most relaxed speech style (where the maximum use of non-standard forms would occur) when talking to a linguistic investigator, particularly if, as has usually been the case, the investigator is male. In fact, some recent studies where the investigator was female found that differences in the use of non-standard forms depended not only on the sex of speakers but also on the degree to which they were integrated into the local culture (see Milroy, 1980; Cheshire, 1982a). Trudgill (1972) found that covert prestige is attached to non-standard features by younger working-class speakers of *both* sexes, and suggested that this reflects adherence to a subculture that is distinct from the mainstream value system of our society.

The analysis of sex differences in language has been useful within linguistics, by helping to explain some of the social mechanisms that are involved in language change (see, for example, Trudgill, 1972; Milroy, 1980). But it also has important implications for education. Children who speak non-standard English are at a disadvantage at school, because their variety of English is not the same as the variety used by the teachers and in school reading books. They have to choose, perhaps at an unconscious level, whether to use the standard English forms that are linked with mainstream culture and the school, or the non-standard English forms that symbolize solidarity with the vernacular culture. It is sometimes thought that boys are more likely than girls to reject standard English and the values of the school, because "female" values and female teachers predominate there (see, for example, Shuy, 1969). In fact, however, girls who are integrated into the peer group vernacular culture are equally likely to reject the language and the values of the school (see Cheshire, 1982b), and any attempt at teaching standard English should take this into consideration.

Research has also shown that some linguistic features function differently for female and male speakers (see Milroy, 1980; Cheshire, 1982a). One example of this is the non-standard past tense verb form *come*, which occurs in sentences such as "I come here last night". Adolescent boys in the town of Reading, in Berkshire, invariably use this non-standard form in both formal and informal speech; adolescent girls, on the other hand, use the form intermittently, varying it with the standard English past tense form *came*. We would expect, therefore, that boys will have more difficulty in replacing the non-standard form with the standard form, in their school writing. This kind of differentiation, then, also needs to be given careful consideration by educationists and teachers.

Some researchers have carried the analysis of sex differences in language a stage further, by looking at female and male roles in conversations. It has been suggested, for example, that in conversations between men and women, it is women who initiate the conversation and encourage men to speak, while men control the topics. It has also been claimed that men interrupt more often than women (see Zimmerman and West, 1975; Acker, 1980). As yet there is no valid empirical confirmation, but if these differences do exist, the knowledge could have some useful social applications, perhaps in counselling or therapy, or even, as Kramer *et al.* (1978) suggest, as an unobtrusive measure of sexual inequality.

Evaluation of speech

Sex differences in the evaluation of speech have been analysed from the point of view of the hearer (in other words, analysing the way in which men and women evaluate speech) and from the point of view of the speaker (focussing on the way in which judges evaluate men's speech and women's speech). Elyan *et al.* (1978) found clear differences in the way that women and men evaluate speech. Women rated speakers who used Received Pronunciation more highly than men, in terms of status, intelligence, independence and egoism; and they gave lower ratings than men to speakers with regional accents. These findings have implications for education, for they imply that female teachers might form different stereotyped views of their pupils than male teachers. The way that children speak is thought to affect teachers' evaluation of their academic potential (see Seligman, Tucker and Lambert, 1972) and this, in turn, can affect academic success (Rosenthal and Jacobson, 1968). There could be serious consequences in other areas, too: in trial by jury, for example, in job interviews, and in politics.

As Smith (1979) points out, it is difficult to analyse how women's and men's speech is evaluated, because judges may be reacting to the sex of speakers, rather than to their language. It has been suggested that women's speech is characterized by a number of linguistic features, such as a more frequent use of tag questions, fillers, intensifiers and "empty" adjectives (for example, *divine* or *lovely*) (see Lakoff, 1973), but this has not been confirmed by empirical studies. It is now thought that the linguistic characteristics described by Lakoff typify a more general "powerless" variety of speech, used by speakers who have little social prestige (see Lind and O'Barr, 1979), and, therefore, associated more often with women than with men. Lind and O'Barr set up simulated legal hearings, and found that jurors of both sexes rated witnesses using the "powerless" variety of speech as less competent, trustworthy, convincing, socially attractive and socially dynamic than witnesses who did not use this variety, irrespective of their sex. Although these findings do not bear directly on sex differences in language use, they do show that using certain linguistic features can affect the way in which speakers of both sexes are evaluated, and are relevant in all areas where language plays a central role. Those speakers who have low social prestige may reveal this in their speech, and be evaluated negatively in job interviews, legal proceedings and other important social situations. Thus, although the initial impetus for this research came from an interest in sexual inequality, the results have wider implications that could affect all sections of society that are treated unequally.

Conclusion

Changes that take place in society are reflected in language, though language change tends to lag behind social change. Sex roles in the USA and in Britain have been changing during the course of this century, and we would normally expect these social changes to be accompanied by gradual changes in language. We have seen, however, that research into the relationship between language and sex has led to conscious attempts to change discriminatory and stereotyping language. These practical applications are accelerating the rate at which language is changing and this should, in turn, accelerate the rate at which society is changing.

We have also seen that research in this area has implications for education and for legal proceedings and job interviews. It has potential applications for many other areas also: in the field of language pathology, for example, where it seems that sex-role stereotyping could account for some language disorders in male speakers (see Kramer, 1974).

The main application of work on the relationship between language and sex has, of course, been in attempts to change our use of discriminatory language, in order to remove sexual inequality from society. It has wider applications also, however, that have been only briefly mentioned here: it helps our general understanding of the way in which language reflects and maintains social divisions, and of the way in which our thinking is often unconsciously moulded by our language. An understanding of this will help to eliminate not only sexual inequality, but inequality in all areas of social life.

References

Acker, S. (1980). Women, the other academics. *British Journal of Sociology of Education*, **1**, (1), 81–91.

Adams, C. and Laurikietis, R. (1976). "The gender trap: a closer look at sex roles", Book 1: Education and work. Book 2: Sex and Marriage. Book 3: Messages and Images. Virago, London.

Aitchison, J. (1981). "Language change: progress or decay?", Fontana, London.

Arnold J. (1973). "The Cook and the Carpenter", Daughters, Houston, Texas.

Austerfield, V. and Turner, J. (1972). What are little girls made of? *Spare Rib*, 3 September.

Avery, G. (1978). "Huck and her time machine", Armada, London.

Bawden, N. (1967). "A handful of thieves", Gollancz, London.

Bodine, A. (1975). Androcentrism in prescriptive grammar: singular 'they', sex-indefinite 'he', and 'he or she'. *Language in Society*, **4** (1), 129–146.

Byars, B. (1976). "The Midnight Fox", Penguin, Harmondsworth.

Cadogan, M. and Craig, P. (1976). "You're a brick, Angela: a new look at girls' fiction 1839–1975", Gollancz, London.

Cheshire, J. (1982a). "Variation in an English dialect: a sociolinguistic study", Cambridge University Press, London.

Cheshire, J. (1982b). Dialect features and linguistic conflict in schools. *Educational Review*, **34** (1), 53–67.

Conklin, N. (1974). Toward a feminist analysis of linguistic behaviour. *University of Michigan Papers in Womens Studies*, **1** (1), 51–73.

"Daily Telegraph Careers A–Z", (1981). William Collins, London.

Delamont, S. (1980). "The Sociology of Women", George Allen and Unwin, London.

Dixon, B. (1977). "Catching them young: sex, race and class in children's fiction", (Vol. 1), Pluto Press, London.

Dodson, F. (1975a). "How to parent", Star books, London.

Dodson, F. (1975b). "How to father", New American Library, New York.

Ekstrom, R. B. (1979). Intervention strategies to reduce sex-role stereotyping in education. *In* "Sex-role stereotyping: collected papers", (O. Hartnett, G. Boden and M. Fuller, eds), Tavistock Publications, London.

Elyan, O. *et al.* (1978). R.P. accented female speech: the voice of perceived androgyny? *In* "Sociolinguistic patterns in British English", (P. Trudgill, ed.), Edward Arnold, London.

Equal Opportunities Commission, (1980). "Ending sex-stereotyping in schools".

Equal Opportunities Commission, (1979). "Do you provide equal educational opportunities?"

Fyson, N. L. and Greenhill, S. (1979). "People talking", Macmillan Educational, London.

Garner, A. (1979). "The Stone Book", Armada, London.

Goffman, E. (1979). "Gender advertisements", Harvard University Press, Cambridge, Mass.

Goot, M. and Reid, E. (1975). "Women and voting studies", Sage, London.

Graham, A. (1975). The making of a nonsexist dictionary. *In* "Language and sex: difference and dominance", (B. Thorne and N. Henley, eds), Newbury House Publishers, Rowley, Mass.

Gripe, M. (1973). "The Night Daddy", Chatto and Windus, London.

Guttenag, M. and Bray, H. (1976). "Undoing sex-stereotypes: research and resources for educators", McGraw Hill, New York.

Harrison, L. (1975). Cro-magnon woman – in eclipse. *The Science Teacher*, April 1975, pp. 8–11.

Hoffman, M. (1981). Children's reading and social values. *In* "Language in School and Community", (N. Mercer, ed.), Edward Arnold, London.

Kemp, G. (1977). "The turbulent term of Tyke Tiler", Faber, London.

Kidd, V. (1971). A study of the images produced through the use of the male pronoun as the generic. *Moments in contemporary rhetoric and communication*, **1** (1), 25–30.

Killian, R. A. (1979). "Managers must lead!", AMACOM, USA.

Komisar, L. (1971). The image of woman in advertising. *In* "Woman in sexist society", (V. Gornick and B. K. Moran eds), Basic Books, New York.

Kramer, C. (1974). Women's speech: separate but unequal? *Quarterly Journal of Speech*, **60** (February), 14–24. Reprinted in Thorne and Henley, 1975.

Kramer, C., Thorne B. and Henley, N. (1978). Perspectives on language and communication. *Signs: Journal of women in culture and society*, **3** (3), 638–651.

Kress, G. and Hodge, R. (1979). "Language as ideology", Routledge and Kegan Paul, London.

Labov, W. (1966). "The social stratification of English in New York City", Center for Applied Linguistics, Washington, D.C.

Lakoff, R. (1973). Language and woman's place. *Lanuage in Society*, **2** (1), 45–79.

Leach, P. (1977). "Baby and Child", Michael Joseph, London.

Lind, E. A. and O'Barr, W. M. (1979). The social significance of speech in the courtroom. *In* "Language and social psychology", (H. Giles and R. N. St. Clair, eds), Blackwell, Oxford.

Lindgren, A. (1971). "Pippi Longstocking", Oxford University Press, Oxford.

Lobban, G. (1974). Presentation of sex-roles in reading schemes. *Forum for the discussion of new trends in Education*, **16** (2), Spring, pp. 57–60.

Lobban, G. (1975). Sex-roles in reading schemes. *Educational Review*, **27** (3), 202–9.

Mahy, M. (1972). "The Man whose mother was a pirate", Dent, London

Marshall, E. and Hample, S. (1966). "Children's letters to God", Pocket Books, New York.

Martyna, W. (1978). What does "he" mean? Use of the generic masculine. *Journal of communication*, **28** (1), 131–138.

Mackay, D. G. (1979). On the goals, principles and procedures for prescriptive grammar: Singular *they*. *Language and Society* **9**, 349–367.

Mackay, D. G. and Fulkerson, D. (1979). On the comprehension and production of pronouns. *Journal of verbal learning and verbal behaviour*.

Merseyside Women's Liberation Movement. (n.d.). "Once and Future Tales", (Snow White, Red Riding Hood, The Prince and the Swineherd). Available from 53, Sandown Road, Liverpool.

Miller, R. (1978). "Equal opportunities: a careers guide", Penguin, Harmondsworth.

Miller, C. and Swift, K. (1977). "Words and Women", Gollancz, London.

Miller, C. and Swift, K. (1981). "The handbook of non-sexist writing for writers, editors and speakers", The Women's Press, London.

Milroy, L. (1980). *Language and social networks*. Blackwell, Oxford.

Moulton, J., Robinson, G. M. and Elias, C. (1978). Sex bias in language use: "neutral" pronouns that aren't. *American Psychologist*, **33** (11), 1032–1036.

National Council for Civil Liberties. (1978). "Sex discrimination in schools: how to fight it".

Nilsen, A. P. (1973). Grammatical gender and its relationship to the equal treatment of males and females in children's books. Unpublished Ph.D. Thesis, University of Iowa.

O'Faolain, J. and Martines, L. (1979). "Not in God's image: women in history", Virago, London.

Pagels, E. H. (1976). What became of God the mother?: conflicting images of God in early Christianity. *Signs: Journal of women in culture and society*, **2** (2), 293–303.

Parke, R. (1981). "Fathering", Fontana, London.

Perl, L. (1978). "That crazy April", Armada, London.

Phelps, E. J. (1981). "The maid of the North and other folk tales' heroines", Holt, Rinehart and Winston, New York.

Piercy, M. (1979). "Woman on the edge of time", The Women's Press, London.

Roberts, H. (1981). "Doing feminist research", Routledge and Kegan Paul, London.

Rosenthal, R. and Jacobson, L. (1968). "Pygmalion in the classroom", Holt, Rinehart and Winston, New York.

Salk, L. (1974). "Preparing for parenthood", David McKay, New York.

Schneider J. W. and Hacker, S. L. (1973). Sex role imagery and the use of the generic 'man' in introductory texts: a case in the sociology of sociology. *The American Sociologist*, **8** (1), 12–18.

Seligman, C. R., Tucker, G. R. and Lambert, W. E. (1972). The effects of speech style and other attributes on teachers' attitudes towards pupils. *Language in Society*, **1** (1), 131–142.

Shuy, R. (1969). Sociolinguistic research at the Center for Applied Linguistics: the correlation of language and sex. *Giornata internazionali di sociolinguistica*, Palazzo Baldassini, Rome.

Smith, P. (1979). Sex markers in speech. *In* "Social markers in speech", (K. P. Scherer and H. Giles, eds), Cambridge University Press, Cambridge.

Snail, M., Kelly, A. and Whyte, J. (1980). "Girls into science and technology", available from 91 Didsbury Park, Manchester 20.

Southall, I. (1971). "Josh", Penguin, Harmondsworth.

Spender, D. (1980). "Man made language", Routledge and Kegan Paul, London.

Spender, D. (forthcoming). "Men's studies modified: the impact of feminism on the academic disciplines", Pergamon, Oxford.

Spender, D. and Sarah, E. (eds) (1980). "Learning to lose: sexism and education", The Women's Press, London.

Sutcliff, R. (1967). "The chief's daughter", Hamish Hamilton, London.

Thorne, B. and Henley, N. (eds) (1975). "Language and sex: difference and dominance", Newbury House Publishers, Rowley, Mass.

Todasco *et al.* (1973). "An intelligent woman's guide to dirty words: English words and phrases reflecting sexist attitudes towards women in patriarchal society, arranged according to usage and idea", Vol. I of "The Feminist English Dictionary", Feminist Writers Workshop, Loop Center YWCA, Chicago.

Trudgill, P. (1972). Sex, covert prestige and linguistic change in the urban British English of Norwich. *Language in Society*, **1**, (1), 179–195.

Trudgill, P. (1974a). "Sociolinguistics", Penguin, Harmondsworth.

Trudgill, P. (1974b). "The social differentiation of English in Norwich", Cambridge University Press, London.

Whitehead F. *et al.* (1977). "Children and their books", Macmillan Education, London, for the Schools Council.

Whyatt, B. (1980). "Myths and legends for young feminists, and for old feminists the original version", available from B. Whyatt, 90, Plane Avenue, Wigan, Lancs. WN5 9PT.

Williams, J. (1979). "The Practical princess and other liberating fairy tales", Chatto and Windus, London.

"Women in Education", Special Issue 1980. Autumn, no. 20: Women and Education Newsletter Group: 14, St. Brendan's Road, Withington, Manchester 20.

Zimmerman, D. H. and West, C. (1975). Sex roles, interruptions and silences in conversations. *In* "Language and sex: difference and dominance", (B. Thorne and N. Henley, eds), Newbury House Publishers, Rowley Mass.

[1] In the 1979 and 1982 editions, however, Leach reverts to using *he* to refer to babies that may be either male or female, on the grounds that most readers prefer this. *She* remains in the text of most charts on the book, and in the captions to illustrations.

4

Sociolinguistic methodology and the identification of speakers' voices in legal proceedings[1]

James Milroy

The work that has so far been carried out on linguistics and the law has been, broadly speaking, of two kinds. The first kind has been concerned with the difficulties experienced by the ordinary citizen in understanding the language used by lawyers and judges in court and is represented by the work of O'Barr (see O'Barr, 1981 and references cited therein). Active research into this field has been carried out mainly in the USA (e.g. in the Law and Language Project of Duke University directed by O'Barr) and may have been largely motivated by the acknowledged cultural pluralism of that country and the problems of minority linguistic groups. In Britain there does not seem to have been as much active research into this particular area, although similar problems of cultural and linguistic diversity are now present (see e.g. Furnborough *et al.*, 1982).

Research into the language attitudes of the professions (law, medicine, dentistry, civil service, journalism) would, however, be of the greatest interest. In some professions there is an ancient tradition of linguistic obscurity that can be justified on various grounds, usually those of technical precision and clarity. Legal proceedings, for instance, were conducted in French until after 1362, even though the majority of the people of England had never been native speakers of French. Writers on medicine before 1600 who dared to write in English rather than Latin still had to preface their work

APPLIED SOCIOLINGUISTICS
ISBN: 0-12-701220-6

with an apologia, as it was thought that forbidden knowledge of private bodily functions should not be imparted to the lewd and vulgar populace. A famous work on paediatrics (Thomas Phaire's *The Boke of Chyldren*, 1545) strongly and memorably attacks the Latinism of medicine:

> . . . how long wold they haue the people ignorant? why grutche they phisyke to come forth in Englyshe? Woulde they haue no man to know but onely they?
> (ed. Neale and Wallis, 1955)

In subsequent centuries, the professions have continued to build up an extensive vocabulary based on Greek and Latin that is not immediately accessible to the layman. This can be seen as part of the functional elaboration in vocabulary involved in the long-term process of language standardization. It is, however, clear, in the law at least, that some difficulties may arise from this historical fact: O'Barr recommends that a training in language matters should be part of the curriculum of law-schools, and Gumperz (1976) reports that efforts have been made in the USA to implement this kind of recommendation.

The second area in which linguistics has been relevant to the law is in the identification of voices on tape-recordings. In the USA, controversy has raged on the matter of "voice-prints", i.e. spectrograms or other visually interpretable print-outs of a person's speech. It has been claimed that "voice-prints" are as individually identifiable as finger-prints (indeed the use of the term "voice-print" instead of "spectrogram" is intended to imply this). Without wishing to deny that phonetic instruments may be of value in forensic matters, most linguistics and phoneticians are very sceptical of the strongest claims that have been made for "voice-prints", and generally feel that such claims take advantage of the wishful thinking and credulity of those who are not experts in phonetics and linguistics. One expert, Peter Ladefoged, has appeared in a large number of court cases and has examined thousands of spectrograms: he states (1975, p. 187) that claims for the accuracy of voice-prints are greatly exaggerated. One reason for this is that (as Bolinger, 1980, p. 112, points out) "voiceprint identification is not refined enough to establish guilt" (although it may help to establish innocence): indeed visual print-outs merely substitute visual expertise for aural expertise on the part of the analyst. The phonetician is likely to be wrong part of the time whether he uses visual or aural techniques, and there is at present no obvious way of determining absolutely whether instrumental methods of voice-identification constitute an advance on the refined ears of phoneticians. A second reason, which is partly connected with the first, is ultimately statistical. No one can define a finite population from which the data-sample to be analysed is drawn; therefore, there is no way of knowing how many individuals have similar vocal characteristics. If "voice-prints" were as reliable as finger-prints, this might not be a serious problem. As it is, this is far from the case. One prominent forensic phonetician (Hollien, as reported in Bolinger, 1980, p. 112) claims that voiceprinting is "a fraud being perpetrated upon the American public and the courts of the United States".

It has been necessary to consider voice-printing briefly, even though the court-case that forms the basis of this chapter made no use of spectrographic evidence. The claims made in favour of voice-prints exemplify very clearly the natural human desire to be absolutely certain about matters in which certainty may not always be possible. They also demonstrate a tendency to be naïvely optimistic about advances in instrumental techniques. The most important point for the linguist, however, is that these claims, together with more impressionistic claims made by witnesses in court, demonstrate the general ignorance (shared by the public and some experts alike) of the complexity of language. To consider voice-quality alone, it is known that the voice-quality of an individual can vary from time to time for a number of reasons, from the effect of emotional or sexual arousal, throat-infections, hangovers and menstrual periods, for example (see, in general, Laver, 1980). This takes no account of a host of other ways in which an individual's speech can vary. But this general gullibility seems to have the effect of motivating people to try to establish *guilt* rather than to prove innocence (or at least fail to establish guilt). In the case to be discussed, the linguistic evidence fails to establish guilt; yet, the accused was convicted on the unsubstantiated opinions of witnesses on voice-identification (the expert evidence that was offered was set aside). The procedures used by the police and in court in this case may also seem rather surprising to the reader: the law may well reply that these procedures were perfectly correct in law; yet, it can also be said that in this case certain evidence taken into account should have been ruled inadmissible for reasons known to field linguists and phoneticians, but not (apparently) to the law.

Dialect variation

The case to be discussed (Regina *vs* Mullan, tried in Belfast in 1980) depended on voice identification by witnesses. Positive identification was taken to suggest guilt, and the jury's decision (by a majority verdict) that the accused was guilty was based mainly on the fact that several witnesses had sworn under oath that the voice (or voices) heard on several tape-recordings was/were one and the same voice, and that the voice was that of the accused. Ladefoged writes (1975: 189), on the basis of his forensic experience:

it is completely irresponsible to say, as I have heard witnesses testify in court,

"The voice on the recording is that of the accused and could be that of no other speaker".

We cannot know how many other speakers in the population may have voices so similar to that of an accused person that they sound virtually identical on rather poor tape-recordings.

For the linguist, however, the Mullan case does not involve only the identification of voices by differentiating voice-qualities: it raises quite clearly the question of dialect and accent differences between speakers. Expert dialect evidence has been in the news in recent years, especially in the notorious "Yorkshire Ripper" case. At one stage, the voice on a tape sent to the police was identified by the dialectologist, Stanley Ellis, as being from the Sunderland area. The fact that this tape turned out to be a hoax should not blind the police and public to the potential value of expert evidence in such cases.

It is common knowledge that there is considerable dialectal diversity within the British Isles, a much greater diversity than within the United States. There can often be some clear differences between the speech of two places that are only a few miles apart, and of course gross and obvious differences over a distance of forty miles or so (compare Liverpool with Manchester, Leeds with Teesside). It is obvious that in a legal case where two accents are grossly different (say, a suspect's London accent and a Manchester accent on a tape-recording), the police would not normally pursue the case, as they would know that no one could be persuaded to believe that the two accents were those of the same speaker. However, when two accents sound broadly similar to the layman (but showing consistent differences that can be specified by the expert), it may be that some people do not notice the differences. On the other hand, they may be aware of differences in a vague way. In the Mullan case we are dealing with two different accents, and the case raises the rather interesting issue that people may be aware of an accent different (defence counsel seems to have been well aware of it), but may be prepared in court to dismiss this possibly subliminal awareness for various reasons.

The Mullan Case

Seamus Mullan, of Garvagh, Co. Londonderry in Northern Ireland, was sent for trial in the summer of 1980 accused of blackmail. He was convicted and sentenced to ten years in prison. The circumstances leading to his conviction read rather oddly, but the conviction depended on two vital pieces of evidence:
(1) that the voice of Mullan was the same as that of an armed and masked

man who broke into the home of the Barton family of Kilrea (near Garvagh) on the evening of 7 September 1979, that the masked man's voice was the same as that of Mullan overheard being questioned in a police station, and that Mullan's voice (and that of the masked man) was/were also the same as that of a telephone caller or callers (tape-recorded at the Barton's home, later in September) who made five threatening phone-calls demanding a large amount of money (£45 000) from the Barton family:

(2) that, apart from evidence on voice identification, Mullan was the man who made the fifth telephone call, as he was alleged to have been observed apparently making a call from a telephone-box in Draperstown, Co. Londonderry, at the same time as the fifth threatening phone-call was received by the Barton family (about 3 p.m. on 21 September 1979).

It is not clear how Mullan became a suspect in the first place. Although the case was not defined as a terrorist case (it was tried by an ordinary jury, as terrorist intimidation of juries and witnesses was not considered to be an issue), there were sectarian overtones. Repeatedly, according to the transcript and in the tape-recordings, the Barton family are told that they have been singled out for this treatment because they are Catholics and that co-religionists of theirs have been held responsible for killing members of the security forces. The odd thing about this is that Mullan is also a Catholic.

However this may be, the Barton family reported to the police the intrusion by the masked man. On 23 September (*after the threatening telephone-calls had also been received*), members of the family were invited to attend the police station, where they overheard a man being questioned on a different matter in the next room. The man was Mullan, and without seeing him, Mrs. and Miss Barton in response to the policeman's question identified his voice as that of the masked man. At the same time, the police had made a tape-recording of their interrogation of Mullan, and this recording was subsequently made available for linguistic analysis.

Given that there have been severe misgivings about visual identification of suspects (even when they are presented in an identification parade), it is odd that evidence on voice identification of the above kind can be admitted. One might suppose that visual identification is actually easier than voice identi-fication, as many people have voices of similar timbre. The least that one might expect in such circumstances is that an array of similar voices should be presented and that witnesses should be asked to pick out the voice of the miscreant from that array. Clearly, two distressed people might have been predisposed to identify Mullan's voice as that of the masked man. They would be anxious to help in apprehending the criminal. Unfortunately for the defence, Mrs Barton was the first witness called at the trial. She swore under oath that the accused's voice was the same as that of the masked man.

Although the defence barrister (R. A. Ferguson, Q.C.) suggested that she might have been mistaken, he could not go too far in his cross-examination, as the witness was very distressed. A strong cross-examination might well have increased the jury's sympathy for the witness and alienated any possible sympathy for the accused.

Miss Maureen Barton was then questioned, and her examination included details of the five threatening telephone calls which were received between 18 and 21 September, more than ten days after the intrusion by the masked man. The important point to note here is that Miss Barton testified that the voice on call 1 was the same as the masked man and that all five telephone calls were by the same person (the masked man). With reference to the first call, the court transcript reads thus:

Q. Did you recognize the voice in that?
A. After a very, very short conversation with the telephone caller I immediately recognized his voice as the man who had come into our kitchen armed and masked. I have no doubt in my mind that it was exactly the same voice, exactly.

Miss Barton was also certain that the voice on call 2 was the same as the voice on call 1.

It was exactly the same voice as the voice of the caller who had rung me four hours earlier, exactly the same voice. I have no doubt in my mind, the fear and the terror that that voice put into me.

Later, prosecuting counsel asked the witness what she would say if it were suggested to her that the phone calls were by more than one person. Although court transcripts do not indicate changes in voice quality, it is clear that Miss Barton's response was highly emotional.

Listen the voice that was in our kitchen and the voice on those telephone calls is from the same person. That voice it has haunted me. It does haunt me and I know that for the rest of my life I will never forget that voice. The fear and the terror I will never forget it. It was the same voice.

The tape recordings, when analysed, indicate that Miss Barton is mistaken in certain important particulars: the speaker on call 2 can hardly be the same as the speaker on call 1 (see further below). It is obvious, however, that it would have been extremely difficult for the defence to cast much doubt on her evidence without alienating a jury's sympathy. In fact, the defence believed that they had a trump card. Hoping, no doubt, that expert voice identification might help to establish guilt, the police had called in Dr J. R. Baldwin of the Department of Phonetics and Linguistics, University College London. Dr Baldwin had analysed the tape-recording of Mullan in the police station and the recordings of the telephone calls. He was prepared to testify that the voice on calls 1, 3, 4 and 5 differed from the one in call 2, and that only the caller in call 2 had a voice similar to Mullan's. In other words, Baldwin's evidence tended to establish innocence, and not guilt. The police made this evidence available to the defence, who hoped that it would be sufficient to cast doubt on Mullan's guilt, as indeed it is.

Before Baldwin was called, however, many witnesses had testified that there was only one telephone caller and that his voice was that of Mullan. Detective Inspector Houston, for example, had listened to the two calls recorded on 18 September. In answer to the question "Did you recognize the voice of anyone on that tape?", the officer replied that he recognized the voice of Mullan. Furthermore, the prosecution then established that Detective Inspector Houston was already familiar with that voice: thus, it was implied that his opinion was reliable. Other witnesses replied that Mullan's voice and that of the caller were "one and the same", or in words to that effect.

There is another peculiar circumstance, to which I have already referred. At the time of phone call no. 5 (about 3 p.m. on 21 September), Mullan had been observed apparently making a call from a telephone kiosk in Draperstown. A Mr Carron, who was a soldier in plain clothes, had been deputed by the police to observe Mullan's movements on that day and testified to this effect. Oddly enough, the voice on call no. 5 appears to be the same as the voice on calls 1, 3 and 4, and that is the voice that cannot reasonably be shown to be that of Mullan (as we shall see).

The police had in fact consulted *two* expert witnesses, Dr Baldwin, and Dr Peter Roach of Leeds University. For some reason, Dr Roach was not called as a witness, but it is difficult to believe that his opinion could have been substantially different from that of Baldwin. The latter testified that only the voice on call no. 2 was similar to Mullan's, and that he was not sure that even that voice was Mullan's. In cross-questioning, the prosecution managed to suggest that Baldwin's evidence was not as reliable as those of the other witnesses, and the jury apparently gave it little weight in reaching their verdict.

There are two reasons why it is a very serious matter that Mullan should have been convicted on evidence that is based solely on the *unsubstantiated* opinions of witnesses on voice identification. First, it is not as easy as the layman believes to identify voices on the telephone or on poor tape-recordings. Second, apart altogether from differences of voice-quality, there may be *accent* differences between speakers. These differences are systematic and not random. In this case, it is odd that the witnesses had not noticed that there were two different accents on the telephone calls: it is of course possible that they had noticed subliminally, but had underestimated the importance of this difference.

Identifying voices on the telephone and on recordings

Any field-linguist who has collected and analysed large amounts of conversational talk from different people (as in our own research reported in
Milroy, 1978 etc.) will know that the limitations of human memory are such
that it is difficult to identify who is speaking at any given point. People who
are all from the same area and social group speak in a similar accent and also
have broad similarities of voice quality and intonation. For instance, the
habitual posture of the larynx is similar in a local population and varies in a
general way from region to region: some accents have "raised larynx" voice,
others may have a lowered larynx. Some accents (e.g. Belfast) have nasal-
ization, others (e.g. Liverpool) are denasalized (see, e.g. Wells: 1982,
pp. 91–3).

In sociolinguistic fieldwork and analytic practice (in which 50–100 voices,
or more, are involved), it is important for the linguist to listen to his tapes
immediately after they have been collected and make a note of who is
speaking at different points on the recordings, solely because it is impossible
to distinguish reliably on voice quality alone. In our own research (J. and L.
Milroy, 1978; L. Milroy, 1980; J. Milroy, 1981), we have followed this
practice, as (by definition) all speakers, being from the same area and of the
same social group, have broadly similar accents. Part of the point of the
research was to show that within this homogeneous population, quite subtle
but consistent differences of accent could nevertheless be demonstrated. In
prior identification of speakers, however, we could not quantify accent
differences, and we could not rely on voice quality (except in differentiating
male from female, old from young), as we knew that speakers of similar age
and the same sex would usually have similar voice-qualities. When (as was
usual) five or six voices were recorded on the same tape, we relied, not on
voice-quality, but on short-term memory of the field-work itself, memory of
the content of the conversations and the views expressed by the different
speakers. If we had delayed in this work of identification, long-term memory
of who was speaking at different points would have become less reliable, and
memory of differing voices would only have helped in rare cases of extreme
and obvious differences (the lady who had no teeth, for instance, was always
easily identifiable).

In any situation in which visual cues are absent, listeners rely on a large
number of factors besides voice-quality. In particular, listeners may identify
a telephone caller by their knowledge of the kind of business that the caller is
engaged in, by memory of topics of conversation enjoyed by the caller and
by shared knowledge in general. In practice, however, telephone callers
usually identify themselves immediately. There are good reasons why a

ritual of identification is customary in telephoning. The visual cues by which we normally identify people are absent, and many people share similarities of voice quality and accent. Furthermore, there may be distortion on the line, and many distinctive acoustic features of voice are cut out on the telephone. A person's voice does not sound the same on the telephone as it does in real life. Thus, it is normal for the caller to identify himself/herself immediately. If, for any reason he does not do so, it is quite likely that the listener will enquire as to his/her identity with some question such as "Is that George speaking?" If it were really a simply matter to identify a telephone caller, there would be no need for these "opening sequences".

However, as Brown (1980) points out, listeners are conditioned by their *expectations* as to who is likely to be telephoning much more than by idiosyncratic differences of voice. When the telephone rings, the caller may literally be anyone in the world, but everyone knows that there are greater or lesser probabilities as to who is calling. Thus, if the telephone rings in my office there is an immediate presumption that the caller is telephoning on some matter of professional business. He or she is therefore most likely to be someone in the university who has academic business to discuss with me; he is less likely to be a professional colleague from another university, and I shall be very surprised if he turns out to be someone (now living in Canada) with whom I was friendly twenty or thirty years ago. In the Mullan case, it is clear that the listener's expectations had been narrowed down to such a degree that they were convinced that the caller could only be one person: the armed and masked man who had broken into their house. Their expectation would naturally be that there would be only one caller identical to the masked man: there would be no reasonable expectation that anyone else would telephone to blackmail them. Thus, it should be understood by courts that witnesses' expectations in such cases will lead them to answer as these witnesses did. It would be surprising if they actually testified otherwise. As it is, their testimony is only of value if their opinions are backed up (or at least not contradicted) by objective analysis of the recordings.

Before we proceed to our linguistic analysis, it should be noted that the witnesses' identification of Mullan's voice "live" in the police station is also subject to the same reservations. Here they had been led to expect that there was quite a high probability that the person being questioned was the masked man: they would reasonably presume that the police would not ask them to identify the voice of anyone not believed to be the man. It is clearly unfair to narrow down the possibilities in such a case to only one voice, as no one can define the size of the population who may have similar voices (there could be tens of thousands of people who have voices and accents similar to Mullan). To hold a voice identity parade which narrows down the possibilities to, say, ten voices might be judged a fairer procedure provided that all ten voices were similar in voice quality and accent. It is extremely worrying that voice identification evidence of this kind, obtained surreptitiously and without the accused's knowledge or permission, should be admissible in any court of justice. There is a very high probability of wrong identification.

Linguistic analysis of the evidence

The tape-recorded evidence consists of two recordings made of Mullan's voice at the police station and five recordings made of the anonymous telephone calls. Of these, the police station recordings are quite short (amounting to five or six minutes in all) and of poor quality. They are not good enough for instrumental analysis. The first three telephone calls are much longer (about eight to ten minutes each); call 4 is shorter and call 5 is the shortest of all. Dr Baldwin analysed all these tapes: in response to a question by defence counsel (R. A. Ferguson, Q.C.) he answered as follows:

> . . . I came to the conclusion that the suspect's speech was least like the caller on the four telephone calls (viz. calls 1, 3, 4, 5) and most like the speaker on call 2, but that there were significant differences between the suspect and the speaker on call 2 . . .

In this, Baldwin was absolutely correct, and his conclusions should have been enough to cast considerable doubt on the purely impressionistic views of other witnesses. However, it does not seem to have been made clear in the questioning that Baldwin's views were based on *facts* about systematic differences in voice and accent that had been analysed by an expert phonetician, not on unsubstantiated opinion. No substantive analysis of these differences seems to have been presented at the trial, nor does the jury seem to have been instructed that objective expert evidence based on facts cannot be lightly set aside.

Cross-questioning by the prosecution concentrated on suggesting that Baldwin's opinion was no more reliable than other witnesses, and the prosecution seems to have convinced a majority of the jury. Unfortunately, at one point, Baldwin answered a particular question in a way that the prosecution was able to exploit. In answer to the question: "And the accent was similar in all of the telephone messages?", he said "Yes, that is correct". A preferable answer would be: "No, that is not correct". The witness could have explained that, to a layman, that the accents might appear to be similar, but that – despite these similarities – there are clear, consistent and systematic differences between call 2 and the other calls, which are obvious to a phonetician, dialectologist or sociolinguist, and particularly obvious to a linguist familiar with Northern Irish accents.

My analysis of the recordings used the methods pioneered by Labov (1966) in New York City, and now familiar in British sociolinguistics (used by Trudgill, 1974, in Norwich; Macaulay, 1977, in Glasgow; Milroy and Milroy, 1978 etc., in Belfast). These methods, as is well known, crucially involve isolating from the great mass of talk a series of recurrent linguistic variables. These are usually phonological or morphological (e.g. as in Trudgill's study of deletion of the 3rd person singular inflexion in present tense verbs: *he go* as against *he goes*). A number of *variants* of particular variables are then identified. Sometimes, two variants are sufficient, as in the Belfast variable (th): this measures presence or absence of the consonant [ð] in a set of words of the type: *mother, rather, bother*; in other cases, several variants can be identified, as in the Belfast variable [a], which ranges from low-front [a] to central [ä] to low-back [a] to mid-back-round [ɔ], in words like *that, grass, have, man* (Milroy and Milroy, 1977, 1978).

The Labov methodology also depends on quantification. Large numbers of tokens are counted, and it is usually found that the incidence of particular variants differs for individual speakers and groups of speakers (classified according to social class, region, age or sex). Most people associate Labov's methodology with differentiating speakers according to social class; however, it has been successfully used to differentiate individuals and groups within the same social class and region. Milroy and Milroy (1977, 1978; see L. Milroy 1980; J. Milroy, 1981) studied a population in three close-knit areas of inner-city Belfast, in which it could be presumed that all persons sampled had roughly the same regional and social background (i.e. to the layman their accents would appear to be very similar indeed, if not identical). Even in this project, clear and significant differences were repeatedly shown between groups of speakers classified according to age, sex and area of the city: furthermore, all *individual* speakers had different quantitative scores on each of the ten variables studied, except in cases where a few speakers shared a 100% score on one variable out of the ten (L. Milroy, 1981, pp. 204–5).

Quantitative work of this kind depends on a knowledge of linguistics that the average person does not possess. In general, it depends on the knowledge that a language is a highly complex phenomenon that is sytematically structured, and that variation within a language is also largely systematic and not random. It is, of course, better known that phonological differences are *indexical* (Abercrombie, 1967); in particular, everyone knows that specific phonological differences are indices of different regional accents, and that you can guess where a person comes from by his accent: that is to say that certain variables mark regional differences (as in the Mullan case). However, phonological differences can also be markers of social class, age and sex of speaker, or of variation according to the situational context in which a person is speaking.

In a country where regional dialect differences are marked and where specific phonological variables can readily be identified (e.g. the glottal stop in Glasgow – Macaulay, 1977; /h/-dropping in Norwich – Trudgill, 1974), the quantitative methodology is highly promising as a means of demonstrating that, in some particular case, two recorded voices are probably *not* those of the same speaker. For example, if over a series of variables, one recorded voice consistently had scores markedly different from another voice, it might well be unreasonable to conclude that they were the same speaker. In the Mullan case, the differences on prominent variables as between Mullan's voice and that of telephone caller 1, 3, 4 and 5 is enormous: the incidence is 100% in one case to zero in the other. This establishes as a matter of verifiable fact (not a matter of opinion) that the two accents are completely different. I shall return to this point below.

I am not aware that the quantitative methodology has been used before in cases of this kind. In the present state of our knowledge, it would appear to be more capable of being applied forensically than are instrumental techniques. Notice that even if instrumental techniques were more advanced than they are, it would still be possible for one analyst to *select* from the data certain "voice-prints" that might tend to suggest that two speakers were the same, and another analyst to select from the *same* data other "voice-prints" that might indicate the opposite. The quantitative methodology, however, requires that, for given variables, *all* the relevant data *must* be accounted for: the analyst is not permitted to ignore relevant data that might not suit his argument.

Finally, the selection of variables depends crucially on the linguist's prior knowledge of regional variants in the area to be studied. In a case like the present one, this means that the linguist should know before he begins what features are likely to be diagnostic in differentiating Ulster accents; he should have a good professional knowledge of Ulster dialect. We consider this point more fully in the next section.

Ulster dialect

Quantitative sociolinguistics of the type pioneered by Labov has always depended on isolating a small number of variables to be studied from a very large number of possible variables. In New York, for example, Labov studied post-vocalic (r), i.e. presence or absence of /r/ in all words of the types represented by *guard, water*; (th), i.e. variation between /d/ and /ð/ in

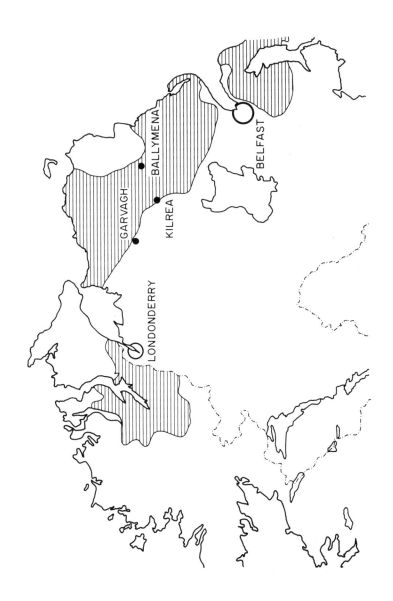

GARVAGH

BALLYMENA

KILREA

BELFAST

LONDONDERRY

the first consonants of words like *this, that, there*; and three other variables. Depending on his prior knowledge of New York speech, he selected those variables that he believed might be diagnostic of social differences and which were also likely to occur frequently on the tapes. There might have been many other "sounds" in New York speech that would either not occur frequently or not show as much variation. My selection of variables in this case also depended on similar factors:

(1) (most importantly) prior knowledge of Ulster dialects, which enabled me to isolate those features that would be diagnostic of regional differences and ignore those features that might be more similar as between two regional dialects;

(2) relative frequency of incidence of particular variables. Thus, variation between the glottal stop and [t] was very frequent (in words like *not, later*)

As I have already indicated, the differences of accent between the tape-recordings of Mullan and the anonymous speaker on telephone calls 1, 3, 4 and 5 are considerable and they are easily identified by a trained analyst. It is clearly desirable, however, that the analyst should have prior knowledge of the features that are likely to distinguish different *Ulster* accents: an expert from outside Ulster may, in the first place, notice those features that do not differentiate these accents (e.g. fronted pronunciations of /u/, which are common to almost all Ulster dialects, but not found in most of England); it may therefore take such an expert some time to identify the variables that are diagnostic, and he may have less confidence in his conclusions than an analyst familiar with variations in Ulster.

Dialectologists (Gregg, 1964, 1972; Adams, 1964) have traditionally distinguished two broad dialect areas in the northern counties of Ireland. The first, which comprises North Down, Central and North Antrim, North Co. Londonderry and a large part of East Donegal, are Ulster Scots in type: the Ulster Scots areas in fact extend more widely than is indicated on the map on page 63 (based on Gregg, 1973) and include the North-East corner of Ulster. In the core Ulster Scots areas, the most extreme rural dialects are barely distinguishable from those of Galloway and Ayrshire (see Gregg, 1964; J. Milroy, in press). Most of the area west and south of the Antrim and Derry Scots areas (as marked on the map) is known as the mid-Ulster (Adams, 1964) or the Ulster Anglo-Irish (Gregg, 1972) dialect area. Although most Ulster dialects are affected by Scots, there is a sharp dialect boundary between Ulster Scots and Mid-Ulster dialects, and many features of pronunciation distinguish them. These are discussed by Adams and Gregg, and those relevant to Belfast English are listed in J. Milroy (1981, p. 25). The following major differences are relevant in this case:

(1) The historic short vowels /ɛ, a, ɔ/, before voiceless stops (as in *pet, pat, pot*) tend to be long or half-long in Ulster Scots areas, clearly distinguished from one another. In Mid-Ulster they are noticeably short, and may merge or overlap in various patterns. In particular, the Ulster Scots vowel in words like *cot, pot, stop, rock*, is [ɔ˙] whereas the mid-Ulster vowel is unrounded and advanced to [ä].

(2) Before velar stops and the velar nasal, there is a marked tendency for historic short /a/ to be raised to [ɛ] in Ulster Scots. Thus *back, bag, bang* sound like *beck, beg, beng*. This is found to a certain extent in Belfast, but is not generally characteristic of Mid-Ulster, west of Lough Neagh.

(3) The glottal stop for post-vocalic [t] is very characteristic of Antrim and Derry Scots, and has a much lower incidence outside of Ulster Scots areas. Sometimes, in Ulster Scots, the [t] is present, but has strong glottal reinforcement

In other possible situations, other variables might be relevant: e.g. Belfast dialect and many of those to the south and west fail to distinguish between /w/ as in *wine* and /hw/ as in *whine*. It is not known at present how far north of Belfast this merger extends. In the tapes of the Mullan case, all speakers recorded distinguish between /w/ and /hw/; therefore, there may also be quite fine phonetic differences that we have not studied. It is not necessary to go this far, as the differences between Mullan's speech and that of telephone caller 1, 3, 4, 5 are perfectly clearly established on two variables which show gross phonetic differences. Mullans' speech is Mid-Ulster, that of telephone caller 1, 3, 4 and 5 is Ulster Scots.

Recall that Mullan is from Garvagh and the Barton family from Kilrea. Both these places are at or near the dialect boundary as defined by Gregg. It would be unwise to be too precise about this boundary, but it is quite clear that telephone-caller 1, 3, 4 and 5 is from a place within the Ulster Scots area. My opinion is that he is from an area well within this boundary: somewhere east or north of Kilrea, possibly from the area around Ballymena, Ballymoney and Coleraine. Mrs and Miss Barton have mid-Ulster accents, but Miss Barton's brother Joe (who answered some of the calls) has an accent that is more Scots in type. It is, however, less heavily Scots than that of the caller. It happens that the mid-Ulster accent is spreading at the expense of Ulster Scots (Gregg, 1972), and this sex differentiation within the Barton family demonstrates very nicely the tendency for male speakers to be more conservative in accent and for females to adhere to more innovative forms.

The variables

The most obvious diagnostic in this case is incidence of the glottal stop [ʔ] or glottalized /t/, [ʔt], in three positions:

(1) in final position in words of the type: *not, it, what*;
(2) medially between vowels in words of the type: *later, butter*;
(3) in other post-vocalic positions, e.g. before the consonant in the frequently occurring word *Patsy* (the Christian name of Mr Barton senior).

The statistics in this case are easy to report. The incidence of glottalization in these positions in the accent of caller 1, 3, 4, 5 is 100% (about 120 tokens); in the accent of Mullan (15 tokens) the incidence is zero; in the accent of telephone caller 2 (40 tokens), the incidence is also zero.

Typical examples (from call no. 1) are [paʔtsi, geʔ, ɪʔ, weʔt, nɔ ʔ t, nɔ ʔ , hwäʔ] for *Patsy, get, it, wait, not* (twice), *not, what* (twice). All tokens of /t/ that can be glottalized or replaced by a glottal stop *are* glottalized or replaced by a glottal stop. Mullan, as recorded in the police station *never* uses glottalization or a glottal stop in these environments: *not* and *what* are [nät, hwät], except that final /t/ is sometimes flapped (as would be expected in mid-Ulster speech), when it is followed by a vowel in connected speech, thus: [hwär]. The same applies to caller no. 2. Caller 1, 3, 4, 5 never uses the flap: being Ulster Scots, it is not to be expected that he would.

In articulatory, auditory and acoustic terms, the phonetic difference between /t/ and /ʔ/ is gross. In articulatory features, they can be said to differ in all features but one (+ stop). It is inconceivable that a single speaker can consistently maintain such a difference over a stretch of talk.

Among the several vowel differences that differentiate the speakers, the most frequently occurring diagnostic variable is (ɔ), measuring the incidence of [ɔˑ] as against [ä] before voiceless stops in words of the type *what, clock, stop*. Again, the phonetic differences are numerous:

[ɔ] can be described as:

+back
+low
+mid
+round
+long

whereas [ä], a low central to front vowel, is:

−back
+low
−mid
−round
−long

The two vowels can be said to differ in four features out of five.

Again the statistics are decisive. Mullan and telephone caller 2 *always* use [ä], whereas caller 1, 3, 4, 5 *always* uses [ɔ]. Thus Mullan has [hwät, stäp, kläk] for *what, stop, clock*; caller 2 has [nät, hwät] for *not, what*; caller 1, 3, 4, 5, however, has [stɔp, drɔp, n ɔ ʔ, gɔʔ, hwɔʔ] for *stop, drop, not, got, what*. Mullan uses the word *stopped* four times in quick succession: it is always [stäpt].

These variables alone are convincing, as they both have scores of 100% for caller 1, 3, 4, 5 against scores of zero for Mullan and for caller 2. They demonstrate that we are dealing with two quite different accents. But there are other distinguishing variables also – of a kind which are predictable to the student of Ulster dialects. Telephone speaker 1, 3, 4, 5 consistently raises /a/ to [æ] or [ɛ] before velar consonants: thus, he says [kəntrɛktər, kəntɛkt] for *contractor, contact*. Telephone speaker 2 also uses relevant words (e.g. *contact, attack*), and does *not* raise /a/ to [æ] or [ɛ]. Mullan has a palatal glide after initial [k] in the word *Kelly's* (repeated): this is a well-known mid-Ulster feature. Caller 1, 3, 4, 5 has no such glide in relevant words such as *Catholic*. Caller 1, 3, 4, 5 also has Ulster Scots lengthening of most short vowels before /p, t, k/; Mullan does not have this lengthening; Caller 1, 3, 4, 5 has a relatively high (Scots) monophthong [e ·], in words like *wait, days*; Mullan has a lower vowel. There are other differences.

It is not a matter of opinion that these two accents are different: the differences are audible, verifiable and consistently maintained. When these differences are demonstrated, a court should be willing to accept that since the accent difference between Ulster Scots and Mid-Ulster is of the same order as differences between Newcastle and Leeds, and much greater than the differences between Leeds and Sheffield, then the likelihood that Mullan is the same speaker as caller 1, 3, 4, 5 is so minimal as to be not worth considering. It is not even remotely likely that a brilliant mimic could maintain these differences consistently (there would be variation and some "mistakes"). In any case, this hypothetical mimic would presumably have no reason to alter his accent completely in call 2.

An experienced phonetics teacher will know that speakers who do not normally use glottal stops cannot easily be persuaded to produce them in isolated words, let alone use them in prescribed environments in a long stretch of talk. It would probably be a simple matter to demonstrate that a speaker like Mullan is unable to utter the sentence "What a lot of little bottles" with glottal stops in the "right" places. This kind of evidence could be obtained, but in this case it was not.

Conclusions

My two major conclusions concern the status of linguistic evidence in cases of voice identification, and the potential uses of linguistics in forensic matters.

As we have seen, Miss Barton testified first that telephone caller 1 was the masked intruder who had threatened the family. It is quite possible that she was correct in this. There is no recording that is known for certain to be that of the masked man; therefore, his speech cannot be analysed and compared with that of Mullan and the telephone speakers. However, if caller 1 was the masked man, then Mullan could not be the masked man, as caller 1 cannot reasonably be said to be Mullan. Miss Barton further testified that telephone caller 2 was the same speaker as telephone caller 1, and furthermore that all the telephone calls were by the same speaker. It is inconceivable that any linguistic analysis could support her opinion. In short, whereas Miss Barton expressed an unsubstantiated opinion influenced by certain expectations, a linguistic analysis is based on audible and verifiable differences between accents. Furthermore, it shows that the differences are not merely random variations in pronunciation of occasional words, but that they are consistent and systematic. The details analysed point to structural differences between dialects that are of a high order of generality and abstraction: for example, the Ulster Scots vowel-length system (as evidence in calls 1, 3, 4, 5) differs from the Mid-Ulster one not merely in one particular vowel, but throughout the whole vowel system. Abstract systematic differences of this kind are never obvious to ordinary speakers; they can be described only by trained phonologists who have carefully observed the different systems.

It would appear, however, than an expert witness can still be said to be expressing an "opinion" if he concludes that the demonstrable accent difference implies that different *speakers* are involved. But this opinion is of much greater value than an unsubstantiated opinion, as the probability that an ordinary speaker can switch from one non-standard accent to a perfect imitation of another is infinitesimal. Clearly, in such a case, it should be incumbent upon the prosecution to prove that the accused is a mimic of unparalleled talents. As for caller no. 2: his accent is similar to Mullan's. There are some general indications that he is *not* Mullan, and a closer phonetic analysis might tend to support this.

We must conclude that caller 1, 3, 4, 5 is not Mullan, even though Mullan was observed to try to make a telephone call at the same time as call no. 5 was received. In call no. 5, glottal stops and other Scots characteristics are as prominent as they are in calls 1, 3 and 4. It is a great pity that only one linguistic expert was called in this case, and that the prosecution managed to imply that his evidence was not conclusive. If others had been called in addition, the linguistic evidence – compelling as it is – could hardly have been ignored. Indeed longer recordings could have been made of Mullan's speech and linguistic tests administered to him. These too could have helped.

It follows from all this that linguistic evidence of various kinds may be more helpful in legal proceedings than has been realized, but specifically in differentiating voices, not in proving identity of voices. We cannot entirely blame the legal profession or the juries for being unable to weigh up the linguistic evidence if we are slow to come forward to help them, even though juries have been willing to believe quite extraordinary things, e.g. that virtually inaudible tape-recordings are recordings of the voice of some accused person (J. Anthony, personal communication). Similarly, it is odd that (as in this case) very doubtful voice identification procedures can be used by the police.

In the United States the role of expert linguistic evidence has been more readily recognized than in the UK. In one recent case, the "Black English case" reported by Labov (1982), there has been a significant breakthrough as far as applied sociolinguistics is concerned. A number of linguists of different persuasions were all able to testify to the effect that BEV (Black English Vernacular) differed radically in a number of systematic ways from Standard English. Their evidence was in this case decisive: probably for the first time, jurists have recognized that dialects differ from one another at an abstract systematic level, and, further, that these differences have specifiable social and educational consequences. The Mullan case, it seems to me, is no less significant than the Black English case. It is important that the consequences of conscious or unconscious discrimination against non-standard dialects should be understood (as in the "Black English case"), but in a different way, it is equally important that an individual should be protected from conviction when that conviction is mainly based on mis-identification of his voice. However we view it, there must be many potential legal cases where linguists of both the "armchair" and the "field" varieties can be of more help than they have been to date. It is somewhat unedifying for linguists to debate so-called general principles (e.g. whether or not linguists should consent to be expert witnesses) when it can be specified exactly how useful they can be in cases like the present one. It should certainly be emphasized that they can often show that speakers are different, but cannot necessarily show that the voices on two recordings are the same.

Postscript

At the time of writing (September–October 1982) Seamus Mullan has served two years of his ten-year sentence. Believing that he had been wrongly convicted, Mullan attempted to draw public attention to his case by going on hunger-strike in the autumn of 1980. Unfortunately, a number of other persons in Northern Ireland started a hunger-strike at about the same time for purely political reasons, and the publicity given to their political strike drew attention away from Mullan. Mullan's lawyers (Mr F. McNicholl and Mr R. A. Ferguson, Q.C.) promised to apply to the House of Lords for leave to re-open the case, and Mullan ended his strike. At the same time, being convinced that there had been a miscarriage of justice, the lawyers appealed publicly for assistance in uncovering new evidence that might help to cast doubt on Mullan's guilt. I offered to analyse the tapes, fully prepared to find that the differences between them were perhaps not decisive. I was horrified to discover that the taped speakers had what I know to be two radically different accents, and that the Ulster Scots accent was already evident in the first full sentence of the first call analysed (no. 1). I was completely convinced that *at least* two different speakers were involved. My report to the lawyers was submitted in January 1981. It does not seem to have been regarded as "new evidence", and leave to appeal to the House of Lords was refused.

Thus, although it is clear that Mullan was convicted and sentenced mainly as a result of misidentification of his voice, his only hope now is that he may be granted a pardon.

Whether or not Mullan actually made phone-call no. 2, at least one very unpleasant blackmailer remains at large, and the "guilty" verdict on Mullan will stand for ever.[3]

References

Abercrombie, D. (1967). "Elements of general phonetics', Edinburgh University Press, Edinburgh.

Adams, G. B. (1964). Ulster dialects. *In* "Ulster dialects: an introductory symposium", Ulster Folk Museum, 1–4, Holywood, Co. Down.

Bolinger, D. (1980). "Language: the loaded weapon", Longman, London.

Brown, R. (1980). The role of the listener's expectations in speaker recognition. "Work in progress", (Department of Linguistics, Edinburgh University) **13**, 72–8.

Furnborough, P., Jupp, T., Munns, R. and Roberts, C. (1982). Language, disadvantage and discrimination: Breaking the cycle of majority group perception.

In "Language and Ethnicity", Linguistic Minorities Project and British Association for Applied Linguistics, London.

Gregg, R. J. (1964). Scotch–Irish urban speech in Ulster. *In* "Ulster dialects: an introductory symposium", Ulster Folk Museum, 162–91, Holywood, Co. Down.

Gregg, R. J. (1972). The Scotch-Irish dialect boundaries of Ulster. *In Patterns in the folk-speech of the British Isles*, pp. 109–39. (W. F. Wakelin, ed.), Athlone Press, London.

Gumperz, J. J. (1976). Language, communication and public negotiation. *In* "Anthropology and the public interest: fieldwork and theory", (P. Sanday, ed.), Academic Press, New York and London.

Labov, W. (1966). "The social stratification of English in New York City", Center for Applied Linguistics, Washington D.C.

Labov, W. (1982). Objectivity and commitment in linguistic science: The case of the Black English trial in Ann Arbor. *Language in Society*, 11, 165–201.

Ladefoged, P. (1975). "A course in phonetics", Harcourt, Brace, Jovanovich, New York.

Laver, J. (1980). "The phonetic description of voice quality", Cambridge University Press, Cambridge.

Macaulay, R. K. S. (1977). "Language, social class and education: a Glasgow study", Edinburgh University Press, Edinburgh.

Milroy, J. (1981). "Regional accents of English: Belfast", Blackstaff, Belfast.

Milroy, J. (1982). Some correspondences between Galloway and Ulster Speech. *Scottish Language*, 1.

Milroy, J. and Milroy, L. (1977). Speech community and language variety in Belfast. Report to the Social Science Research Council, London.

Milroy J. and Milroy, L. (1978). Belfast: change and variation in an urban vernacular. *In* "Sociolinguistic patterns in British English", (P. Trudgill, ed.), Edward Arnold, London.

Milroy, L. (1980). "Language and social networks", Basil Blackwell, Oxford.

Neale, A. V. and Wallis, H. R. E. (eds) (1955). "The boke of chyldren", by Thomas Phaire. E. and S. Livingstone, Edinburgh.

O'Barr, W. M. (1981). The language of the law. *In* "Language in the U.S.A." (C. A. Ferguson and S. B. Heath, eds), Cambridge University Press, Cambridge.

Trudgill, P. (1974). "The social differentiation of English in Norwich", Cambridge University Press, Cambridge.

Wells, J. C. (1982). "Accents of English", 3 vols. Cambridge University Press, Cambridge.

Notes

Details of the case reported in this chapter are from transcripts and tape-recordings of Regina *vs* Mullan. I am extremely grateful to Mr Francis J. McNicholl, solicitor, and Mr R. A. Ferguson, Q.C., for drawing my attention to the case, and for making these materials available. In details of the case, I have used real names, except that I have used a fictitious name for the threatened family, to save them possible embarrassment. I am also grateful to Lesley Milroy for her assistance and criticisms at all points.

[2] As a result of intimidation (and in some cases murder) of juries and witnesses, the Government introduced the "Diplock Courts" for terrorist cases in 1976. Such cases are similar to the Special Courts in the Republic of Ireland except that they are tried by a single judge, sitting alone. It has been suggested that in this case, Mullan would not have been convicted by a Diplock Court, owing to the inconclusive nature of the evidence.

[3] The Mullen case was re-opened by the Secretary of State for Northern Ireland. In September 1983 the appeal was rejected on the purely technical grounds that the defence should have sought expert evidence before the trial commenced (R. A. Ferguson, Q.C., pers. comm.). Although this evidence cast doubt on Mullen's guilt, it was not considered relevant by the appeal court.

5

Good copy – bad news
The syntax and semantics of news editing

Allan Bell

Editing is the process by which one text is transformed into another text which is different in form but congruent in meaning. Editing is a very common language activity. Probably most written language undergoes editing, the only obvious exception being personal letters. Editing may be done by oneself, the original writer, or by others. It may range from the most cursory re-reading of a text, resulting in a few minor alterations, to the multiple re-workings which a poet gives to a work. Editing is the intra-language equivalent of translation or interpreting, a process by which a text in one language is transformed into another language.

The study of editing

The application of linguistic analysis to editing may serve three purposes. First, it can provide insights into the nature of linguistic structure. The editing process often results in minute changes which put language structure under the microscope in a way which usually occurs only in the arm-chair linguist's intuitions. This motivation is purely internal to the discipline of linguistics. Although it applies linguistic analysis to an object to which it is not normally applied, it is not *applied* linguistics in the sense of addressing issues beyond the discipline itself.

APPLIED SOCIOLINGUISTICS
ISBN: 0-12-701220-6

Secondly, linguistic analysis of editing may provide information on issues relating directly to language use or ability. Comparison of the edited text with the original reveals any stylistic differences between the two. We may then draw inferences concerning the motivations of author and editor (or even their identities if these are unknown) or concerning the kinds of readerships for which the texts were intended. Already such a study moves away from applied (unhyphenated) linguistics to applied socio-linguistics, since we seek here a link between linguistic facts and extra-linguistic factors.

This kind of analysis may serve, for instance, to test the authenticity or authorship of a text. In much biblical or Shakespearean scholarship, the received text is compared with possible sources, or competing versions are compared with each other, in order to establish a canonical text. Editorial overlays are peeled away to reveal the presumed original text. If authorship is in doubt, stylistic comparison with other texts is used to support arguments for or against various contenders. Where the purpose for which a text was edited is known, analysis of input and output can establish whether that purpose has been achieved. If a text has been edited for a particular readership, comparison with the original can show whether the edited version is in fact more suitable for the readership than the original. Texts are often re-written for learners, whether foreigners or children, according to read-ability formulas. The study by Davison *et al.* (1980) indicates how writing to such formulas does not necessarily produce a text suitable for the target readership.

Editing analysis constitutes a description of what copy editors do in their professional role (cf. Crystal, 1981, p. 18). Editors focus on language options. Changes they make in the original result from a focussed choice, rejecting the alternatives taken by the author. It seems justified to impute considerable significance to social factors which may correlate with an editor's choices – more than when the choice is among open alternatives, as it was for the original author.

A third purpose of editing analysis is to identify meaning differences between the original and the edited versions. Here the focus is on the content of the text rather than language and its use. We may compare, for instance, the final and rough drafts of a poem. The forms which a poet has tried but rejected can throw into sharper relief the expression finally chosen. Its significance might have been obscure or even unnoticed without the contrast of the poet's deliberate alteration.

Usually our interest in comparing the content of texts is to establish whether the edited version is a faithful rendering of the original. We acknowledge authors' rights to change the meaning of what they originally wrote, assuming they have changed their minds on the matter. Outside editors are not given the same licence. They are expected to transmit faithfully the meaning of the original text. In many cases, it may not matter if an editor takes liberties with the content of a text. If details of a story are changed in re-writing for children, it is unlikely to matter. However, more substantial changes may, even in fictional writing, remove the edited version unacceptably far from reality or from the author's original. Adding and deleting information or restructuring connections in a text can produce a misleading version (Davison *et al.*, 1980).

Most editing goes on in the realm of "facts" not fiction. In diplomacy, government and commerce, inaccurate editing (and especially inaccurate inter-language translation) can cause misunderstanding and conflict. Reports and documents are edited and summarized for busy decision-makers who lack time to read the full version. If the edited text does not faithfully represent the original, decisions may be taken on mistaken information.

The classic case of editing is news. Millions of words of news pass daily through the hands of many copy editors throughout the world. A single news text may be edited five or more times. If news editors do not faithfully pass on the content they receive, the consumers of news, both the public and decision-makers/governments, will be misinformed. While the basic analysis here is a *linguistic* comparison of texts, the findings take on a pattern only in the light of social factors. Any inaccurate editing which we find will be accountable largely in terms of the social systems and ideologies in which the editors work.

This chapter serves the second and third purposes, and the first only incidentally. Although the following editing analysis puts a number of linguistic facts in an unusual light, I will focus on the pattern of syntactic changes, and inaccurate semantic changes, made in the course of news editing. The analysis provides evidence on issues of news style and accuracy which both news professionals and society at large treat as significant.

Sample

The data used in this study are drawn from a large random sample of news collected in New Zealand in 1974. All news broadcast on the six radio stations in Auckland, New Zealand's largest city, was recorded on five days (approaching 400 000 words). Over one third of the analysable sample was international news, which the stations received from a common source. At this period, all staple international news entered New Zealand at Wellington (the capital) on the Australian Associated Press-Reuter wire from Sydney, Australia. AAP received most of its copy from Reuters, some from Associated Press and United Press International, and a little from Agence France

Presse, Tass and other agencies. In Wellington, AAP copy was received by two separate internal wire services: the New Zealand Press Association, and the General News Service of the public corporation, Radio New Zealand (Fig. 1).[1] The two public radio news networks which broadcast from Wellington, YA and ZB, received their AAP copy direct, selected by the General News Service editor (who works in the same newsroom). This editor also edited the copy for transmission on the GNS wire to Radio New Zealand stations outside Wellington, including ZBR and ZM in Auckland.

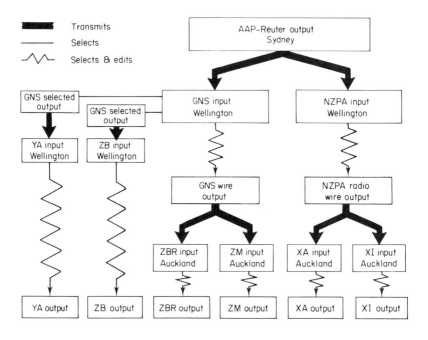

Fig. 1. The flow of international news to New Zealand radio stations:

AAP   Australian Associated Press-Reuter wire service, Sydney, Australia;
GNS   General News Service, Wellington, New Zealand-wire service of the public
            corporation, Radio New Zealand;
PA   New Zealand Press Association, Wellington;
YA   National Programme of Radio New Zealand, prestigious news service;
ZB   Radio NZ Community Network news – both YA and ZB are relayed through
            Auckland stations, but originate in Radio NZ's Wellington studios;
ZBR   Local Radio NZ community station;
ZM   Radio NZ rock music station – both ZBR and ZM broadcast from the
            Auckland studios of Radio NZ;
XA   Radio Hauraki, private rock music station, Auckland;
XI   Radio i, private community station, Auckland.

The Press Association edited AAP copy for transmission to privately owned radio stations, including XA and XI in Auckland. Figure 1 diagrams the flow of international news from the AAP-Reuter wire to the six radio stations heard in Auckland. (On the structure of international news agencies and flows, see Boyd-Barrett, 1980, p. 73 ff.)

The main selection of news is made by the GNS and PA editors. In the two-stage flow, GNS and PA also do the basic rewrite, and the recipient stations (ZBR, ZM; XA, XI) make usually minor alterations. I obtained much of the AAP copy for the five sample days, and rather less of the copy transmitted by GNS and PA. Actual edited wire copy for many stories was available from all but one station. ("Story" is used throughout in its journalistic sense of one report/dispatch on one topic).

The editing process

News editing is the archetypal editing situation. A television or radio news-caster is only the last of several people who have handled the news copy which is read out. Between the original journalist and the newscaster there may be five or more copy editors.[2] These are language professionals with a threefold function:

Select

From the stories that come off the external wires or from internal journalists, the copy editors select some few for the next edition. The copy editor limits the volume of news largely by rejecting entire stories. For broadcast news, from which I draw my data in this study, the selection process is drastic. At BBC news, the "copy taster" discards 90% of news agency material (Schlesinger, 1978, p. 60). In New Zealand, the main overseas wire carries about 100 000 words daily, which would occupy ten hours of continuous radio broadcasting. Again, about 10% gets through the gate.

Cut

A second way the copy editor limits news output is to abbreviate the stories which are accepted. This is particularly necessary in broadcast news. The average radio news item is less than 100 words long, but international wire services are intended mainly for newspapers, so some stories reach 2000 words. The copy editor has to cut, usually by accepting the first page of copy and throwing the rest away.

Alter

It is the copy editor's third operation that is really interesting to the linguist.

Selection leaves the form of accepted stories untouched. Cutting deletes matter, but does not otherwise change what remains. But alteration changes the actual language form of news accepted for broadcast. So while the object of much content analysis of news is what gets left out (e.g. Cutlip, 1954), the focus of this study is the fate of what is left in. Editing alterations serve two purposes. They reduce the amount of news copy even further, because editors delete individual words and phrases as well as the complete sentences rejected in cutting a story. The second purpose is stylistic. The linguistic form of copy originating both outside and inside the news organization must be made to conform to "house style". Most obviously, house style is codified in the "style book" which newspapers and broadcast stations issue to news-workers. However, such manuals tend to deal with only the most obvious points of style, and copy editors in any case rarely consult them. For broadcast news, editing is also intended to restyle written language to a form more suitable to be read aloud. Both radio newsworkers and the official style books lay great stress on the differences between "writing for the eye" and "writing for the ear".

Methodology

The news editing process was analysed in four steps. This methodology is applicable, with appropriate adjustments, to analysis of all types of editing. In many cases, there is no problem in identifying what was the original version on which an edited text is based (step 1). Steps 2 and 3 are the syntactic and semantic analyses of editing changes: the heart of any such study. At step 4, the precise methods used to identify patterns in editing changes will depend on the kind of questions which the study addresses.

Step 1.

Establish which agency story is the input to a given output story. In the world of news, identifying the source text is a major problem. International wire systems are massive and complicated, and the copy is hard to obtain (cf. Boyd-Barrett, 1980, p. 103). Figure 1 shows only a fragment of how news flows in one small country. Newsworkers and managers usually know only their small link in the system. And the systems are constantly changing. The only foolproof method of identifying what is the input to a given output story is when the input copy bears the editor's actual markings. However, editing increasingly occurs at video display terminals. Copy is fed in on tape, displayed on a screen, and edited on the tape without necessarily ever being printed out. The spread of this technology is rapidly eliminating blue-pencilled wire copy and the sure external evidence of identity which it offers.

Physically edited copy was available for many stories analysed from my sample (Figure 2 is a page of wire copy with a recipient editor's markings.) For most of the other stories used, the input was identified through internal evidence. These were once-off stories, or reports containing idiosyncratic phrasing or information (such as figures). In other cases, it is impossible to decide whether an output story is in fact derived from a certain input wire. Big stories may have 10–20 continually updating wires, with a broadcast news item which is a rewrite combining several wires. The form of a few input wires was reliably reconstructed by comparing several output versions. In all cases, the necessary principle followed was: when in doubt, omit. When the output is broadcast news, we use the form actually read out by the newscaster and tape-recorded, which often differs from the edited script. The eventual data for this study included 290 international stories, with both input and ouput copy.

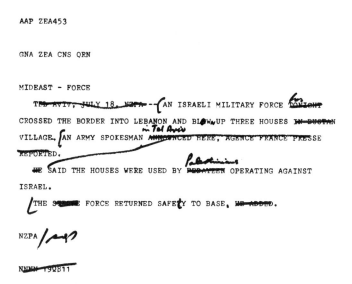

Fig. 2. A page of AAP-Reuter wire copy, with markings by a recipient New Zealand editor. Note the slip in line 3, failing to delete *village*.

Step 2.

Describe the syntactic and lexical changes by which the output copy can be derived from the input.   What copy editing does is put up for re-negotiation the syntactic and lexical choices made by the original journalist (or previous editor). The editor can reverse these choices, or take options which the journalist refused. Linguistically, the editing process can be described by means of rules, which are formally similar to the ordinary rules of linguistic theory. Editing rules cover all types of linguistic operations, and often perform major surgery on the syntax of the input copy. They take as input one well-formed sentence and turn it into another, semantically congruent, well-formed sentence of news English.[3] There is thus a Syntactic Condition on the application of editing rules:

> *After all editing rules have been applied in a sentence, the resulting structure must be syntactically well-formed.*

Each step by which the output form is derived from the input must be specified precisely by a separate rule or group of rules. As many as 100 rules may be needed to derive an output version several sentences long from its input form. Below I sketch something of the work which editing rules perform, and the extra-linguistic factors which influence their application.

Step 3.

Examine all editing rules to identify any which have introduced inaccuracy. As well as meeting the Syntactic Condition, copy editors must also satisfy the Semantic (or Accuracy) Condition:

> *No editing rule may be applied if its effect is to make the meaning of the output story in any way non-congruent with that of the input.*

Editing inaccuracy is an incongruence of output copy with input. We do not require that editors retain *all* the information contained in the original: that would mean no editing whatever. Rather, the output must faithfully represent the content of the input. There may be gaps in the output information, but no mismatch with the input. Any change made in output copy requires a *warrant* in the input copy. Our standard of accuracy is therefore the input copy. For the purposes of editing analysis, the input story is treated as an accurate and adequate representation of the real-world facts. This is of course an idealization, which the results presented below seriously question. Nevertheless, we are concerned here only with incongruencies introduced at a given editing step. Each successive copy editor has to work on the same principle: that the input copy received is accurate. The researcher likewise exercises this suspension of disbelief for the editing stage being scrutinized.

   We test for inaccuracy by turning the edited version into a question, in the frame *Is it the case that X?*. If this can be answered *Yes, it is the case that X* from the original story, then the Accuracy Condition has been successfully met. If the answer is *No*, then the edited version contains something which is incongruent with the original.

Step 4.

Look for patterns in, and propose explanations of, the distribution of editing rules and editing inaccuracies. At this stage, we have a detailed analysis of editing rules, and of the meaning inaccuracies which some rules have introduced. We now proceed to see if there is a pattern in the syntactic or semantic aspects of editing.

On the syntactic side, the editing process allows us to see a language variety in the making, actually on the production line. We identify what kinds of structures are typically affected by editing rules, and what operations the rules perform. We can see whether the application of any rules is influenced by extra-linguistic factors. Do certain editors, or certain radio stations, favour paticular rules? Are editing rules merely optional, or are they variable rules? The next section deals with these questions.

In the semantic analysis, I identified some 150 editing incongruencies in the sample. These grouped under five classes of inaccuracy, and we see how specific editing rules tend to result in certain kinds of inaccuracy. We can move from this description to prescriptive guidelines on what changes editors should and should not make. Analysis of which stories were inaccurately edited shows that certain categories of news suffer more than others. We can quantify the seriousness of inaccuracies, and relate these to various extra-linguistic factors. Do certain individuals or stations edit less accurately? Are certain kinds of news more liable to inaccurate editing? I present evidence on these questions in the last section of this paper.

Syntactic surgery: the art of editing

The scale of operations which a copy editor performs on the surface of a news item can be major (Bell, 1977, p. 227 ff.). Here is the original text of an item of sports news transmitted by AAP-Reuter from Sydney, followed by the version as edited by the New Zealand Press Association (the arrow denotes "is rewritten as"):

(1) AAP/S1   The waterlogged conditions that ruled out play yesterday still prevailed at Bourda this morning, and it was not until mid-afternoon that the match restarted.

       S2   Less than three hours' play remained, and with the West Indies still making their first innings reply to England's total of 448, there was no chance of a result.

       S3   At tea the West Indies were two for 139.

→   PA/S1   Waterlogged conditions ruled out play this morning, but the match resumed with less than three hours' play remaining for the final day.

S2   The West Indies are making a first innings reply to
England's total of 448.

S3   At tea the West Indies were 139 for two, but there's no
chance of a result.

The Press Association preserves most of the information, but attacks the
syntax on a broad front. Bits of sentences are amputated and re-attached
elsewhere; core constituents are transplanted or transformed. The output of
the operation is syntactically very different but still well formed, and
remains semantically congruent with the input. The main editing rules
needed to describe the derivation of PA/S1 are:

(a)   Place adverbial (*at Bourda*) deleted.
(b)   Time adverbials (*yesterday, still*) deleted.
(c)   Main verb (*prevailed*) deleted.
(d)   Relative clause (*that ruled out play yesterday*) raised to main clause.
(e)   Relative pronoun (*that*) and definite article deleted.
(f)   Clefting reversed (*the match did not restart until mid afternoon*).
(g)   Time adverbial deleted (*not until mid-afternoon*).
(h)   Lexical substitution made (*resume* for *restart*).
(i)   Alternative co-ordinator substituted (*but* for *and*).
(j)   Main clause of S2 (*less than three hours' play remained*) embedded into
S1 under *with*.
(k)   Finite verb goes to non-finite (*remaining*).
(m)   Time adverbial (*for the final day*) inserted from another version.

All these changes are entirely typical of the editing process, and their effect
on the syntactic structure of the input is considerable. We can distinguish
three broad categories of editing rules:

Information deletions remove information from a sentence (rules a, b, c, g
above, plus information addition by rule m).

Lexical substitutions replace one or more lexical items with another
congruent item or group of items (h, i above).

Syntactic rules perform various kinds of operations, with minor or major
effects on the structure of a sentence (d, e, f, j, k).

Information deletions

Cutting the length of stories remains the broadcast editor's main task even
with the severely reduced volume of copy which the selection process
retains. The copy editor makes the main additional cut by deleting entire
sentences. The news agencies are press-orientated, and often transmit

stories containing 40 or more sentences. Some stories which are only 2–5 sentences long may be broadcast without sentence deletions. Long wires with more than a dozen sentences run to three or more pages of teleprinted copy, and usually the first page only is used. For medium-length wires, often the first 2–3 sentences are used, together with one or more sentences from the middle or end of the story. Most sentence deletions can be performed without requiring any changes in the remaining sentences of a story. The most common consequent change occurs when the deleted sentence contains the antecedent of a pronoun which occurs in a later sentence and which must then be depronominalized.

Another type of deletion takes out constituents within a sentence. It is unusual for any sentence, except in the shortest wires, to pass the copy editor without some constituent(s) being deleted. The editor treats detailed information as superfluous, or at least unwarranted in the few sentences available to tell a story. Often omitted are personal details of age, occupation, nationality, or even the person's name if the focus of a news item is what happened rather than who it happened to. One of three defendants in a murder trial was referred to as: *a third girl, Josephine Kona Burton, 20, masseuse*. In broadcast news, description plus name plus age plus occupation is too much in a row for both newscaster and listener, so the copy editor left simply: *a third girl aged twenty*.

The simplest deletions are those, like the above, which drop a single node, and any dependent structure, without requiring other changes to structure. Time and place adverbials are often deleted (as in rules a, b and g above), especially from the lead sentence of a story. Also common is the deletion of non-head items within an NP – adjectives, numerals, embedded PPs, relative clauses:

(2)   16 per cent of the 143 166 smallpox cases
    →   16 per cent of the smallpox cases
(3)   the image of the title she won in November
    →   the image of the title

In co-ordinate structures, one or more of the co-ordinated constituents can be deleted, provided that one element remains to keep the sentence well-formed. In this example, the copy editor was able to take out all the detail and link up the final clause without even having to insert *and*:

(4)   They say she died after being brutally beaten around the head,
           kicked, and stabbed with a pair of scissors, and finally strangled.
    →   They say she died after being brutally beaten and strangled.

All these are pure deletions, which leave behind structures unaffected by the removal of optional constituents. There is a second class of constituent deletions where the structure assigned to the input copy differs from the output in more than the mere absence of the deleted constituent(s), yet the linear surface of the sentence remains unruffled. In example (1) above, the radical structural changes effected by rules a–g result solely from judicious deletion by the editor:

(5)   The waterlogged conditions that ruled out play yesterday still
             prevailed at Bourda this morning and it was not until mid-
             afternoon that the match restarted . . .

This is an unusually complex instance of a very common phenomenon. Higher nodes of a derivation are deleted, which automatically raises and re-attaches the lower constituents without requiring any further changes. This occurs particularly in complex NPs (6), or with time or place adverbials embedded in a subordinate clause (7):

(6)   for pickpocketing offences
    →   for pickpocketing
(7)   who was killed last week while practising in South Africa for the
             Grand Prix
    →   who was killed last week in South Africa

The motive for these deletions is abbreviation. But the *form* which the deletions take is governed by the physical process of copy editing. Editors favour changes which are easy to make on a page. Re-ordering material is disfavoured; minor insertions are more acceptable; and words or phrases that can be crossed out and still leave a good sentence are a gift to the overworked copy editor. There is probably no time to retype the copy before the next deadline. If something can just drop out and the linear surface be rejoined, it is much faster than shifting bits of sentences around.

    In studying processes like editing or translation, the practical limits and strengths of the technology used need to be remembered, as well as linguistic factors. For example, the advent of video editing may well be changing the patterns of deletion. What is easiest to delete by pen on paper may not be so easy on video screen.[4] Explaining editing changes in grammatical depth must be complemented by examining the surface of the text on which a copy editor works.

    In the third type of constituent deletion, the sentence which remains is ungrammatical and needs repair. Such repairs may require minor structure-mending rules, as when the tense must be changed in reported speech, or a determiner reinserted in an NP:

(8)   Scotland Yard solicitor Neil Denison
    →   *Scotland Yard solicitor →
    →   a Scotland Yard solicitor

When the deletions are major, they may require surgery before they meet the Syntactic Condition. Subject NPs are deleted, main verbs disappear without trace, transitive verbs are left without objects. The copy editor then has two options: transplant the surviving structure into another sentence or, less probably, rebuild the original sentence until it is a well-formed structure again. Contrary to popular belief, broadcast news very rarely contains ungrammatical sentences. In a transplant, the recipient sentence normally remains almost untouched, with only a preposition or conjunction inserted under which the new structure can be embedded. The donor sentence, however, often undergoes quite radical changes to fit it easily into the recipient structure:

(9)   ZB/S1   In London, the soccer star George Best has been remanded on bail on charges of stealing a fur coat and other items from the former Miss World, Marjorie Wallace, because she hadn't arrived from America to give evidence.

The ZB editor keeps all of AAP's first sentence (down to . . . *Marjorie Wallace*). But the clause *because she hadn't arrived from America to give evidence* is all that survives of AAP/S2:

(10)   AAP/S2   Scotland Yard solicitor Neil Denison had sought the adjournment from the court because Miss Wallace, the main witness, was still in the United States.

In the earlier example (1), rules j and k voluntarily transplant the main clause of AAP/S2 into PA/S1 as a subordinate clause. Because the editor also transplants *there was no chance of a result* (into PA/S3), the remains of S2 are a non-sentence. The editor applies structure-mending rules to rebuild this into a full sentence:

(11)   AAP/S2   . . . and with the West Indies still making their first innings reply to England's total of 448 . . .
  →   PA/S2   The West Indies are making a first innings reply to England's total of 448.

Lexical substitutions

These rules replace one lexical item, or several items, with one or more alternative items. We can group lexical substitutions according to the level of semantic equivalence between the input and output items. Some items are virtually equivalent as dictionary entries: *resume* for *restart* in (1) above, *lawyer* for *solicitor*, *in jail* instead of *behind bars*. Other substitutions are equivalent in the immediate sentence context:

(12)   completely ready for full *nationhood*
   →   *independence*

Still others do not mean the same thing but prove to be true in the context of the whole story:

(13)   she was *later* sacked
   →   *recently*

On occasions, substitutions are made which violate the condition of semantic accuracy, so that the output story says something different from the input. Inaccuracies such as (14) are the subject of the second half of this chapter:

(14)   emergency measures were being taken to aid flood victims . . .
   →   emergency law is being enforced

Syntactic editing rules

Most editing rules are syntactic rules rather than information deletions or lexical substitutions. I have already outlined how rules are applied to re-pair ungrammatical structures after constituents have been deleted. Such structure-mending rules are obligatory and often accomplish major re-organizations of surface constituents. They are required particularly but not exclusively after deletion rules. Depronominalization commonly becomes obligatory after deletion of its antecedent; without such deletion, depro-nominalization would be an optional reversal.

The kinds of operation by which structure is optionally reorganized in (1) above are entirely typical of those used in the 290 stories I have analysed. Variations on co-ordination and de-co-ordination, relativization and de-relativization are particularly common. Attribution sentences have different sentences embedded as their complements; an NP of one sentence is embedded under a preposition as PP in another sentence; relative clauses are de-embedded to become main clauses (15), or re-embedded into other sentences; main clauses are embedded as relative or time clauses in other sentences (16).

(15)   Miss Wallace, the main witness, is still in the United States.
   →   Miss Wallace is still in the United States and is the main witness.
(16)   He said the funeral is to take place next Friday, and Miss Wallace
             is attending.
   →   He said Miss Wallace is attending the funeral, which is to take
             place next Friday.

In (16), the subject NP of the one co-ordinate clause (*the funeral*) is copied as object of the second co-ordinate clause, and the first co-ordinate then embedded under the NP as a relative clause.

In copy editing, the syntactic choices made in the input text are re-negotiated. Syntactic editing rules are either *applications, reversals,* or *alternatives*. If the original version chose not to apply any particular rule of grammar, the editor may reverse this choice and apply the rule. All the optional rules of a normal grammar are potential editing application rules. Particularly common are auxiliary and negative contractions, *there* insertion, passivization, agent deletion, and relative clause reduction. Such rules belong in any grammar of English, and all the copy editor does is take options which were not applied previously.

A second group of rules reverses choices which have already been made. Complementizer *that* is reinserted; co-ordinate sentences are de-co-ordinated; sentences are de-passivized and agents reinserted; clefting is reversed, and *there* re-deleted; NPs are de-pronominalized. A wide range of optional rules is subject to editing reversal.

So-called "optional rules" are not the only syntactic rules which offer choice. Obligatory as well as optional rules may produce several alternative outputs. In editing, the choice is open to select an output that was not chosen in the original. Such rules are among the copy editor's most common tools. Lexical substitutions are in fact a choice of alternatives, as is the substitution of one tense or aspect by another, and the choice of an alternative article or complementizer.

The nature and range of editing changes which I have described in this section appear to be common to all kinds of editing practice. The study by Davisson *et al.* (1980) compared four texts re-written for US school children with the original. Their independent categorization of editing changes is strikingly similar to mine, particularly in the rules needed to describe the "splitting" and "merging" of clauses.

Patterned variability in editing

The analysis so far has been purely linguistic: applied to text comparison, but nevertheless not seeking any social explanation of the linguistic facts. The re-styling function of editing, however, can only be described in a sociolinguistic framework. Editing rules are not simply optional: they are variable rules. Like the standard variable rules of sociolinguistic theory (e.g. Cedergren and Sankoff, 1974), they are constrained by linguistic and social factors. I will examine briefly one variable rule and the social factors which influence its application.

Determiner deletion is the rule which deletes the determiner in a descriptive NP which precedes a name NP in apposition to it:[5]

(17)   the fugitive financier Robert Vesco
     →   fugitive financier Robert Vesco

Copy editors can handle determiner deletion in three ways. They may leave the copy exactly as they found it. That is, if the determiner is present in the copy, leave it in; if it is absent, having been already deleted by a previous editor, then leave it absent. As active alternatives, a copy editor may delete a determiner which was retained in the input copy; or reinsert a determiner previously deleted. We can formalize this process through two editing rules: the editing rule of determiner deletion, which is formally identical to the ordinary linguistic rule of determiner deletion; and the editing rule of determiner re-insertion, which precisely reverses the deletion rule.

   Table I presents data on determiner deletion for two New Zealand radio stations, the AAP-Reuter news agency from which they received their international news, and the NZPA agency which edited AAP for the private station XA (cf. Fig. 1). In "national" news originating within New Zealand, both stations have low determiner deletion. Station YA, the prestigious "National Programme", permits no determiner deletion at all. Station XA, a rock music station, has a level of 14% deletion. However, in inter-national news the picture is different. AAP, the source of international news for the other three, has 59.7% deletion, a much higher level. To shift the style of the international copy, YA, PA and XA start applying the editing rule of determiner reinsertion, putting back in the determiners previously deleted in AAP copy (Fig. 3). YA reinserts almost all the deleted deter-miners it receives to reach a level of 4.5% in the international news it broadcasts. The PA agency brings the AAP level down slightly to 53.5% in the copy it sends out. That frequency is then the input to station XA, which reinserts rather more determiners to reduce the level further to 40%.

Table I.   Total determiner deletion on 2 news agencies and 2 radio stations, New Zealand.

	National news	International news
AAP-Reuter news agency	–	59.7%
Station YA	0%	4.5
NZPA news agency	–	53.5
Station XA	14.0	40.0

   These shifts are influenced by one clear factor. The frequency of deter-miner deletion in a station's own internal copy represents a target level. Copy editors "know" the frequency of deletion in external input copy, "know" the target level in their station's own copy, and apply editing rules to shift the input towards that target.[6] The further a station's target level is from the frequency in the input copy received, the higher will be the level of application of the editing rule needed to adjust that frequency. In addition, no *editing* rule of determiner deletion occurs in the sample. The shift is always to reinsert the determiners, and never to delete more, because the target is a low level of deletion. But the editor does not reinsert all the deleted determiners, so that even after editing the style of external copy is not identical to internally-originated copy. Editors are prepared to sanction in external copy forms they would not accept from their own journalists.

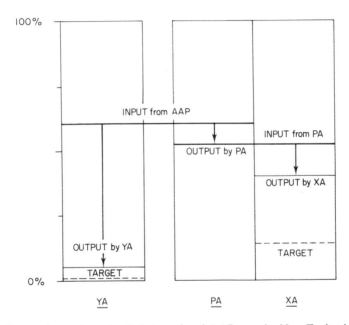

Fig. 3. Determiner reinsertion in international AAP copy by New Zealand editors on 3 news media: station YA, agency PA, and station XA.

The relative frequency of application of variable rules in a station's news language correlates only with the social composition of the station's audience (Bell, 1982a). Variable editing rules thus function to shift the style of the input text closer to the style which the station deems suitable for its kind of audience. This shows how a number of divergent styles can be derived from a single text. The same set of international news analysed here was received and edited by two internal news agencies and six different radio stations in

Auckland. These diverse stations have widely differing audiences, and language styles to match. They take a common input and apply variable editing rules to shape the style towards their own audience. We can formalize the goal of copy editing for style in the following axiom:

> *If the probability of a linguistic variable on a given station differs from its frequency in input copy, editing rules operate to approach the input frequency to station probability.*

Semantic butchery: the failures of editing

This research was begun as a purely formal study of how editors change the language they work on. However, I was soon struck by the fact that, in the process of editing news for length and style, copy editors often altered the meaning of news to something different from the original. This second section examines inaccurate editing, using the techniques outlined above in steps 3 and 4 of the methodology.

News-makers, workers and consumers all have a warm, sometimes passionate, interest in the accuracy of news. Accusations of bias or in-accuracy in the news media are so commonplace in the political life of Western countries that they need little documentation. In Britain, the tensions have surfaced most recently over the 1982 Falklands/Malvinas war with Argentina. The government criticized coverage of the war by the BBC and some newspapers as "over-neutral". The *Sun* newspaper (editorial of 7 May 1982) accused the BBC, *Daily Mirror*, and the *Guardian* of treason. Simultaneously, the Glasgow University Media Group was documenting the BBC's coverage as overwhelmingly pro-British (*Sunday Times*, 16 May 1982).

Internationally, debate on this issue has become increasingly sharp in the past decade. The nations of the "South" or Third World have accused the media of the "North" of consistent bias in reporting about their countries. The question of news accuracy is thus important and salient both within societies and between nations.

Disputes over news bias are, however, rarely resolved satisfactorily. Opposing parties bring their overt opinions and unexamined ideologies to an interpretation of the news. The media traditionally maintain that criticism by two opposing sides means they must be getting it right in the middle. The issue in all such debates invariably turns on one point: What is a true account of the situation? What is the standard against which particular reports can be measured? Who is to judge what were the real-world facts: source, reporter, researcher, an independent expert, a neutral panel of judges?

Studying inaccuracy

In mass communication studies, the investigation of news accuracy was pioneered by Charnley (1936), who clipped stories from local newspapers and sent them to sources mentioned in the report to identify inaccuracies. This and subsequent studies have found on average about one error per story, with usually about half the stories rated fully accurate. Most researchers have been aware of the risk of having the accuracy of a report judged by the person being reported on, and some have developed other measures to identify inaccuracy. Lawrence and Grey (1969) interviewed the reporter as well as sending questionnaires to the reported.

These developments reflect the problem of how to decide what is an error. Step 3 of the methodology described earlier solves this by treating the input copy as if it were fully accurate, and identifying any non-congruence in output copy as bias or inaccuracy. We thus limit our field to the smaller compass of copy editing stages (rather than a final report versus "the facts"), but by that means sharpen our focus and strengthen our inferences.

A second strand of research emerges in recent work in Britain and Australia. Here linguistic analysis is used to draw inferences concerning the ideological biases of certain media. The most publicized research (e.g. *The Listener*, 29 July 1982) is that of the Glasgow University Media Group (1976, 1980). The Group periodically gets into debate with BBC television over bias in the BBC's industrial news, or alternatively, in the Glasgow Group's views. The Group has noted (1976, p. 256) inaccurate editing changes between successive news bulletins which are of precisely the kind present in my data.

Research by Kress and Trew is more linguistically oriented. Trew (in Fowler *et al.*, 1979) analyses contrasting reports in different British national dailies, and the development over time of reports and editorials about a single event. Kress and Trew (1978) make independent use of a methodology similar to that developed here to study the London *Sunday Times*' rewrite of a crucial industrial text. Kress (e.g., 1983) discusses the ideological bases of journalistic rewriting of news, and compares different reports of one story in two Australian papers. This research all involves close work on the language of news reports, and is strongest when it contrasts actual texts (Bell, 1977, p. 266 ff.). At its best, such analysis can show convincingly how language is a vehicle of covert interpretation in supposedly neutral reporting.[7]

The third line of research relevant to our study deals with news flow and selection patterns. White (1950) pioneered research on the "gatekeeping" performance of copy editors. Some studies have directly questioned gatekeepers on their reasons for accepting or rejecting stories (Gieber, 1956).

Others (Hester, 1971) have combined interview with content analysis of input and output news. Some have analysed only the news flow, comparing what stories editors received with what stories are transmitted (Cutlip, 1954). From imbalances in selection, inferences are drawn concerning the news values of gatekeepers or their institutions at any stage of the news flow from wire service to newspaper. Such research has concluded, for instance, that gatekeepers tend to reduce the proportion of news from the countries of the South, and to select negative rather than positive news (Peterson, 1981).

This work focusses on patterns in the selection of entire stories. There is little research on the significance of editing changes *within* stories accepted for publication. McNelly (1959) stresses the importance of the copy editing role of wire editors, and points out that the term "gatekeeping" is inadequate to describe this function. Gatekeepers who are not solely "copy tasters" operate a filter as well as a gate. Once a story is through the selection gate, it must then pass the cutting and altering filter, and will probably emerge in a different form. Garrison's research (1979) on the effect of video technology is the only major study of copy editing. He concentrated on interviews and observation of copy editors, and compared input and output copy of 15 stories. The kinds of copy changes were categorized, but too broadly to bear comparison with my study.

Five types of inaccuracy

I have formalized the requirement for accuracy under step 3 of the methodology. Any meaning change requires a warrant in the input copy. The Semantic Condition is that no editing rule may be applied if its effect is to make the meaning of the output story in any way non-congruent with that of the input. Such a condition corresponds to Grice's Co-operative Principle of conversation, category of Quality (1975, p. 46): "Try to make your contribution one that is true". Accuracy is not strictly a goal of copy editing: the goals are to cut and to re-style. Accuracy is rather a condition on the application of editing rules, a *sine qua non* of editing. Most of the editing alterations described in the previous section do not and need not falsify the content of a news story. But some do, when applied injudiciously.

The inaccuracies identified in my sample fall into five categories. We can state five sub-conditions of editing accuracy, each of which defines a type of inaccuracy:

(a) No editing rule shall make the information in the output copy non-congruent with that in the input copy (inaccuracy type: *falsification*).
(b) No rule shall increase the assertive strength of a linguistic unit beyond the warrant of the input copy (*over-assertion*).

(c) No rule shall redefine the scope of a unit beyond the warrant of the input copy (*over-scope*).
(d) No rule shall reorder or delete information so that the focus of events becomes non-congruent with that in the input copy (*refocus*).
(e) No rule shall add new information not contained in the input copy (*addition*).[8]

The input copy is thus treated as a canonical text. Potential violations of the sub-conditions a–e are tested at successively higher levels of the input copy: constituent, sentence, story; then other available copy, and real-world knowledge. The basic information unit of news is the story rather than the sentence. Apparent inaccuracies at the level of the sentence are frequent, but usually they merely increase or reduce redundancy, or incorporate information from other sentences of the input. Sometimes a change which may still appear inaccurate in the context of the input story is warranted by information in other wires on the same topic. On rare occasions, we must seek a warrant in sources beyond the news, for instance to check on geography.

Falsification

Falsification, the first type of inaccuracy, is non-congruence between information in the output and input copy. We test for falsification by turning the edited version into a question and treating the input copy as its answer. Any unit to which we must give the answer *No, it is not (quite) the case that X* is a falsification:

(18)   Jose Lopez Rega, an astrology follower
    →   Jose Lopez Rega, an astrologer

Questioning the output copy in the frame *Is it the case that Lopez Rega is an astrologer?* we must reply *No, it is not the case: Lopez Rega is an astrology follower.* Most believers are, after all, not themselves priests.

The most extreme case of falsification in my data saw *not* being deleted, to leave the outgoing sentence saying the polar opposite of what came in. But this occurred in interestingly mitigating circumstances. Two independent editors were misled by the double negative in *did not deny*:

(19)   AAP   The spokesman could not say how many people had
                   died but *did not deny* a report by a journalist who
                   claimed more than 1500 had perished . . .
    { →   ZB   *denied*
       →   PA   *has denied*

Many "errors of fact" seem to be slips of the tongue or pen – by which *53 people* became *83 people*, and *April 24* went to *April 25*.

Time and place deictics are traps for unwary editors. In overseas news entering New Zealand, *today* in the original wire story usually needs to become *yesterday*. Copy editors have to resist the temptation to give these stories a greater but unwarranted immediacy. One item that originated in London about 6 a.m. New Zealand time was broadcast in Auckland at 6 p.m.:

(20)   AAP   Nineteen of those victims – eight of them children – still lay in hospital *last night*. (Sydney: 0951 N.Z. time)

→   GNS   Nineteen of the victims – eight of them children – are still in hospital *today*. (Wellington: 1039)   →

→   ZBR   *late today* (Auckland: 1800)

Successive changes were made as the day passed, first by the GNS wire service, then at the next editing step by station ZBR. They wrongly claim greater recency for an event which is in fact retreating into the past. The accurate change would have been to <u>*early today*</u>.[9]

Inaccurate approximations of time adverbials usually imply that an event is more recent than it actually is. Copy editors often reduce detail by rounding specific figures, or approximating them with quantifiers such as *many, several, some*. Occasionally such time approximations are unacceptable, again claiming greater immediacy:

(21)   Mrs Peron . . . was a cabaret dancer *14 years ago*
→   *some years ago*[10]

One of the most regular editing rules changes simple past tense to present perfect, which increases the immediacy of an event, normally without falsifying meaning. However, this rule operates on the presupposition that the events described have only just taken place – within about the last 24 hours. In one interesting case this presupposition fails:

(22)   AAP/S5   Mrs Peron *granted* salary rises to workers on her first full day in office.

S6   General Peron's widow, as Vice-President to her husband, assumed the chief executive's spot after he died on July 1.

{ → ZB   *has granted*
{ → GNS   *has granted*
{ → PA   *has granted*

This sentence occurs well down the wire (dated 8 July) describing Mrs Peron's appointment of a secretary the previous day. A trap has been set in the middle of this story, probably because at an earlier editing stage two wires have been combined. AAP/S5 above is old news, since S6 repeats what the copy editor should have known – that Mrs Peron became President on 1 July 1974. Her first full day was 2 July: a week before this story. The only outlet which avoided this pitfall was station YA, which deleted the whole sentence. ZB, GNS and PA (the other three outlets which received the AAP copy direct) all changed simple past tense to present perfect.

Expressions of place are generally less of a problem than time. A New Zealand copy editor clearly needs to change *here* in the lead sentence of a wire datelined London or Addis Ababa. However, editors do sometimes claim greater proximity of place. In a story about the siting of a nuclear power plant, *about 50 miles south of here* [Boston] was edited to *just south*. *Just* does not seem a congruent approximation of *50 miles* in such a delicate matter. In (23), a spatial *at*-relation becomes *beyond*, which *reduces* the importance of the site of wreckage from a minor aircraft accident in Sydney, Australia:

(23)   over a wide area of the city's northern suburbs
   →   over a wide area north of the city

It is a common feature of reference in news items that a first reference is by name and second reference by description, with no surface marking of the identity:

(24)   The assassination attempt on the President in *Washington, D.C.* today has shocked many people in *the capital*.

A correct reading depends on the knowledge that Washington, D.C. is a capital city. With countries less well known than the United States, the editor's geo-political knowledge may fail:

(25)   AAP/S1   Rebel troops and police arrested top-ranking military and civilian officials in *Asmara* today . . .

          S2   Armed mutineers led by junior officers held the radio station, airport and key intersections in *the northern provincial capital of Eritrea*, and manned road blocks outside the town.

   →   PA/S1   Rebel troops and police in *the Ethiopian city of Asmara* have arrested top ranking military and civilian officials . . .

          S2   Armed mutineers led by junior officers have seized *the city's* radio station, airport and key intersections.

          S3   They have also seized control of *the northern provincial capital of Eritrea* and are manning road blocks outside the town.

PA/S2 correctly maintains the identity of *Asmara* and *the city*. However, the editor transplants the place adverbial *in the northern provincial capital of Eritrea* from AAP/S2 to become object NP of a new sentence. PA/S3 bears the second, incompatible reading that *the northern provincial capital of Eritrea* is a city other than *Asmara* (or *Eritrea* may be taken as the name of the city rather than of the province, on the pattern of *the city of Boston*). A two-city interpretation is made possible because the editor has split the original AAP/S2 into two sentences. Insertion of *also* in PA/S3 then forces the reading that this is a second city, different from that in PA/S2. This is in spite of the form *the city* in PA/S2, a one-city interpretation of the original source phrase which should have made the error of PA/S3 impossible.

For a recipient who knows that Asmara *is* the northern provincial capital of Eritrea, the PA story becomes just uninterpretable. S3 repeats information from S1 and S2, while claiming (by *also*) that it is new information. Repeating identical information is highly deviant in a news story. In broadcast news, maxims such as "Be brief" and "Be informative" (cf. Grice, 1975) are near-absolutes. At the next editing step, station XI received PA's version and used it in successive news bulletins. The first three broadcasts made no significant change, but by the fourth the XI copy editor noticed something wrong and re-edited PA/S3 to:

(26)   They have also seized control of *a northern provincial capital* and
            are manning road blocks outside the town.

XI solves the non-sense by deciding that S3 is indeed new information and editing to make the two-city reading fully consistent. But in the process, the last remaining clue to PA's misreading disappears.

One of the hidden traps of copy editing is that almost any syntactic change may initiate a semantic change that is not immediately obvious (cf. example 22). XI's version seemed a perfectly legitimate piece of editing but, because it operates on already inaccurate copy, it compounds the error. We have been able to identify this case only because an earlier editing step was available. International news heard on New Zealand radio has passed through the hands of 3–5 gatekeepers. It is certain that earlier editors have made inaccurate changes which are compounded at later editing stages. Without access to the earlier versions, such errors cannot be identified by later editors or researchers, let alone by the audience.

Over-assertion
The second class of inaccuracy occurs with changes which go beyond the evidence of the input copy. Lexical items, constituents or whole sentences may be intensified beyond the point warranted by the input. So we might

rank items within the lexical field of *walking*, roughly from least to most intense:

shuffle → amble → stroll → WALK → stride → rush → race.

It is generally illegitimate to replace one term of this set with another term to its right. We identify over-assertion when we have to answer *No, it is not necessarily the case that X* to a question about some editing change in the output copy. A falsification is something contrary to the evidence. Over-assertion is a change which further evidence could prove to be warranted, but that warrant is lacking.

Over-assertion is yielding to the ever-present journalistic (and academic) temptation to make things sound a little better than you know them to be. In (27), it is not necessarily the case that a *horde of newsmen* was present:

(27)   reporters keeping vigil
    →   a hoarde of newsmen [sic]

Two complementary types of change result in over-assertion. First, a copy editor may *insert an intensifier* not warranted by the input copy. Mrs Peron was reported to have granted salary rises to *workers*, which one editor changed to *all workers*. Again, in the finely-balanced world of Middle East diplomacy, inserting *only* into this story regarding the status of the PLO was unwarranted:

(28)   The joint communique declared that the PLO was "*the legitimate representative* of the Palestinians, except Palestinians living in the Jordanian Hashemite Kingdom".
    →   *the only legitimate representative*

Second, and more commonly, an editor may *delete linguistic hedges*: devices which tone down the strength of what is asserted. The original wire in (29) is careful to hedge its guess about the purpose of the patrol. The output version strengthens a speculation to an assertion:

(29)   Paratroops believed loyal to the government patrolled the air force base at Debre Zeit, near Addis Ababa, *in an apparent attempt to prevent dissident airmen* from joining in the revolt.
    →   *to prevent airmen*

As Rosenblum points out in his perceptive, insider's book about the work of the international news agencies (1979, p. 114), correspondents may choose their words very carefully to cover both what they know and do not know. If copy editors find the account fuzzy, they may rewrite it into a clearcut but distorted story. Here is the end of a wire story describing how a piece of wing broke off an aircraft approaching Mascot airport in Sydney, Australia:

(30)   AAP   Mr W. A. Norton of Dent Street, Lindfield, saw the
                        incident on his way to work.
                        He said the jet continued towards Mascot without any
                        apparent problem.
     ⎧ →   ZB   The jet continued to Mascot without any apparent
     ⎪   problem.
     ⎨ →   GNS   The aircraft apparently landed without any trouble.
     ⎪ →   PA   The jet landed without any trouble.
     ⎩

The original is a sourced eye-witness account that sticks scrupulously to
reporting what Mr Norton actually saw. It hedges this around with the words
continued, towards and *apparent*, and makes no commitment on whether the
aircraft eventually landed safely. But the three separate editors who used
that story started chopping out the hedges. ZB replaced *towards* with *to*.
GNS took it further and used *landed* for *continued*. The PA editor removed
the last remaining hedge, *apparent*, and stated bluntly that *The jet landed
without any trouble.*

   This version goes well beyond the original wire, and has been made
possible only because the copy editors have removed all reference to the
eye-witness. The first AAP sentence, and consequently the attribution *he
said* in the second sentence, have been deleted. If the editors had tried to
make their changes without deleting the source, they would have seen that
the resulting sentence was unacceptable:

(31)   Mr W. A. Norton of Dent Street, Lindfield, saw the incident on
            his way to work.
            He said that . . .
     ?   the jet continued to Mascot without any apparent problem.
     *   the aircraft apparently landed without any trouble.
     **   the jet landed without trouble.

Mr Norton was in no position to say anything of the kind, because he was ten
miles from the airport on the other side of Sydney harbour.

   The most common device by which journalists hedge their assertions is
quotation and attribution. Wire stories frequently carry direct quotations
from spokespersons or public figures. Copy editors usually delete quotation
marks and often this does not matter. For read-aloud news, direct quotation
is obviously a problem. Frequently quotation marks remain in edited copy,
and it is then the newscaster's responsibility to pick this out through
intonation. Sometimes quotation is marked syntactically:

(32)   Egypt and Jordan today agreed that the Palestine Liberation
            Organisation (PLO) should attend the Geneva Middle East

peace conference *"at the appropriate stage"* as an independent body.

→   *at what they call the appropriate stage*

The function of quotation markers is to dissociate the sender from direct responsibility (cf. Kress, 1983). When they are deleted and not marked by intonation, the broadcasting station adopts the expression as its own:

(33)   AAP   They said the Israelis left behind leaflets warning local
                     inhabitants against cooperating with *"terrorists"*.
{→ ZB   *terrorists*
{→ YA   *the terrorists*

Many news stories involve someone being quoted: an eye-witness, spokesperson, observer, or other source. As we have seen, copy editors often take out these attributions. However, attribution deletion gives a false air of impersonal authority to what is said. And it usually sets off a chain reaction of deletion or alteration in later sentences of a news story, where it may be even less acceptable than in the earlier sentence. A news story can be seen as embedded under a stack of attribution sentences:

(i)   Station XA reports in Auckland at 1200 that
(ii)   PA reported in Wellington at 1100 that
(iii) AAP reported in Sydney at 1000 that
(iv)   Reuters reported in London at 0900 that
(v)   Correspondent PQ reported in Jerusalem at 0800 that
(vi)   An Israeli military spokesman said in Tel Aviv at 0700 that . . .

Sentence (i) is always implied in the very fact of station XA broadcasting the story. We do not expect all the other editing steps to be explicitly acknowledged, but source (vi) and agency (iv) should be.

When a statement is attributed to a source, the listener is explicitly alerted to the fact that this is one individual's description and viewpoint. The practice of deleting attributions becomes particularly undesirable when a story involves sharply opposed groups. Here it is vital to know which side is the source of information so we can make allowance for its viewpoint:

(34)   Israeli naval units tonight raided three Lebanese ports sinking
           about ten vessels in each of them, *the Israeli military spokesman
           announced.*
    →   Israeli naval units have raided three Lebanese ports sinking
           about ten vessels in each of them.

It is a common feature of war reporting that one event produces two irreconcilable versions, and sets of statistics, from the opposing sides.[11] Other (unused) reports gave the Lebanese account of this incident: 21 boats sunk, not 30. Neither figure may be correct: certainly both cannot be. Preferably both counts should be reported, but at least the statistic should be anchored to its source.

On a higher level of attribution, most wire stories are sourced to the originating news agency (iv above). This is almost invariably deleted on New Zealand radio, for obvious reasons. Repeating the source would slow down news presentation. Attributions like *according to Reuters* or *Associated Press reports* can be easily removed without adjusting the rest of the lead sentence or even altering its remaining structure. But by deleting all attribution of a story to its source, the editing station makes itself responsible for the content of that item. It says *We tell you here and now that X*, and takes responsibility for errors inherited from the wire copy. The significance of this becomes clear in analysis of the two-step editing process from AAP to PA to XA and XI. Over 80% of editing errors between the AAP wire and XA/XI's broadcast versions occur at the PA stage. But XA and XI vouch for this previous editing, first by virtue of broadcasting it, and then by removing any explicit disclaiming attribution.

Over-scope

In the third type of inaccuracy, the scope of information is mistakenly broadened beyond the warrant of the input copy (or sometimes narrowed: "under-scope"). If place or time adverbials are shifted or deleted, the scope of the sentence or phrase may be over-extended or over-restricted. We identify over-scope by questioning the time or place adverbial in the frame of the output sentence.

An interesting group of scope redefinitions occurred in a story about flooding in southern Brazil. Most of the details in the early sentences of the original report concern only one state, and one city in the state, while the floods also affected at least six other states of Brazil:

(35)   AAP   Serious flooding in southern Brazil was today reported
                        to have brought a heavy death toll in the town of
                        Tubarao, cut off by swollen river waters . . .
                        Authorities in Santa Catarina State where Tubarao is
                        situated have declared the state a disaster area . . .
                        The death toll could be over 1500.
    →   ZB   A possible death toll of more than a thousand is
                        reported from Brazil in the flooding in the south of
                        the country.
                        The area's been declared a disaster area . . .

In the attempt to abbreviate the story, specific reference to Santa Catarina state and Tubarao city has been deleted from the early part of the output version, but the other facts stand as if they referred to the whole situation. So the floods appear less serious than they are: the death toll of *more than a thousand* actually applies to one city of many hit by the floods. Later paragraphs of the AAP wire show that large areas of northern, western and eastern Brazil were also flooded, with great devastation. On the other hand, *Santa Catarina State* has been quasi-pronominalized to *the area*, which then appears in ZB's version to refer to the whole of *the south of the country*. The rule has been applied where there is no true identity, thus over-generalizing the extent of the official disaster area. So ZB's alterations both over-restrict and over-extend the scope of the place adverbials.

Other editors treated the story to imply that the flooding was more limited and its consequences less disastrous than in fact. One version deleted all specific place adverbials:

(36)   PA   More than 1500 have perished in the city of Tubarao
                    in southern Brazil.
→   XA   More than 1500 people have perished.

We can often identify over-scope by questioning the output copy in a frame such as:

(37)   Is it the case that 1500 people have perished *in general*?

Using the input to (36) as answer, we must say that it is not the case in general, only in Tubarao. Hardly a single New Zealander would know the name of that city or state. South America is very remote from New Zealand, not so much in distance (they are after all "neighbours" across 6000 miles of the Pacific Ocean) as in consciousness. Yet, it would be unthinkable for a copy editor to treat so casually the geography of more distant but better-known regions such as the United States or western Europe.

Time over-scope occurred in the editing of a story about a visit to a British regiment in Germany which Princess Anne made shortly after her car was ambushed in London (March, 1974):

(38)   AAP/S4   It was her first trip abroad *since the abortive kidnap
                    attempt in London last week* . . .
S6   British army and West German police security men
                    worked together round-the-clock in providing
                    maximum security for Anne.
S7   A helicopter, plain-clothes detectives, German police
                    with tracker-dogs and British military police with
                    submachine guns were constantly on guard around
                    her.

→   PA/S3   It was her first trip abroad *since the abortive kidnap attempt in London last week.*

        S4   A helicopter, plain-clothes detectives and military police with submachineguns have been constantly guarding the Princess *since the kidnap attempt last week.*

Most of the really serious editing errors (e.g. 25) require the copy editor to adopt a single-mindedly perverse reading and make a cluster of changes for the interpretation to stick. This example is no exception. The offending rule copies a reduced version of the time adverbial *since the abortive kidnap attempt in London last week* from the first sentence on to the last, over-generalizing the information in the last sentence. The original twice specifies *British army* and *West German police*, and indicates explicitly that the precautions described were in force only on Princess Anne's three-day trip to Germany. To make its transference of the time adverbial acceptable, PA has to delete AAP/S6 completely, and cut from S7 all reference to *German* police. The resulting version gives the quite false (but rather more sensational) information that, since the time of the ambush, for the four days in Britain as well as in Germany, Princess Anne was provided with this intense security.

Refocus
Refocus and addition are the two less frequent types of inaccuracy. Refocus involves the reordering or deletion of information so that the balance of a story is no longer congruent with the input copy. Such distortion is classically difficult to "prove" when looking at a report in isolation, but it is made far more visible when editing actively refocusses a story. Refocus is the prime cause of non-congruency in the following story:

(39)   PA/S1   Argentina's new president – Isabel Peron – has named her late husband's former aide as her personal secretary.

        S2   He's Jose Lopez Rega, an astrology follower, who also managed Mrs Peron when she was a cabaret dancer fourteen years ago.

        S3   He was a constant companion of the late General since 1965 . . .

→   XA/S1   Argentina's president – Isabella Peron – has named her personal secretary – an astrologer who managed her career when she was a cabaret dancer some years ago . . .

        S2   Isabel, who takes over in Argentina following the

death of President Juan Peron last year – ah, last
week. [sic]

S3   The new personal secretary is Jose Lopez Rega, a
close companion of the late president and his wife
since 1965.

There are three refocusses in XA's version:

(a) The relative clause *an astrology follower who also managed Mrs Peron
when she was a cabaret dancer fourteen years ago* has been shifted from
the second sentence to the lead sentence.

(b) The information that Lopez Rega had been Mrs Peron's *late husband's
former aide* has been deleted from the first sentence.

(c) The pronoun *he* is replaced in S3 by the full noun phrase *the new
personal secretary*, repeating material from the first sentence.

Together with no less than seven other changes which affect the meaning,[12]
these highlight the astrology and cabaret dancer motifs (a), and refocus
Lopez Rega's past relationship from General Peron to Mrs Peron, streng-
thening the innuendo of sexual liaison (b, c). These editing alterations have
a considerable cumulative effect on the tone of the story. Argentina is made
laughable: a country run by an astrologer and ex-cabaret dancer who share
an invitingly illicit degree of personal intimacy.

Addition

Lastly, information addition occurs surprisingly often, but only occasionally
is the editor's new information wrong. In (40) there is no warrant for the
insertion of *police* in either of the output sentences:

(40)   Miss Brice's body was found . . .
          She had been brutally beaten.
  →   Police found the body . . .
          They say she died after being brutally beaten.

One editor, exasperated with the inconclusiveness of a five-day cricket
match in Guyana which was continually interrupted by rain, prejudged the
result and rewrote a story to say the match had ended:

(41)   AAP   Play was again *held up at the start* of the final day of
                   the Fourth Test between the West Indies and
                   England here today.
  →   PA   In the West Indian city of Georgetown the final day of
                   the Fourth Test between the West Indies and
                   England has been *washed out by rain, resulting in a
                   draw.*

However, the match did resume – had in fact already done so before PA received this wire in Wellington. Two hours later the same editor unblushingly put through an update wire saying that the game was underway. And once again, station XI suffered from PA's bad editing, and compounded the error unawares by repeating at the end of the inaccurate item: *That result again – a draw*.

Inaccuracy and news values

The examples of inaccuracy cited include a few of the worst among some 150 editing errors in the sample of 290 stories. We now turn to identify what are the patterns in these inaccuracies (step 4 of the methodology). What kinds of stories are poorly edited? Do any social or political factors seem to promote inaccurate editing? What sorts of semantic effects do editing changes have? Why do editors make inaccurate changes?

The semantic effect of inaccuracies can be largely described under one heading: they make a story more newsworthy. I have already noted in passing that many changes to time adverbials make a story sound more recent than it really is. The concept of recency is just one news value or factor which media researchers such as Galtung and Ruge (1965) suggest are influences on the selection of news. In my data, we see these factors influencing the *editing* of accepted news, as Galtung and Ruge hypothesized they would (1965, p. 71). In almost every example given above, the inaccuracy clearly enhances the story's value on some news factor. Here I can only sketch findings relevant to a few of the factors:

Frequency includes what I have called "recency". Certain inaccuracies serve to make events conform to the established cycles of news work, e.g. by prejudging the result of a cricket match (example 41) or claiming events as more recent (20, 22).

Unambiguity is an asset which promotes the selection of a news story. This has two repercussions on editing. Firstly, unambiguous, clearcut stories are less liable to be badly edited. If a story is ambiguous, complicated, diverse, it is more likely to suffer, as did the complex, updating wires on the Brazil floods. And second, copy editors are likely to commit inaccuracies in the process of making complicated stories less ambiguous. Maybe's become certainties (29, 30), open sets are closed (28). Attribution deletion is the classic case, since acknowledging a viewpoint, and particularly conflicting viewpoints, necessarily makes a story ambiguous (33, 34).

Negativity of a news story is frequently increased during editing: from the potential chaos of Peron's government (39), to the threat to Princess Anne's safety (38), to broadening the scope of the Ethiopian rebellion (25) or the Brazilian floods (35).

Consonance of a story with preconceptions about a nation or region affects which stories are badly edited. Many inaccuracies serve to shift stories towards greater consonance with stereotypes, particularly for the Latin American examples cited (14, 19, 39).

Recent research shows how the unwitting "frame" or ideology of news workers affects the selection and form of the news (e.g. Tuchman 1978, Glasgow University Media Group 1976). The findings presented here make it clear that the frame, and the news factors which are part of it, influence the transmission as well as the creation of news. Editing inaccuracies are not unpatterned accidents. They serve to make news stories more newsworthy, however unconscious copy editors may be of the errors and their effect.

News of the "South" and the New Information Order

The bias becomes even clearer when we quantify inaccuracies. I score the seriousness of each editing error by assigning it a value on a scale from fully accurate (at 0) to wildly inaccurate (at 6), in the manner of the semantic differential (Osgood *et al.*, 1957). A news story fully accurately edited scores 0. A story with one very serious editing inaccuracy, or several smaller errors, scores 5–6, with two very serious inaccuracies about 10–12.[13] We can then examine the data on parameters such as originating source, topic classifications, country of origin, or the news factors mentioned above. I present data on only one dimension here: country of origin.

Grouping stories by country of origin, we sum the scores of editing inaccuracies in news about each country, and divide the total by the number of stories about that country. This yields a measure of editing inaccuracy per story concerning these countries. Table II presents indexes of editing inaccuracy for those countries with an adequate number of stories in the sample. News about Brazil, Ethiopia and Argentina has been exceptionally badly edited: 2.2–3.7 on the 0–6 point scale, the equivalent of one serious error per story. Individual stories about these countries score very heavily: 12 for PA's editing of the Brazil floods, 14 Ethiopian revolution (PA), 10 Mrs Peron (XA). These scores represent the equivalent of two or more extreme inaccuracies per story. The other countries were all Western except the Soviet Union, and were all passably well edited.

Clearly, there has been a considerable difference in editing quality between news about the nations of the North and of the South. This finding accords with studies on the quality of gatekeeping of Third World news. Hester (1971) has analysed how US copy editors select from the Associated

Table II. Indexes of editing inaccuracy per story for news from 12 countries (0–6 scale). A low score indicates relatively accurate editing, a high score inaccurate editing.

	Inaccuracy index	Number of stories
Brazil	3.7	9
Argentina	2.7	7
Ethiopia	2.2	9
France	1.4	9
United States	1.1	44
Great Britain	0.9	56
Australia	0.7	34
Soviet Union	0.6	14
South Africa	0.5	9
Canada	0.3	10
Netherlands	0.2	12
Rhodesia (now Zimbabwe)	0.1	8

Press wires they receive. "Developing" countries accounted for less than one third of the news on the AP wire, and this proportion was further reduced at each editing stage. The wire editors whom Hester interviewed asserted that reader interest in Latin America and Africa was especially low. Hester (1974) analysed the flow of news from Latin America to the United States. The "criminal/violent" category of news made up 14% of what was sent from Latin America, but 48% of the Latin American news that Associated Press passed on to its client newspapers. Peterson (1981) studied how *The Times* of London selects its foreign news. She concluded that even this elite among newspapers tended to ignore nations of the South unless conflict occurred there.

The North's reporting of the South has been the subject of increasingly vigorous argument in international forums such as Unesco over the past decade. Nations of the South have accused the Western media, especially the "Big Four" international news agencies, of under-reporting their countries and concentrating on negative news. Western media have in turn accused their opponents of advocating censorship and destroying the freedom of the press. The debate resulted in the MacBride Report (1980) presented to Unesco by the International Commission for the Study of Communication Problems and in Unesco's adoption of a New World Communication and Information Order.[14]

Editing inaccuracy is cumulative. We have seen how an error at one editing stage may be compounded at later stages. Quantifying inaccuracies for the New Zealand agencies/stations shows that the PA agency averaged 2.1 per story on the 0–6 inaccuracy scale. Radio station XA scored 0.9. If we add the two scores, we have an inaccuracy index of 3.0 for these two successive editing steps within New Zealand. To put this in perspective, recall that New Zealand hears its international news only after it has passed through 3–5 editing filters. If the earlier steps are no more nor less accurate than the last two, the average international news item broadcast on New Zealand radio may contain the equivalent of one very serious inaccuracy as a result of copy editing alone, quite apart from the reliability of the original report. If some wires are any indication, a few stories will contain as many as three or four major editing errors. My findings on editing inaccuracy lend support to the criticisms the South has made. The results are more specific and persuasive than much of the evidence available on news proportions, selection, etc. News about the South has been distorted during editing, however unintentionally.

The editing steps I have analysed are only the last in the news flow. Here inaccurate editing has patterned according to the same factors which bias news selection. Since these factors have also been shown to affect selection at the earlier stages of international news flow, it is likely that they influence how the international news agencies *edit* their copy. From accounts such as Rosenblum (1979, p. 113), the scale of rewriting at the agencies' own desks in New York (AP, UPI), London (Reuters) or Paris (AFP) seems to be greater than at the later editing stages I have analysed.

The contribution of sociolinguistics

We have applied (socio)linguistic analysis to news editing and found evidence for the kind of inaccuracy of which news media are so often accused. What can sociolinguistics do to help solve the problem? There are three components to the problem of inaccurate editing: practical, technical/linguistic, and social/ideological.

The practical problem is the time/space pressure on editors: the time before the next deadline, and the space available for news. Radio editors handle large amounts of copy under the pressure of often hourly deadlines. They receive copy which is intended for newspaper use, and re-style it to be read aloud. Above all, they have to abbreviate. Stories of 2000 words are cut to 50–100 words, complexities simplified, detail removed. Some errors result from ignorance (e.g. of geography), others are pure slips of the pen. These are matters of working conditions and ethos. Sociolinguists can do nothing here except point to the evidence of inaccuracies apparently caused by haste (e.g. example 19) or over-abbreviation (35).

On the linguistic component of inaccurate editing, linguists can offer something. "Technical" failure presumably plays a part in all inaccurate editing, in some cases very obviously (e.g. 25, 38). We can move from description to prescription, and propose linguistic guidelines by which copy editors can avoid certain inaccuracies. A very small percentage of the hundreds of changes made by copy editors result in inaccuracy. There are few editing rules which are essentially bad, which in themselves necessarily cause inaccuracy. Deleting or inserting negatives are such non-rules, for the obvious reason that a statement and its negation cannot be compatible. And few rules are obligatory, e.g. updating time adverbials.

Most inaccuracy results when legitimate rules are applied without regard to the congruence of output copy with its input. From the analysis and examples above, we can identify particular editing rules which typically lead to one of the five types of inaccuracy. Under the five conditions for accuracy (a–e, page 92), we can group a number of specific positive and negative guidelines for copy editors (with examples where the guidelines were violated):

To avoid falsification:

(i)   *Don't delete or insert negatives* (as in example 19).
(ii)   *Do delete or update time adverbials, or convert to non-deictics* (20). *Today* in the lead sentence of a wire story must usually be updated (to *yesterday*), converted to a non-deictic (*on April 25*), or deleted altogether.
(iii)   *Don't approximate time and place adverbials with non-congruent expressions* (21).
(iv)   *Don't substitute non-congruent lexical items* (18).
(v)   *Don't delete or insert expressed agents.*
(vi)   *Don't reverse the transitivity of verbs.*
        Copy editors often change an active intransitive verb into its passive transitive equivalent, or vice versa. This implies either the insertion or deletion of an agent, which may not always be warranted by the input copy. PA's version in (42) deleted the expressed agent: the legislative acts which increased police powers in South Africa. The transitivity of *increasing* is now ambiguous. XA's subsequent change to active in-transitive implies that police powers increased by natural growth.

(42)   AAP   various new acts which had increased police powers
      →   PA   an increasing of police powers   →
      →   XA   increasing police powers

To avoid over-assertion:

(vii)   *Don't delete attributions* (30, 34).
        I have argued that copy editors should retain source and agency attributions. It is most important that source attribution (eyewitness,

spokesperson, etc.) should be retained. This reminds listeners that the news has a specific, human source. It is a report, just one version of events. Agency attributions are less obviously vital, but in my view still important. If agency attributions were always retained, audiences would have the chance to recognize two facts: that most of the world's news originates in the Big Four agencies, and that most overseas news enters New Zealand on a single wire. In many other countries, both news sources and outlets are more diverse. In New Zealand, the public can read a story in the morning paper, hear a parallel account on radio, and watch it again on evening television news. Multiple reinforcement from apparently independent outlets makes the story and its details seem unassailably authoritative. But many witnesses do not make one truth when they are all second-hand accounts based on a lone wire containing unknown errors of fact and interpretation. Attributing a story to its source agency would at least make this situation explicit. Finally, the problem of non-attribution is aggravated when there is double deletion, of both agency and spokesperson. In (43), the Press Trust of India has taken particular care not to give its own backing to the statement:

(43)   Thousands of Indians were reported homeless today as flood waters continued to rise in the north and northeast, inundating large areas of standing crops, *the Press Trust of India said.*
The Agency quoted officials as saying several thousand hectares of jute and rice crops have also been destroyed . . .

→   Thousands of Indians are reported homeless as flood waters continue to rise in the north and north east.
Several thousand hectares of jute and rice crops have also been destroyed.

Retaining attributions will slow down broadcast news presentation, but it need not be repetitive. The copy editor has a wide choice of lexical variants, and several syntactic options: foregrounding (*PQ said that X*); backgrounding (*X, said PQ*); passivizing (*PQ is said to be X*); relativising (*PQ, who is said to be X*); reduction to *according to PQ*. A lead sentence can credit the agency, perhaps sometimes in headline form: *a report from Reuters.*

(viii) *Do mark direct quotations by syntactic devices or intonation* (33, cf. 32). As with attribution deletion, this is especially necessary in conflict situations.

(ix)   *Don't delete hedges.*
In pursuit of less ambiguity, editors are tempted to delete items like *try* or *attempt* (29), or to describe incomplete actions as accomplished

(41). Hedging devices tend to cluster, and they are often deleted in clusters as in (30), thus compounding the over-assertion.

(x)   *Don't insert intensifiers* (28).

(xi) *Don't intensify lexical items beyond what the input story warrants* (27).

To avoid over-scope:

(xii) *Don't pro-form non-identical referents* (35).

(xiii) *Don't delete, shift or transplant constituents which define the scope of a sentence or constituent* (36, 38).

To avoid refocus:

(xiv) *Don't!*

To avoid information addition:

(xv) *Don't!*

The scale of this study is too small to produce adequate guidelines for accurate editing, yet following the guidelines given here would eliminate many inaccuracies. The prime rule of thumb for working editors must be: when in doubt, don't. As Rosenblum (1979, p. 112) notes, "any alteration increases the chance for inadvertent error". Severe copy editing *can* be compatible with accuracy. Station YA edited heavily but very accurately (index 0.5 on 0–6 scale). But one PA editor who edited as heavily scored a quite astonishing 4.2 for inaccuracy, an extreme error per story. Editors who make few alterations give themselves less chance to produce an inaccurate version.

Yet inaccurate editing is not mainly a practical or linguistic problem. Reducing time/space pressures and upgrading language skills should reduce the amount of inaccuracy over-all. But it will not redress the imbalance in where the inaccuracies occur. If inaccurate editing were purely a practical or linguistic matter, all types of news would be affected alike. Yet we have seen this is not so: inaccuracies are not randomly distributed, but concentrate in certain categories of news (e.g. about some countries), and distort news in consistent ways (to make it more newsworthy). This can only result from the frame or ideology within which the editors are working.

Here sociolinguistic analysis can make its second contribution. It provides harder evidence than is possible in other methods of investigating inaccuracy. Newsworkers are noted for receiving researchers and their findings with hostile disbelief.[15] But editing inaccuracy constitutes a failure by the copy editor's own professional standards. The copy editors who introduced them would themselves condemn these inaccuracies if made aware of them in retrospect. Pointing out the bias in where and how the inaccuracies occur should stand a little better chance than most arguments of persuading newsworkers that there is indeed a problem.

The third contribution would be in further studies of news editing in a wide range of media and places. The accuracy of international news editing, especially by the major agencies, is important if nations are to have a fair picture of each other. The bad editing of news about the nations of the South is of particular urgency and significance for the issues surrounding Unesco's New World Information and Communication Order. Research in this area can promote justice in news reporting between the South and the North. More studies can gather more evidence to present to newsworkers. And the findings need to be publicized so that audiences are alert to the human fallibility of news.

Conclusion

The methodology of this study limits its range to defined stages of news transmission, concentrating on the paired texts of input and output copy. It examines not just selection among arguably equal alternatives, but the active, purposeful intervention of the copy editor in the form and meaning of news copy. Copy editors do not merely chose among an open set of options. They actively, if unconsciously, substitute alternatives already rejected, reverse choices already made by the source journalist.

Because this process is one of active intervention, where copy alteration is the subject of a focussed choice, the force of the patterns which emerge is much more striking. In the syntactic analysis, we saw how editing can re-style a text towards a target considered suitable for a particular audience. In the semantic analysis, we saw the active substitution of meanings which are incongruent with the original. Inferences of bias according to social/ political factors made on this evidence are specific and persuasive.

Any situation where one text is transformed into another can be subjected to this kind of analysis. It can be applied to any stage of the news flow; to the effects of news censorship; to the editing of other mass communication content such as books or television scripts; to interpretation and translation from one language to another in news transmission, diplomacy, business; to re-writing texts for L1 or L2 learners; to the captioning of TV programmes for the deaf. Such research depends on social and political conditions to define its issues, on a sound and detailed linguistic analysis for its evidence, on media sociology for its interpretation, and on newsworkers for its application.

References

Bailey, B. (1971). Jamaican Creole: can dialect boundaries be defined? In "Pidginization and Creolization of Languages", (D. Hymes, ed.), pp. 341–8. Cambridge University Press, Cambridge.

Bell, A. (1977). The Language of Radio News in Auckland: a Sociolinguistic Study of Style, Audience and Subediting Variation. Unpublished Ph.D. thesis: University of Auckland (University Microfilms, Ann Arbor, Michigan, 1979).

Bell, A. (1982a). Radio: the style of news language. *Journal of Communication* **32**, 1, 150–164.

Bell, A. (1982b). This isn't the BBC: colonialism in New Zealand English. *Applied Linguistics*, **3**, 3, 246–58.

Berry, F. C., Jr. (1967). A study of accuracy in local news stories of three dailies. *Journalism Quarterly*, **44**, 3, 482–90.

Boyd-Barrett, O. (1980). "The International News Agencies", Constable, London.

Burns, T. (1977). "The BBC: Public Institution and Private World", Macmillan, London.

Cedergren, H. and Sankoff, D. (1974). Variable rules: performance as a statistical reflection of competence. *Language*, **50**, 2, 333–55.

Charnley, V. M. (1936). Preliminary notes on a study of newspaper accuracy. *Journalism Quarterly*, **13**, 4, 394–401.

Crystal, D. (1981). "Directions in Applied Linguistics", Academic Press, London.

Cutlip, S. M. (1954). Content and flow of AP news – from Trunk to TTS to reader. *Journalism Quarterly*, **31**, 4, 434–46.

Davison, A., Kantor, R. N., Hannah, J., Hermon, G., Lutz, R. and Salzillo, R. (1980). "Limitations of Readability Formulas in Guiding Adaptations of Texts" (Technical Report No. 162). Center for the Study of Reading, University of Illinois at Urbana-Champaign.

Fowler, R., Hodge, B., Kress, G. and Trew T. (1979). "Language and Control", Routledge & Kegan Paul, London.

Galtung, J. and Holmboe Ruge, M. (1965). The structure of foreign news. *Journal of Peace Research*, **2**, 1, 64–91.

Garrison, M. B. (1979). The Video Display Terminal and the Copy Editor: a Case Study of Electronic Editing at the Milwaukee Journal. Unpublished Ph.D. dissertation: Southern Illinois University at Carbondale.

Gieber, W. (1956). Across the desk: a study of 16 telegraph editors. *Journalism Quarterly*, **33**, 4, 423–32.

Glasgow University Media Group. (1976). "Bad News", Routledge & Kegan Paul, London.

Glasgow University Media Group. (1980). "More Bad News", Routledge & Kegan Paul, London.

Grice, H. P. (1975). Logic and conversation. *In* "Speech Acts" ("Syntax and Semantics", Vol. 3) (P. Cole and J. L. Morgan, eds), pp. 41–58. Academic Press, New York and London.

Hester, A. (1971). An analysis of news flow from developed and developing nations. *Gazette*, **17**, 1, 29–43.

Hester, A. (1974). The news from Latin America via a world news agency. *Gazette*, **20**, 1, 82–98.

Klima, E. S. (1964). Relatedness between grammatical systems. *Language*, **40**, 1, 1–20.

Knightley, P. (1975). "The First Casualty", Andre Deutsch, London.

Kress, G. (1983). Linguistic processes and the mediation of "reality": the politics of newspaper language. *International Journal of the Sociology of Language*, **40**, 43–57.

Kress, G. R. and Trew, A. A. (1978). Ideological transformation of discourse: or how the *Sunday Times* got *its* message across. *Journal of Pragmatics*, **2**, 4, 311–29.

Lawrence, G. C. and Grey, D. L. (1969). Subjective inaccuracies in local news reporting. *Journalism Quarterly*, **46**, 4, 753–7.

MacBride, S. *et al.* (1980). "Many Voices, One World", (Report by the International Commission for the Study of Communication Problems). Unesco, Paris, and Kogan Page, London.

McNelly, J. T. (1959). Intermediary communicators in the international flow of news. *Journalism Quarterly*, **36**, 1, 23–26.

Osgood, C., Suci, G. and Tannenbaum, P. (1957). "The Measurement of Meaning", University of Illinois Press, Urbana, Illinois.

Peterson, S. (1981). International news selection by the elite press: a case study. *Public Opinion Quarterly*, **45**, 2, 143–63.

Righter, R. (1978). "Whose News? Politics, the Press, and the Third World", Burnett Books/Andre Deutsch, London.

Rosenblum, M. (1979). "Coups and Earthquakes", Harper & Row, New York.

Schlesinger, P. (1978). "Putting 'Reality' Together: BBC News", Constable, London.

Smith, A. (1980). "The Geopolitics of Information", Faber & Faber, London.

Tuchman, G. (1978). "Making News: a Study in the Construction of Reality", Free Press, New York.

White, D. M. (1950). The "Gatekeeper"; a case study in the selection of news. *Journalism Quarterly*, **27**, 4, 383–90.

Notes

Allan Bell was Leverhulme Visiting Fellow in 1982 at the University of Reading, England, on leave from New Zealand, where he works as an editor and sociolinguist. Parts of this paper were presented at the Second New Zealand Linguistics Conference, Wellington, 1978; the Center for Applied Linguistics, Washington, D.C., 1981; and the 10th NWAVE Conference, Philadelphia, 1981. Thanks to Walt Wolfram and Joy Kreeft for their comments on earlier drafts. I am grateful for the financial support of the Leverhulme Trust, and the hospitality of the Department of Linguistic Science, University of Reading, especially Peter Trudgill.

[1] I use the post-1975 label "Radio New Zealand" for the radio division of the former New Zealand Broadcasting Corporation. Since 1974, a further private station has been added, otherwise the Auckland radio scene is not much different today. The wire system, however, has changed in one major respect. NZPA no longer edits the AAP-Reuter wire for private radio stations, which now take a Reuters wire direct. For information on the flow of news in New Zealand and for access to wire copy, I am

indebted to staff members of Radio New Zealand (especially Ken Gibson), Radio Hauraki, Radio i, Radio Windy/Wellington (Fraser Folster), N.Z. Press Association, *N.Z. Herald*, and *Auckland Star*.

[2] The term "copy editor" is used rather than the normal New Zealand (and British) "sub-editor" (or just "sub"). The label "sub-editor" is opaque to non-newsworkers everywhere, who understandably misinterpret it to mean a deputy editor. In many news organizations, the person who selects stories to pass to the sub-editors is called a "copy taster". Research on news flows (e.g. White, 1950) labels these people the "gatekeepers". Remarkably few people are involved in the editing process: perhaps only 5–10 even at major "gates" in the system (Boyd-Barrett, 1980, p. 78).

[3] Editing rules have similarities to rules proposed in two other studies. Bailey (1971) suggested that the distance of a text from standard Jamaican English and from Jamaican creole could be measured by counting the number of rules necessary to turn the text into one or other dialect. Klima (1964) proposed a class of "extension rules" to be added to the grammar of one style to generate other styles.

[4] I would expect the use of video technology to alter the pattern of sentence deletion, for instance. Video makes certain kinds of actions (e.g. viewing later pages of a wire) harder to perform, so that a story of several pages cannot be laid out and seen at a glance. Video editing may encourage even further the rejection of later pages of copy. Interestingly, Garrison (1979) found that many copy editors liked to work from printed copy as well as the video screen, especially for substantial rewriting.

[5] For detail on the rule and its social significance, see Bell (1977, 1982b). As well as deleting the determiner, the rule subordinates the (first) descriptive NP to the (second) name NP. Variable syntactic constraints include determiner type, and presence and complexity of embedding in the descriptive NP.

[6] On the precise nature of the copy editor's linguistic knowledge I do not wish to speculate here. While it is clearly closer to the surface of consciousness than is most language use, it is by no means as self-aware as it may appear. Copy editors work largely by unexamined intuition. In my experience, they prove to be frustratingly unaware of the details of their linguistic function. Copy editing may be a deliberate process, but editors have in mind only a very general notion of style for their station's news. Style books are not much more precise. And when a style book does pronounce on structures (not just lexical items), actual practice tends to ignore it. Some style books prohibit determiner deletion or negative contraction, but the stations still delete or contract up to 60%.

[7] The Glasgow Group's studies are regrettably flawed. Their linguistic analysis and sociological methods (cf. Schlesinger, 1978, p. 47) are both rather inept, which leaves their case vulnerable to counter-attack. This is a pity, since the broad lines of their critique are sound, but inadequately supported by analysis of their evidence. Kress's and Trew's work is far more linguistically sophisticated. Again, however, the detail is less convincing than the general impression. They treat ideology as a far more conscious thing than the unexamined frame of mind which Tuchman (1978) finds in newsworkers. This leads them to a conspiracy theory of writers' motives for applying rules like agent deletion in passives and nominalizations. Such a strong view of linguistic processes seems to me only justified where a rule is subject to a deliberate, focussed choice, as it is in the editing changes studied here. Nevertheless, Kress and Trew's work is linguistically able and addresses the socially important questions.

[8] Note that sub-condition (a) corresponds to Grice's first sub-maxim (1975, p. 46) "Do not say what you believe to be false". The second sub-maxim "Do not say that for which you lack adequate evidence" corresponds to my conditions (b) and (c).

[9] International time differences can trap a copy editor who attempts to add a little colour to a story. Rosenblum (1979, p. 112) tells of the US news agency editor who brightened up a hijack story with description of the aircraft sitting on a "sun-baked runway" in Dacca. He forgot that while the sun shone in New York, it was night in Bangladesh.

[10] The reading of *some* as roughly equivalent to *a few* is, I think, standard in New Zealand English, and makes the approximation of *fourteen* by *some* unacceptable. However, in some (!) dialects of American English, *some* has to be at least eight or ten (I am indebted to Dwight Bolinger for this observation). The *fourteen* of the original is in fact already an error, since Mrs Peron was a cabaret dancer in 1956, eighteen years previously.

[11] This was demonstrated again in reporting of the Falklands/Malvinas conflict in 1982. The war produced a textbook crop of irreconcilable statistics from the two sides, Argentina and Britain. Phillip Knightley (1975) of the London *Sunday Times* has chronicled the inglorious history of war reporting from the Crimea to Vietnam in a book that proves truth is indeed the "First Casualty" of war. Knightley shows that official war statistics are rarely to be taken at face value. The Falklands/Malvinas war also threw light on the practice of censorship. Censorship is a form of editing, and its effects can be assessed by the methodology used here. Normally the pre-censorship text will not be available. However, during the Falklands/Malvinas war, there was some assessment of the effects of censorship. *The Economist* (22 May, 1982) examined how the censors cut one particular text. Our methodology enables us to assess (a) whether censorship achieves its aim of withholding information useful to an enemy, and (b) whether and where it distorts meaning and thus misinforms the public.

[12] (d) *astrology follower* to *astrologer* (XA/S1)
   (e) *fourteen* to *some years ago* (XA/S1)
   (f) *also* deleted (PA/S2)
   (g) *and his wife* added (XA/S3)
   (h) *constant* to *close companion* (XA/S3)
   (i) *managed Mrs Peron* to *managed her career* (XA/S1: softens the innuendo)
   (j) Mrs Peron referred to as *Isabel* (XA/S2: unprecedented in the data for a head of state).
On this particular story, note Rosenblum's anecdote (1979, p. 114) that "one news agency desk insisted on adding 'former cabaret dancer' to every mention of Isabel Peron".

[13] Most newspaper inaccuracy studies have simply counted errors. However, to treat a mis-spelt name and a major refocus of a story as equally serious seems inadequate. "Objective" errors of fact (Berry, 1967) such as age or date may be quite wrong in an absolute sense, but not do much harm to the content of a news item. "Subjective" errors of emphasis may be hard to specify as wrong at all, but have significant effects on the meaning of a story. Ideally errors should be judged by a panel, but in this study I have been the sole judge. I therefore claim only reasonable internal consistency for the scores, not an absolute validity.

[14] The course of the debate on the New Information Order is hugely complex, and the literature is multiplying to match. Righter (1978) and Smith (1980) are good introductory surveys and chronologies. Articles appear in journals such as *Gazette*, *Inter Media*, and *Journal of Communication* (especially **29**, 2, 1979). Boyd-Barrett (1980) is the basic text on the structure and workings of the "Big Four" international news agencies: Reuters, Associated Press, United Press International, and Agence

France Presse. These agencies provide most of the world's media with most of their international news, and set the agenda of what other media regard as newsworthy. Besides selection and editing, an additional obstacle to the flow of accurate international news is inter-language translation. Especially for non-English speaking countries, much news must be translated at one of the gates in the flow. Interlanguage translation is even more liable to inaccuracy than intra-language editing.

[15] This has been the experience of many media researchers: e.g. Burns (1977), the Glasgow Group (1980, p. 417). It was also the reaction from some quarters to the present research, and not just to the obviously threatening inaccuracy findings. Seemingly harmless observations on radio language style met an equally defensive response.

Educational Issues

6

Applications of the social psychology of language: sociolinguistics and education

John Edwards and Howard Giles

It can be argued that, as a distinctive and robust branch of sociolinguistics, the social psychology of language has only really emerged in the 1970s as a coherent entity with its own conceptual, theoretical and methodological traditions (Giles, *et al.*, 1980), although there have been earlier proponents (e.g. Brown, 1965; Lambert, 1967). As in other sociolinguistic disciplines, the topics investigated by social psychologists of language are diverse and, despite the short history of the area, it has already been seen to have relevance to a wide range of applied social settings. These include the clinical-medical (e.g. Pendleton *et al.*, 1982; Scherer, 1980), legal (e.g. Danet, 1980; Line and O'Barr, 1979), occupational (e.g. Kalin, 1982), educational (e.g. Gardner, 1982; Robinson, 1978) and language planning policy (e.g. Ryan, 1981; Taylor and Simard, 1981). There is, however, the possibility of selecting one area of sociolinguistic interest which in itself may contain information of wider generality. Thus, in this chapter, we examine sociolinguistic issues in an educational context, with the intention of discussing matters of wider importance and of showing how a social psychological perspective can shed new light on some old problems.

In choosing the educational setting, we have not been completely arbitrary; a number of points can be made in support of this choice. First, of all the areas to which sociolinguistic study is relevant, education is clearly one of the most intrinsically important. As an institution of the middle class,

APPLIED SOCIOLINGUISTICS
ISBN: 0-12-701220-6

school is one of the obvious places in which to investigate language and class contact. Second, home–school and teacher–pupil interactions can be seen as microcosms of wider social interaction. Here, we might think of the school as an arena in which minority–majority relations are reflected, in which general issues of social mobility are first encountered, and in which social policy of the broadest kind (cultural pluralism or assimilation, for example) is first brought to bear upon individuals. Third, many general sociolinguistic matters are particularly susceptible to interpretation in educational terms. Issues like the validity and acceptance of dialects, the position accorded to standard usage, and the relationships between language and identity can all be profitably explored and, to a certain extent, understood in educational terms.

Obviously, these points do not reflect watertight or mutually exclusive categories. Rather, they represent variations on the basic theme that sociolinguistic issues can legitimately be considered in an educational framework. We shall endeavour to justify this theme, and to demonstrate that attention given to education-related matters has an importance extending beyond the school. In this chapter, we follow the child, as it were, from home to school. We consider, first of all, aspects of pre-school life and language, then comment upon the home–school transition and, thirdly, treat aspects of school life itself. Following this, we introduce two social psychological models which we believe make theoretical sense of some of the important processes underlying the complex relationships among language, class and education. Finally, we attempt to indicate how future social pyschological studies in the educational context may inform sociolinguistics in general, and advance some modest pragmatic orientations for the classroom.

The sociolinguistics of language and education

Before school

It is not our purpose here to review the psycho- and sociolinguistics of first language development (see for example Bruner, 1981; Hamers and Blanc, 1982; Robinson, 1981a). It is enough to say that, well before school age, normal children develop a well-formed system of language. The ease with which language is developed, in the absence of direct instruction, and in circumstances in which uniformity of support and reinforcement (especially from parents) cannot be assumed, has been a continuing source of inspiration for linguists and others for a very long time. It has, in fact, prompted a revival of Cartesian rationalism in linguistics, which explains the rapidity and the complexity of language learning through brain readiness or "prewiring". This is not the only theoretical stance possible, of course. However, whether one accepts Chomskian or Skinnerian explanation (to put the matter at its most simplistic level; see Love, 1981), the debate is not over *what* the child learns, but *how* (Wells and Robinson, 1982).

We used the term "normal children" above. What *is* the normal child in this context? The linguistic and anthropological viewpoint here is, and has been for some time, that any child not handicapped by one of the recognized syndromes in speech pathology learns the language of its speech community without formal instruction (see, however, Berko-Gleason (1980) on direct instruction in certain sociolinguistic skills). Thus, although the specifics of what is learned obviously vary enormously, the process itself is entirely natural to the human species. Given that it is possible to argue, as Trudgill (1975) has done, for example, that "all normal adult native speakers know and therefore use their own dialect of English perfectly" (p. 45), it would seem that, whatever the specifics may be, virtually every child is, by an early age, well on the way to becoming a fluent speaker.

While not a logical requirement of the preceding viewpoint, it is nonetheless true that those subscribing to it also generally hold that the language variety learned by the normal child is itself of complete linguistic validity. That is, not only will the child become fluent in the prevailing language variety, but also the variety itself, insofar as it is the regularly-used pattern of communication of the community, possesses the linguistic range and complexity associated with fully-formed systems. Thus, Sapir (1949) tells us that "the gift of speech and a well-ordered language are characteristic of every known group of human beings" (p. 1). The linguistic and anthropological evidence is most relevant here, in that it rules out the possibility of "primitive" or "debased" or "illogical" or "substandard" varieties (Trudgill and Giles, 1977).

With regard to *languages*, such a view has some longevity. Gleitman and Gleitman (1970), for example, reject entirely the notion of the primitive language, incapable of expressing ideas communicable in some other language (see also Lenneberg, 1967). This does not mean, of course, that all languages are the same in their complexity, nor exactly equivalent in expressive power. At the least, however, we can take it that languages, while differing because of different varieties of the human condition, cannot be seen in terms of "better" or "worse". So far as *dialects* are concerned, however, the position is somewhat more involved. Although linguistically no dialect can be seen as inferior or superior to another, the popular viewpoint is often at odds with this. While few would want to argue, perhaps, that French is "better" than German, many can be found who would claim that standard English is "better" than Cockney, say (Edwards, 1982), or that Quebec French is "worse" than Parisian (Bourhis, 1982), or that Mexican-accented Spanish is "worse" than Castillian (Carranza, 1982). This is an important point, worth re-emphasizing: linguistic data notwithstanding, there is abundant evidence of prejudice towards certain dialects, and this seems to be almost universal among languages in which standard dialects have emerged (Giles and Edwards, 1983; Ryan and Giles, 1982).

This implies that, in the eyes of many, not all normal children can learn "proper" language. This perception can arise in two ways: (a) a given dialect is seen to be somehow not as good as another (e.g. Cockney is viewed as inferior to standard English); (b) a given speech pattern is not seen as a valid dialect at all (e.g. the perception of black English as some haphazard, illogical, substandard approximation to "proper" English). These two possibilities are not always clearly separable in the arguments of those who have claimed that some children suffer from "verbal deprivation". The classic examples here are surely the pre-school programmes of compensatory education, usually having a central language component. For example, Bereiter and Engelmann (1966) constructed a programme of intensive instruction in "correct" English for black American children. These children were seen as having "immature" and "rudimentary" language which, in some cases, was actually dispensable. Bereiter and Engelmann attempted, specifically, to break down what they called the "giant word syndrome"; thus, disadvantaged children were seen as unable to recognize single words and, instead, amalgamated words (e.g. "I ain't got no juice" became "Uai-ga-na-ju"; p. 34).

However, as we have already suggested, programmes like this are constructed upon very inadequate appreciations of dialect variation – which includes pronunciation and syntax differences, as well as lexical variation. Bereiter and Engelmann have been criticized by Labov, who is well-known for his demonstration of the linguistic validity of Black English Vernacular (1973, 1976). This rather undercuts the philosophy of intervention and compensatory language programmes for the pre-school child since there is, in effect, nothing for which to compensate.

Generally, the points of view noted above may be seen as the *deficit* and *difference* positions on language (see Edwards, 1979a; Hudson, 1980). The former, fuelled substantially by the writings of Bernstein on elaborated and restricted codes, is more and more giving way to the latter which, as we have seen, has the force of linguistic and anthropological evidence behind it. This does not mean that the deficit viewpoint is entirely without current proponents. As examples, we might cite the work of Tough (1977) in the United Kingdom and Ramey and Campbell (1977, 1979) in the United States, who discuss the developmental (including linguistic) retardation among poor children supposedly deprived of early stimulation and learning experiences.

We will return to these matters in the following sections, for the difference–

deficit issue underlies much of the sociolinguistic investigation in education. We have simply been concerned here to delineate the positions as they bear upon the pre-school child. It is clear that we agree with Gumperz and Hernandez-Chavez (1972) when they state that for all children, regardless of dialect, there exists "control of a fully formed grammatical system" (p. 84) at the time of school entry (although perhaps "well-formed" might be slightly more accurate here).

Going to school

The beginning of a child's school life has some noteworthy sociolinguistic aspects. There is, first of all, the relative degree of continuity/discontinuity existing between the home and the school. For middle-class children whose homes are ones in which standard dialect is used, there need be little linguistic discontinuity; the speech patterns used and encouraged in school will be essentially the same as those of the home (see Ammon, 1977). Additionally, there is evidence to suggest differences in language use among social classes (Robinson, 1978, 1979), differences which will first become salient at school entry. For example, Hess and Shipman (1965, 1968a, 1968b) have claimed that, whereas middle-class mother–child communication is broad and rich in detail, lower-class patterns are often ones of "imperative-normative" control (see also Bernstein and Henderson, 1969; Cook-Gumperz, 1973; Robinson, 1981b; Robinson and Rackstraw, 1972). Working-class language use is geared towards things concrete and specific; middle-class use is more abstract and elaborated. There is, of course, a relation between all this work and Bernstein's notions of *code*. While Bernstein himself has recently been concerned to explain that his codes would be better interpreted as *socio*linguistic than as linguistic, and that his studies were always aimed at elucidating group *performance* differences and not ones of basic competence (e.g. Bernstein, 1972, 1973), his work has quite often been taken as support for the language deficiency argument. Hess and Shipman, for example, see the impact of this work as leading to the necessary "re-socialization" of the child, for whom "the meaning of deprivation would thus seem to be a deprivation of meaning" (1968b, p. 103).

We obviously do not concur with such sentiments, nor do we believe that there is adequate support for them (see Robinson, 1979). We mention this work on class differences in language use only to acknowledge that differences may in fact exist which may prove a hindrance to children's school progess; this is an acknowledgement of *social* deficits rather than substantive cognitive or linguistic ones. And, indeed, there is reason to think that these class differences are themselves not as pronounced as the deficit theorists would have us believe. There is, for example, the general caution that must

124   JOHN EDWARDS AND HOWARD GILES

be attached to any study conducted by middle-class researchers into working-class speech, communicative skills and life-styles, in which differences may be found in rather artificial, unfamiliar or actually alien circumstances (see Edwards, 1979a; Stipek and Nelson, 1980). Also, the work of A. D. Edwards (1976) among 11-year-old middle- and working-class children suggests that "large and consistent speech differences" (p. 108) may not always exist. At the very least, such work indicates how important the context is in any speech study (see also Labov, 1973). Educators must appreciate that children's language behaviour in the classroom is largely determined by their definitions of that context (see Bradac, 1982; Ryan and Giles, 1982; Smith, Giles and Hewstone, 1972) and that these situational construals may be quite different depending upon the ethnic and class background of the children concerned.

To the extent to which dialect differences exist, children may experience a considerable home–school discontinuity. It has been suggested, in fact, that for some children this may amount to "culture shock": the phenomenon many will have experienced upon being immersed in a foreign and unfamiliar context. For immigrant and ethnic minority children particularly, the discontinuity is frequently severe enough to produce this effect, since they are entering a foreign-language environment and a quite different cultural setting (see Abrahams, 1976; Ashworth, 1975; Kochman, 1981). In short, the transition from home to school may, linguistically, be a difficult one for children of certain backgrounds. Although children from all sorts of backgrounds experience anxiety at the home–school transition, working-class, immigrant and ethnic minority children are of particular concern. They are entering a new environment which is very different from the one thay have known, in which the same sorts of behaviour are not valued or normative (McKirnan and Hamayan, 1980) and in which language may for the first time become an issue.

School life

Much of what will be discussed here can be considered to pertain especially to the early years of school life. Given what has already been mentioned, it seems obvious that the first few years of school are of special importance when dealing with sociolinguistic matters. Children arrive possessing a well-formed linguistic system; this much is clear. Difficulties arise, however, because this system may not be the one encouraged and reinforced at school; it may in fact be seen as inferior and substandard. Gumperz and Hernandez-Chavez (1972) have, as noted above, supported the child's basic linguistic competence. They go on to argue further, however, that language differences "do have a significant influence on a teacher's expectation, and hence on the learning environment" (p. 105). This is essentially the crux of the matter. Dialects which, linguistically, are just as valid systems as any other may nevertheless be viewed as invalid. Thus, having ruled out sub-stantive linguistic dialectal deficiency does not, unfortunately, also remove the social deficiencies associated with certain speech styles. This means that, for practical purposes, certain children's speech *is* deficient; we have simply tried so far to point out the aetiology and nature of this deficiency, and particularly to stress the power of social convention and prejudice.

The school is important here because, for most children, it represents the first concentrated evidence of this social deficiency. In addition, of course, there is the fact that schools have traditionally seen themselves as responsible for promoting "correctness" in linguistic matters (Trudgill, 1975). This implies that not only may linguistic discontinuity be noted at school, it may also provoke some action. Typically, as we shall see, this has been of a remedial nature, even though (from what we have already discussed) we can also see that in one sense there is nothing to be remedied. The general issue here, then, is what (if anything) has been done (or should be done) about disadvantaged speech at school. At a very general level, one might say that two broad possibilities exist: either the pupil must accommodate to the ideas and methods of the school, or the school must adapt to the ideas and methods of pupils. Historically, the first of these has prevailed, while latterly we see more evidence of schools changing to deal with different pupil backgrounds. For convenience, we propose to discuss these matters from the perspectives of the teachers, parents and children.

Teachers

Teachers' attitudes have typically been built upon an assumed correctness of certain speech styles, usually those of the middle class. This has led logically to attempts to teach children "proper" linguistic habits, and to the assump-tion that their maternal varieties may not always be completely adequate (see, however, Wiggen's (1978) discussion of the rather different Norwegian situation). As Trudgill (1975) notes, teachers have not been averse to labelling non-standard speech as "wrong", "bad", "careless", "sloppy", "slovenly", "vulgar" or even "gibberish". One can appreciate, of course, that teachers are not alone in these views; they are, after all, widely held, and teachers are members of society too. Nevertheless, teachers' views are of particular importance. Although teachers may express linguistically en-lightened attitudes, they are still "quite likely to be influenced by what they perceive as deviant speech" (Gumperz and Hernandez-Chavez, 1972, p. 105). Also, however they may feel before entering their school career, teachers are soon initiated into the ways of the school. Thus Fuchs (1973, p. 85) has noted that, on the matter of disadvantage generally, the teacher.

unarmed with the strength that understanding the social processes involved
might have given her . . . [is] socialized by the attitudes of those around her . . .
she has learned to behave and think in a way that perpetuates a process by which
disadvantaged children continue to be disadvantaged.

This process, incidentally, tends to undercut the argument that having
children taught by teachers from the same social background, and familiar
with the same non-standard speech patterns, would substantially decrease
linguistic and educational disadvantage. That is, the influence of the school
in linguistic and other matters extends to the teaching staff as well as to the
children.

There is, therefore, some reason to think that teachers' stereotypes and
predispositions may unfairly hinder children's school progress. The work of
Rosenthal and Jacobson (1968) is relevant here. They claimed that, on the
basis of manipulated information provided to teachers, the latter formed
different expectations for what they thought were groups of bright and
not-so-bright children. Rosenthal and Jacobson also claimed that these
expectations were reflected in differential school progress made by the
children. This work has been strenuously criticized (Dusek, 1975, provides a
useful review) and the results have not always proved to be replicable.
However, whatever the verdict on such manipulated expectations, it is
surely beyond doubt that, in the normal course of classroom life, teachers
routinely hold expectations about their pupils. Such expectations are perfectly normal and, in most cases, are probably fairly accurate assessments.
However, in instances in which there are differences between the social
backgrounds of pupil and teacher, we would expect such judgements to be
more fallible. Rist (1970) outlined here a self-fulfilling prophecy originating
from teacher expectations of children. Teachers may feel that certain
children (or groups of children) are less able than others; this may be
communicated in subtle (and, as Trudgill, 1975, noted above, not so subtle)
ways to the children (e.g. by non-verbal reactions; see Rosenfeld, 1978)
who, sensitive to this, respond in ways consistent with the expectation.

The power of social stereotyping in this regard is illustrated by the work of
Snyder (1980) and his colleagues who have shown, in a series of investigations, how people can set up situations non-consciously so as to confirm their
behavioural expectations of others. For example, if a teacher believes that
working-class children are inarticulate and aggressive, he or she might,
when encountering a new class, pose irritating or involved questions that
would unduly tax anybody. Nevertheless, the precise behaviours anticipated
of the children might thereby be elicited, confirming the teacher's negative
stereotype. Although many features may figure in the formation of teacher
expectations, Rist noted that children's speech patterns are of some importance here. The dangers are obvious: a teacher may unfairly (though not out

of malice) categorize a child on the basis of linguistic and other features, this categorization may influence the subsequent school progress of the child, and disadvantage may thus be perpetuated (Eltis, 1980; Seligman et al., 1972).

In this vein, recent research has often shown that reactions are not always based upon objective or portrayed characteristics of the speaker but rather upon characteristics expected by the listener (Aboud et al., 1974). Williams et al. (1971) also provide data supporting this sort of wish fulfillment. In one of their experimental conditions, they asked teachers to evaluate the speech patterns of a black child whom they saw and heard on a videotape recording. Despite the fact that another (white) child's middle-class speech patterns were superimposed on the tape, the black child was nevertheless perceived as sounding "ethnic-non-standard" and was also rated as low in "confidence-eagerness" (see also below). In other words, teachers had biased their perceptions of the speech (and hence their evaluation of the child) in the direction of their stereotyped vocal expectations. Thus, even when listeners' speech stereotypes are disconfirmed in the form of speakers' actual vocal characteristics, discrepancies need not always arise at the listeners' level of cognitive awareness. Instead, listeners may organize the linguistic input according to their own predetermined and valued cognitive structures (Street and Hopper, 1982). Moreover, additional information about a speaker's class and ethnic background can not only bias one's reconstructions of their past performances but can also influence the perceptions of their subsequent behaviour (Ball et al., 1982; Thakerar and Giles, 1981). Of course, the pragmatic implications of such findings are enormous; even if the speech of non-standard dialect children is "improved", there is no guarantee that it will be recognized as such by teachers and others anyway.

Having noted these generalities, let us turn now to some more specific considerations of teachers' views of disadvantaged speech, bearing in mind as we do so the assumption made here of the linguistic validity of all dialects. Some more useful American research has been done by Williams and his colleagues, working with black, white and Mexican-American children (see, generally, Williams, 1976). In a number of studies it was found that when white and black teachers evaluated children on the basis of their speech, along a number of semantic-differential dimensions, two underlying factors emerged (see also above). One of these, labelled "confidence-eagerness", reflected such things as the perceived confidence and social status of the child. The other factor, "ethnicity-non-standardness", was also associated with judgements of social status and, as well, with perceptions of ethnicity and the standardness-non-standardness of the child's speech. These findings were expanded when Williams et al. (1972) asked white and black teachers to evaluate low- and middle-status black, white and Mexican-American children in Texas. First, the teachers were requested to provide semantic-differential evaluations of the three ethnic groups as presented to them via a simple written label – this presumably being a measure of teachers' general and overall stereotypes. Second, teachers evaluated videotaped samples of children's speech and, third, they were asked to estimate each child's classroom achievement.

The first important finding was the confirmation of the previously established two-factor model of judgement. Second, relationships were found between teacher ratings and the status and ethnicity of the children; thus, low-status children were seen as more ethnic/non-standard, and were rated less favourably on the confidence/eagerness dimension. Within this low-status group, white children were seen most favourably. For middle-status children, results were similar with regard to the ethnicity/non-standardness dimension. However, on the confidence/eagerness dimension, black middle-class children were rated slightly *more* favourably than were white children (see Giles and Bourhis, 1976a), and both black and white children were rated more positively than were the Mexican-American children. A third finding was that the teachers' general stereotypes (of the groups overall) correlated reasonably well with their evaluations of actual group members. Williams suggests, then, that the more general teacher stereotypes may have affected judgements made of individual children (and this, of course, is exactly the problem referred to above). Fourth, predictions of children's scholastic achievement were related to the speech evaluations. It is of interest here that the ratings made by black and white teachers were remarkably similar. This work by Williams has been discussed in some detail here since it represents a series of investigations in which similar results have emerged, and since it underlines once again the power of speech patterns to influence teacher ratings specifically.

A study by Edwards (1979b) of Dublin school children provides some further evidence here. Lower-class and middle-class children were tape-recorded reading a short passage, and were then evaluated along a large number of dimensions by teachers-in-training. In this study, the judges were also asked, for each rating made, to indicate how confident they were about their assessment. On every scale, the lower-class children were viewed less favourably than their middle-class counterparts. Factor analysis of all ratings revealed only one underlying factor of importance; that is, all rating scales were interrelated. This finding is comparable to those of Williams in that his "ethnicity" factor is clearly not operative in the Irish context, and it also rather confirms the notion that teachers' judgements of specific children along specific traits proceed from some overall elicited stereotype. We would not wish, of course, to deny that other scales and other situations might evoke other factors (see Day, 1982; Ryan and Giles, 1982); in the school context, however, and on scales relating mainly to language and school ability, teachers' ratings may well be rather unidimensional. It is also of some interest here to note that the teachers-in-training employed as judges were not equally confident about all their ratings. In general, they were more confident when asked to evaluate aspects of personality more or less directly related to the speech sample itself (i.e. scales relating to fluency, reading ability and pronunciation), and less so when asked to judge how happy the child seemed, or his family socioeconomic status. This indicates that some dimensions would appear to have greater face validity than others, and shows judges to have, quite properly, some reservations about making assessments involving rather far-flung matters. Of course, they do make such judgements (Choy and Dodd (1976) even found judges willing to assess, on the basis of brief speech samples, the happiness of the children's marriages) but, as the confidence ratings indicate, they may not be very comfortable with them. This is a useful cautionary note for those engaged in such studies to bear in mind, especially since subjects often seem willing to make ratings along any lines suggested to them by investigators. At the same time, however, it is worth emphasizing that, with regard to the difficulties often involved in generalizing from attitudes to behaviour (Fishbein, 1980), a number of field studies have shown that attitudinal prejudices towards non-standard dialect speakers have been reflected behaviourally (e.g. in lack of co-operation with such speakers; see Bourhis and Giles, 1976; Giles *et al.*, 1975; Giles and Farrar, 1979).

These studies tend generally to suggest that teachers do hold stereotyped impressions of certain children, and that these are related at least in part to children's speech styles. To make the point once again: it is not that teachers are alone in this, for stereotyped reactions to certain accents and dialects are widespread throughout society. However, teachers' views in this regard are rather special since negative evaluations may lead to damaging consequences for children at school. If we consider that many disadvantaged children from materially poor backgrounds, especially if they are members of visible minority groups, have real and continuing difficulties in many aspects of their interaction with mainstream society, then it seems unfortunate, to say the least, that teachers may unfairly add to their difficulties through categorization based upon inaccurate and ill-informed stereotypes and judgements. While we may not be able to hope that schools alone can substantially alter the lot of certain social groups, we should at least hope that they will not exacerbate the problems of the disadvantaged.

Parents
What are the views held by parents with regard to variations in dialect and accent? There are one or two general points to make here first. We must

remember that speech styles, however non-prestigious or non-standard they may be in a wider social sense, are still the maternal and regularly-used varieties for given groups; furthermore, in the absence of intergroup contact, such varieties would hardly be matters of conscious concern at all. There is, however, evidence to suggest that in modern society where cross-group linguistic comparisons are inevitable, low-prestige groups are very much aware of the non-standardness of their speech (Trudgill, 1974). This is the background against which we should consider the views of parents: which is to say, the views of adult members of the child's speech community.

In 1960, Lambert and his colleagues in Montreal studied the reactions of French- and English-speaking students towards French and English speakers (Lambert et al., 1960). English-speaking judges, predictably enough, rated English speakers more favourably than French ones. The French judges' reactions, however, were more intriguing. They too evaluated the English speakers more favourably than they did the French speakers; additionally, they actually gave less favourable responses to the French speakers than did the English judges. Lambert interpreted this as evidence of a "minority group reaction": that is, members of a group seen as inferior in some ways to another adopt the stereotyped views of the dominant group, downgrading themselves in the process (see also Ammon, 1977). Moreover, as Ryan (1981, p. 8) has argued:

> members of lower class minority communities (especially those with distinctive skin color like Blacks and many Hispanics) often feel that their social mobility may be blocked primarily by factors beyond their control. If the minority group is politically powerless and economically disadvantaged, learned helplessness (a low sense of personal control over one's destiny, low expectations for success, maladaptive causal attributions for success and failures) among the children can further limit school achievement (see Brody, 1968; Dweck, 1975; Harari and Covington, 1981; Louden, 1978; Nicholls, 1979).

While there is reason to believe that Lambert's 1960 results would not now be found in Montreal, because of social changes affecting French–English relations (Bourhis and Genesee, 1980), the fact remains that low-prestige groups can and do adopt views of the dominant society (see Milner, 1981, for a critical appraisal of this); that these views are not static only serves to point out how useful language evaluation studies can be in assessing the tenor of intergroup relations (Giles and Marsh, 1979; Giles and Powesland, 1975).

At the same time as a "minority group reaction" may exist, there is also the bonding or solidarity function to be reckoned with (Ryan et al., 1982). That is, one might ask why group members would retain a non-prestigious speech style if they accepted the more general social verdict as to its low prestige? There are several points to be made here. First, and most simply, members of certain visible minorities may find no advantage in changing speech styles; their disadvantage will not thereby disappear. Second, as Ryan (1981, p. 8) has pointed out:

> minority children have relatively few examples available in their communities of individuals who have successfully achieved this goal since these people frequently move away from their speech community phsyically as well as psychologically . . . Also . . . since partial achievement is often downgraded by standard speakers (Ryan and Carranza, 1977; Sebastian and Ryan, in press), only the very high goal of full achievement is worth aiming for.

It should of course be pointed out here that Ryan refers only to members of the group itself; there are many examples of standard dialect speakers (people in the media, teachers, etc.) regularly presented to minority group children. Third, any speech style is characteristic of a particular group's background and life-style, and therefore serves as a bond between group members (Drake, 1980; Giles, 1977; Giles and Saint-Jacques, 1979). This is especially so for groups undergoing a revitalization of group pride (e.g. blacks in the United States, the Chicanos, the Welsh, etc.). But the group bonding function of language extends beyond those groups experiencing some renewed internal vigour. It also provides a group identity which is a known, safe quantity; attempts to alter it may result in marginality: a feeling of no longer belonging to one group and yet not quite fitting in with a new one either (Lambert, 1967). Carranza and Ryan (1975), for example, advert to the Mexican-American notion of the *vendido*: the sell-out, the defector to the other side (see also Khlief, 1979; Kochman, 1976). Fourth, there is the factor of "covert prestige" (Labov, 1966); non-standard varieties, although low in prestige, may yet possess a toughness and a type of masculinity which is appealing and which constitutes a prestige of its own. Indeed, there is some evidence that this prestige is attractive even to those with more standard styles. Thus, Trudgill (1972) noted that some middle-class males in Norwich *claimed* to use non-standard forms more often than, in actuality, they did.

All of this suggests that, when considering the clash of linguistic forms in the school context, there are a number of important elements to bear in mind. These centre upon the fact that a group's speech patterns may be at once generally non-prestigious *and* essential for identity (see also Day, 1982). Here, we should recall some of the findings of Giles and his colleagues (Giles and Powesland, 1975). Drawing upon Lambert's (1967) distinction among the personality dimensions of competence, personal integrity and social attractiveness, it was found that although non-standard dialects and accents typically are evaluated less favourably on scales reflecting the competence dimension, they often evoke higher ratings in terms of the latter two factors. This may be related to the notion of ingroup solidarity, inasmuch as speakers of non-standard forms may be judged as trustworthy, friendly, warm, etc., without necessarily being seen as competent. While this provides some comfort for non-standard speakers, it cannot be denied that the scales relating to competence (e.g. intelligence, industriousness, ambition and confidence) are of some particular importance, especially within educational and other institutional settings (see Kalin, 1982).

In any event, we can note that the speech patterns of non-standard speakers, and of disadvantaged groups, are not without their positive features in a social sense. We have already mentioned that, linguistically, they are valid systems. What, therefore, might we expect to observe in the school context in which the first sustained language contact occurs, insofar as the parents are concerned? Schools are often seen as essentially feminine institutions, and this perception certainly extends to the language patterns used and encouraged there. In fact, this is related to the work noted above on covert prestige: if non-standard English is seen as essentially masculine, then standard English must be relatively more feminine (see also Giles *et al.*, 1980). Right away then a barrier may exist between the home and the school. Parents may see the school as a soft, ineffectual place which their children would do well to leave as soon as possible. This feeling is, of course, often amplified by the desire to have children enter the work-world as soon as possible in order to help support the family.

On the other hand, it is also the case that many working-class parents see in the school an avenue for the upward mobility of their children; far from wanting their children to leave, they may be most supportive of formal education in general and their children's scholastic progress in particular. Labov (1973), Ovando (1978) and others have pointed to the high educational aspirations of lower-class and minority-group parents for their children. How would this translate into perceptions of a sociolinguistic sort? There is some evidence to suggest that parents often adopt a very commonsense and pragmatic view here. They may reject the idea that schools should conduct classes in non-standard dialect, or that schools should provide textbooks written in non-standard forms – suggestions put forward by some recent linguists and educators (see below) – because they wish their children to learn and use what they see to be the dialect of upward mobility. At the same time, however, they do not wish to see a return to the traditional school intolerance for any non-standard usage in class. Covington (1976), for example, has referred to the views of a group of black parents in Washington. They wanted teachers to tolerate their children's use of Black English Vernacular in the classroom, while at the same time they were strongly opposed to texts written in this form, and to teachers using it. In this, the parents were apparantly calling for what many have seen to be the most appropriate course of action (Edwards, 1979a).

Children

As with their parents, children are often caught in some no-man's-land between home speech patterns and the standard forms of the school. Many features other than purely linguistic or sociolinguistic ones are relevant here. First, recall the notion that the school may be seen as essentially feminine by children whose native culture is one stressing action, immediacy, etc. Second, bear in mind that the school and the teachers are seen as outposts of authority, and that different social groups react to authority in different ways. If for parents the discontintuity between home and school is experienced somewhat indirectly, for the children it is direct and immediate. Even at the school itself, the difference between the classroom and the playground, for example, is marked in terms of language use, and represents a contrast which has been ignored at some cost by certain writers on lower-class language (e.g. Bereiter and Engelmann, 1966). Lower-class children may often be torn between a desire to do well at school (with the support of their parents) and the desire to maintain out-of-school peer contacts. In this connection, Labov (1976) has discussed certain Black English Vernacular-speaking children referred to as "lames". Separated from the rest of the peer group because of lack of facility in verbal games (see Kochman, 1981), or because of parental pressure, or because of a perception of the advantages of mainstream culture, these children are more likely to accommodate to the norms (including the linguistic ones) of the school. Their peripheral relation to the non-standard culture opens the way (or perhaps impels them) to greater success in school. In achieving this, they distance themselves from their mates and create, for many black speakers, yet another association between unacceptability and the school. This American example is perhaps suggestive for other cultural settings as well; indeed, we might suspect that wherever discontinuity exists between home culture and that of the school, children may experience difficulties.

However, not all non-standard dialect-speaking children are "lames". What of the majority of those who experience a home-school difference: how is the linguistic difference perceived and dealt with? Evidence suggests that speakers of non-standard forms acquire facility in standard varieties fairly early. For example, Marwit et al. (1972) demonstrated that black second-grade children consistently used more black vernacular forms than did white children; that is, the study supported the notion of Black English Vernacular as a regular and rule-governed dialect. However, when these same children were looked at again in fourth grade, black children showed an increased use of standard forms (although they still used more vernacular ones; Marwit and Marwit, 1976). Marwit (1977) found that this process extended to seventh-grade children as well. The point of these studies is that children possessing a non-standard dialect, and who are in regular contact with standard speakers, may very soon come to use standard forms in their own speech (see also Giles and Bourhis, 1976b).

This does not mean, of course, that children abandon their maternal varieties; peers and community would militate against that. However, children from an early age are aware of the differences, substantive and evaluative, between standard and non-standard (see Day, 1982), and as they develop they become increasingly able to use either as the situation demands. Gay and Tweney (1976) found that black children's production of vernacular forms decreased with age although their comprehension of those forms increased. This rather suggests that the *use* of standard forms need not necessarily eradicate the original variety; at the same time, it does indicate an increasing facility with standard dialect. Gay and Tweney, discussing their experiments with sixth-grade children, report that

> on several occasions when a white adult mistakenly entered a testing room [the experimenter was black], black subjects immediately switched from black English responses to standard English responses when presented with black English stimuli. (1976, p. 266)

Interestingly, Piestrup (1973) reports that when white teachers "punished" black children for speaking in non-standard ways, the children's use of black speech forms increased during the course of their time at school; that is, they accentuated their ethnolinguistic styles. The opposite was true in classrooms in which the teacher did not punish the use of non-standard speech forms and thereby threaten the pupils' positively-valued distinctiveness.

These sorts of findings demonstrate that for non-standard speaking children much the same process operates as for all non-standard speakers; the standard is understood well enough, and it may be produced if the situation is seen to warrant it. We should also point out (with Labov, Williams, and others) that non-standard forms are usually not completely distinct from standard ones: much is shared in common. As Labov (1976, p. 64) put it, "the gears and axles of English grammatical machinery are available to speakers of all dialects". This is a useful point to bear in mind in discussions of this sort; that is, we are considering dialect differences and not language differences. Emphasis upon the features of non-standard dialects which *do* differ from standard varieties may be overdone. In any event, this apparent difference between children's comprehension of standard forms and their production of them is important. It applies to almost all dialects although there may be some few which differ so markedly from the standard that problems are greater (see, e.g., the work of V. K. Edwards, 1979, on West Indian speech patterns in Britain). The pragmatic consequences of these matters are taken up in the last section of this chapter.

Theoretical and empirical considerations

Despite the large literature on language and social class, it can be argued that the area is distinctly atheoretical (at least social psychologically) inasmuch as it gives more attention to the details of the presumed structural and functional differences between working- and middle-class linguistic skills than to systematizing the processes underlying them. In fact, little of value for formulating a substantial theoretical perspective has emerged in the last ten years apart from Robinson's (1979, 1980) and Ryan's (1979) proposals advocating the consideration of ingroup-outgroup dichotomies and identities, respectively. In this section we intend to elaborate upon these proposals by recourse, in the first part, to "ethnolinguistic identity theory" (Ball *et al.*, in press; Giles and Johnson, 1981) which, as the label implies, aims to clarify the relationships between language and ethnic group. This is an issue of considerable importance given our concerns in this chapter with the education of minority group children. The approach is seen to be highly relevant to the role of language in any intergroup context, and aspects of it have been found useful in, for example, the analysis of language in male–female relations (Kramarae, 1981). Hence we shall devote ourselves specifically to extending ethnolinguistic identity theory (ELIT) to any situation involving intergroup discontinuities between the school and the home, whether these be ethnically- or class-based. As well, we shall introduce the possibility that the "intergroup" model of second language acquisition (Ball *et al.*, in press; Giles and Byrne, 1982), itself a natural progression from ELIT, will be useful in understanding the conditions likely to impede or promote proficiency in the standard variety of the language among non-standard-speaking children. It is our belief that until we conduct more basic research from theoretical bases such as these, we cannot hope to develop successful educational policies. Robinson (1979) has underlined here the past difficulties resulting from educational programmes founded on inadequate methods and data.

Ethnolinguistic identity theory

Central to our orientation is a definition of social group membership as those individuals who identify themselves as belonging to the same class or ethnic category (Turner, 1981; see also Barth, 1969; Harris, 1979). This ingroup identification may either be based upon a shared set of ancestral or community traditions, or it may stimulate the *creation* of traditions (Fishman, 1977). In both cases, the main concern is with the establishment and maintenance of distinct group boundaries. It involves a subjective definition of social group membership, and has the advantage of avoiding categorization of individuals solely on the basis of objective criteria (e.g. income and educational level, area of residence, skin colour, etc.). It implicitly allows for the possibility that an individual may act in terms of group membership in some, but not necessarily all, situations. For instance, Tajfel and his associates have distinguished between two kinds of encounters (Tajfel, 1978; Tajfel and Turner, 1979). At one extreme is the *inter-individual* situation, occurring between two or more individuals, fully determined by inter-personal relationships and individual temperaments, and not at all affected by the individuals' social memberships. At the other extreme are *inter-group* situations, involving two or more individuals, completely determined by the individuals' group memberships, and not at all affected by the interpersonal relationships and personalities of those involved. Stephenson (1981) has pointed to the fact that these two extremes might be better conceived of as two separate dimensions, thereby allowing for the possibility that a situation may be defined simultaneously in inter-individual *and* inter-group terms. Therefore, a classroom discussion between a white, middle-class teacher and a black, working-class adolescent may be defined by each of them as occupying, at different times, different positions in two-dimensional space. The more they conceive of the situation in inter-group terms, for example, the more they will tend to treat each other simply as members of an outgroup, rather than in terms of individual characteristics possessed.

Tajfel and his colleagues have developed a theory for understanding behaviour at this inter-group extreme, and this forms the core of ELIT (Giles and Johnson, 1981). It runs as follows: We categorize the social world, and perceive ourselves as members of various groups (class, ethnic, peer, etc.). This knowledge of ourselves as group members is defined as our social identity and it may be positive or negative, according to how ingroups fare in social comparisons with relevant outgroups. It is argued that we strive to achieve a positive identity by seeking dimensions which afford favourable comparison with outgroups (i.e. we strive for positive psychological distinctiveness). Language enters the picture when a group regards its own language, dialect or slang as a dimension of comparison with outgroups (e.g. as something worth having, which the outgroups lack). In this case, the group would be said to have achieved a positive psycholinguistic distinctiveness (Giles *et al.*, 1977). Naturally, and as we have already outlined, there can be cases of dialect being salient for the group but affording them only unfavourable inter-group comparisons (e.g. "we speak sloppily, badly, etc.").

What happens when an individual experiences negative ethnic or class identity? Three basic responses are suggested here, in order of likely priority. First, he or she may apply a strategy of *individual mobility*, trying to pass into the more privileged social category by acquiring its characteristics, and quitting the ingroup so as to attain a new, positive identity (see "lames", above). This is likely if the inter-group boundaries are perceived as soft and permeable (Giles, 1979). Linguistically, the individual will converge on areas where the outgroup's linguistic habits are *believed* to lie (see the notion of "hypercorrection"; Labov, 1966; Trudgill, 1974), and will discard ingroup speech markers (see Thakerar *et al.*, 1982). If individual mobility through language is widespread the ingroup language variety will not, of course, be maintained (see Denison, 1977 on "dialect death").

A second strategy, applicable if individual mobility fails or is thwarted by the existence of impermeable inter-group boundaries, is *social creativity*. This involves a redefinition of the ingroup–outgroup comparison in various ways. These include: referring to other, low-status, groups, or fellow members of the ingroup for social comparison, rather than the outgroup; simply reversing the previous evaluative polarity of existing inter-group comparisons (e.g. "Black is beautiful" in the United States); inventing new, more favourable dimensions of inter-group comparison (see Drake, 1980; Kochman, 1981). The last two sub-strategies occur in linguistic form when individuals flaunt, in a divergent way, their supposedly "debased" or "substandard" speech forms in inter-group contexts (e.g. in certain classroom situations).

The third strategy, outright *social competition*, is likely to be adopted when the previous strategies have failed. Here, members still identify with their subordinate ingroup, and make unfavourable inter-group comparisons, but perceive alternatives to the *status quo* by viewing their subordinate status as illegitimate and unstable. Numerous situations in which language has been the focus of civil unrest can be seen as linguistic illustrations of this (e.g. Quebec, Soweto, Washington).

What does the dominant group do in response to a subordinate group's adoption of any of these sociolinguistic strategies? Assimilation of the subordinate group through individual mobility would threaten the dominant group's psychological distinctiveness, so it would be likely to reassert this by not recognizing the assimilation that had occurred (as, for example, in the Williams *et al.* videotape experiment, 1971), or through creatively divergent counter-strategies (e.g. inventing new ingroup linguistic markers, or even a new dialect; see Elias, 1978; Ullrich, 1971). Subordinate group creativity or competition (strategies 2 and 3) would be likely to elicit reciprocal competition which might include verbal derogation, abrasive verbal humour or overtly political action (for a more detailed discussion, see Giles, 1978, 1979; Giles and Johnson, 1981).

Factors affecting the salience of social group membership
Although a person's membership groups are part of his or her social identity and can be remarkably potent (even by seven years of age; Vaughan, 1978), they will not all be equally salient at any one time. It is only when groups with distinctive linguistic characteristics (often ethnic and social class collectivities) are salient that we would expect accentuation or attenuation of ingroup speech markers as inter-group strategies. Four variables may be suggested as relevant in this regard: perceived ethnolinguistic vitality, perceived group boundaries, multiple group membership and social attributions (cf. Ball *et al.*, in press; Giles and Johnson, 1981). Each of these can be briefly dealt with here.

Giles *et al.* (1977) have suggested that ethnic groups be compared in terms of ethnolinguistic vitality, to which three main groups of factors contribute: status factors (e.g. economic, political and linguistic prestige), demographic factors (e.g. absolute numbers, birth rate and geographical concentration) and institutional support factors (e.g. recognition in mass media, validity of language/dialect in education, government and industry). They proposed that groups with high vitality are most likely to thrive and remain distinct, as well as to act collectively in accord with their group memberships. We will further suggest, here, as the 1977 study implied, that vitality is just as important for other social groups as well, including class collectivities. However, the actions of individual group members are likely to be governed less by actual vitality of their groups than by their *perception* of the relevant factors (Bourhis *et al.*, 1981). Giles and Johnson (1981) suggest that high perceived vitality increases the salience of group identity for members and, therefore, their inclination to accentuate group speech markers to establish a favourable psycholinguistic distinctiveness.

Sociological and anthropological scholars have emphasized the importance of social boundaries in inter-group activity (e.g. Lyman and Douglass, 1973). It is suggested that group members try to maintain a high level of perceived inter-group boundary hardness. When successful, as is the case with many low-prestige dialects (Ryan, 1979), this clarifies social categorization and the norms for conducting inter-group encounters, and thereby increases the salience of group membership. Thus, perceiving an authentic standard dialect as extremely difficult to achieve (hard linguistic boundary) would result in the consequences just noted. Moreover, those who see themselves as belonging to many different, overlapping groups (see Salamone and Swanson, 1979), should possess a more diffuse social identity than persons who view themselves as members of only one or two. That is, class or ethnic attachments should be stronger for those who can identify with few other social categories. Moreover, the favourability of inter-group comparisons offered by these other social membership groups will likely affect individuals' reliance upon their class or ethnic identities, as will their status *within* each group.

The role of the attribution process at the inter-group level (Deschamps, 1977; Hamiton, 1979; Hewstone and Jaspars, 1982a; Pettigrew, 1979) lies in the analysis of how members of subordinate power groups *explain* their inferior social positions and relative states of deprivation (low wages, poor employment prospects, etc.). This application of attribution theory was envisaged by Guimond and Simard (1979), who examined explanations offered by English and French Canadians for their social positions. It was found that English Canadians (the dominant ethnolinguistic group) tended to blame French Canadians themselves for the latter's lower social position. That is, they preferred individualistic causes for economic inequality. In contrast, French Canadians (the subordinate collectivity) offered structural, more social explanations for their inferior standing. Indeed, one regularly witnesses such differential attributions in British and American allocation of responsibility for the social positions of the middle and working classes, by members of those categories. Given the salience of one's own dialect, and the importance of ethnic and class membership, it seems very likely that individual members of subordinate minorities may ascribe their failings to their possession of a certain dialect, or to discrimination by others because of this dialect. The process of ascribing one's failure to membership in the "wrong" social group has been demonstrated by Dion and associates (e.g. Dion *et al.*, 1978).

Seeing the status of one's language and dialect as a possible cause of social inferiority may be strengthened by the operation of the *covariation principle* (Kelley, 1967). This suggests that an effect is seen to be caused by the factor with which, over time, it covaries. It is relatively easy to see how children from lower-status backgrounds might provide themselves with such covariation data. For example, if an individual perceives that almost everyone who uses his or her non-standard dialect occupies a relatively low social position, while almost everyone using the standard dialect occupies a higher one, then dialect might easily be seen as the cause of the differential status. In addition, it is easy to see how this covariation rule would be strengthened by ingroup members who had passed upwards, and were now occupying positions of higher status. At the same time, it is possible to consider other causal explanations for the lack of economic and social success of non-standard dialect speakers; for example, there may exist negative outgroup characteristics. This kind of explanation derives support from a growing literature on intergroup attributions (see Hewstone and Jaspars, 1982a). From this perspective, the individual attributes the behaviour of another to characteristics and intentions associated with the group to which the other belongs, and not simply to individual characteristics. Thus, if the individual is the recipient of negative behaviour by an outgroup member (e.g. being refused employment), then the preferred explanation is more likely to be in terms of negative outgroup attributes (e.g. *"they* are discriminatory") than in terms of negative ingroup characteristics (e.g. *"we* are lazy"). This pattern of attributions has been demonstrated by Hewstone and Jaspars (1982b). Against this background, one might predict that members of lower-status groups might *expect* unfair practices on the part of middle-class standard dialect speakers, and hence they may not bother to acquire the outgroup's dialect at all. To deal with this possibility, we might hypothesize that when the inferior position of subordinate class or ethnic group members is attributed to intransigent and unchangeable discriminatory practices of the outgroup, then their group identification will become more salient (Ball *et al.*, in press). Therefore, the threshold for acting in terms of their social group membership will be lowered, and the probability of accentuating non-standard dialect patterns thus increased.

To conclude this discussion on the theoretical state of ELIT, we advance five propositions (Ball *et al.*, in press; Giles and Johnson, 1981). People will see themselves in either class or ethnic terms, and will strive for positive psycholinguistic differentiation from the standard dialect outgroup, when they:

(1) see themselves strongly as members of an ethnic/class group, with dialect/language an important dimension of this identity;

(2) regard their group's relative status as changeable and attribute the cause of their relatively low social status to advantages taken unfairly by the outgroup.

(3) perceive their ingroup's ethnolinguistic vitality as high;

(4) perceive their ingroup boundaries as hard;

(5) identify with few other social groups – ones which offer unfavourable social comparisons.

Conversely, the opposites of these conditions should lead to erosion of the ingroup dialect, since attempts will be made to become assimilated by the middle class.

The inter-group model of second language/dialect acquisition

Giles and Byrne (19820 have formulated an inter-group model of second language acquisition, which is largely based on foundations just discussed. It is an attempt to place second language acquisition in an *inter-group* context, while maintaining and integrating some of the components of earlier social psychological models (see Clément, 1980; Gardner, 1979). It is our belief that the same processes are involved in the acquisition of proficiency in the standard dialect by non-standard speaking children.

In order to illustrate this, let us designate as subgroup "A" those members of a lower-status group (class or ethnic) for whom the preceding five propositions apply. Those from backgrounds in which the propositions do *not* apply are designated subgroup "B". Subgroup "A" would, we propose, be unlikely to achieve proficiency in the standard dialect. For them, acquiring such a dialect would be "subtractive" to their sense of class or ethnic identity and, even if the acquisition was seen as economically and politically profitable (Ryan, 1981), subgroup "A" members would still experience a fear of assimilation by the outgroup and the likely rejection by their valued ingroup peers (Clément, 1980). Subgroup "A" members would not seek informal acquisition contexts (Fig. 1), and would become proficient only in classroom aspects of the standard dialect, such as vocabulary and grammar. Individual differences in attaining this limited proficiency would reflect intelligence as well, perhaps, as differences in the efficiency of pedagogical techniques.

Subgroup "B", on the other hand, are those lower-status group members most likely to achieve proficiency in the standard dialect. These individuals do not strongly see themselves as members of an ethnic or class group, regard their group's status as unchangeable, attribute their inferior status to inferior group qualities, perceive their ingroup's vitality as low and its boundaries as permeable, and identify with many other social groups offering favourable social comparisons. For such children, acquisition of the standard variety should be "additive" (Lambert, 1974), and their motivation should be "integrative" (Gardner, 1979). Subgroup "B" members would take advantage of available informal acquisition contexts to further their standard dialect skills and would, in addition to formal knowledge, gain high oral competence. As well, positive attitudes towards the middle class and its norms and values would be expected. Anxiety experienced in situations of standard dialect would, for subgroup "B", relate more strongly than intelligence to standard dialect proficiency. Clément (1980) proposed that the kinds of inter-group experiences the second-language learner has with members of the other language community will affect his or her motivation to learn their language. More specifically, he proposed that the more frequent and the better the quality of inter-group contact, the higher will be the learner's confidence in using the second language, and in taking risks in so doing (Beebe, in press). Particularly in this context, however, we would obviously prefer to rely more on the notion that it is the learner's *perceptions* of inter-group contacts that will facilitate or hinder the acquisition process (see Brown and Turner, 1981). In fact, we can argue that the children's attributions about the quality of these inter-group experiences are the critical determinants (Jaspars and Hewstone, in press). If features of external circumstances provide plausible causes for pleasant or unpleasant encounters, children's motivation will be less affected than if no such causes can be found and if, therefore, they are forced to consider that actions of the standard dialect outgroup create unpleasant encounters (see Worchel and Norvell, 1980). The presence or creation of poor environmental conditions is hypothesized to obviate the need for scapegoating (or blaming outgroup members); this in turn prevents the resurrection of previous social group boundaries.

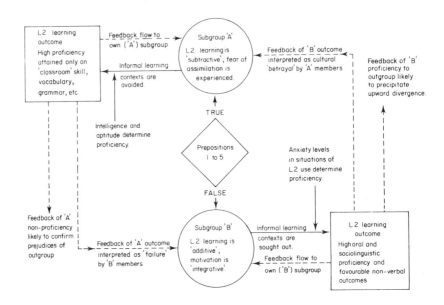

Fig. 1. The intergroup model of second language learning (as schematized in Ball and Giles, 1982).

What would be the collective consequences of the contrasting individual outcomes portrayed above and in Fig. 1? These would depend partly on the relative proportions of "A" and "B" subgroup members in the class or ethnic group. However, both subgroups would, if large enough, feed back information to themselves, to each other and to the standard dialect outgroup. The maintenance of non-standard dialect features by subgroup "A" would probably be interpreted by its members as successful retention of class or ethnic language distinctiveness in the face of cultural or subcultural threat. Subgroup "B" members, on the other hand, would more likely see this as a set of individual failures, due perhaps to socioeconomic or educational inadequacies. And, the standard-dialect middle class (including school staff) would see their prejudices confirmed about subgroup "A". Subgroup "B"'s mastery of the standard variety should fortify its members' integrative motivational tendencies (see Fig. 1). Subgroup "A" members, however, might regard this as class or ethnic betrayal, and become yet more fearful of assimilation and even less motivated to become standard dialect speakers. The outgroup might feel its distinctive identity threatened and might respond by differentiating itself further, perhaps creating a new or altered standard variety.

To incorporate constructs and processes from the second-language acquisition literature into the standard/non-standard educational context, it might also be useful to consider subgroups "A" and "B" in relation to Dulay and Burt's (1978) "socio-affective filter". They suggest that the motives, attitudes and emotional states of learners filter the language input that is processed by them, and affect the rate and quality of acquisition (of standard dialect, in the present discussion). They propose (p. 556) that the socio-affective filter contributes to at least three aspects of selective learning:

> (1) the preferences for certain input models over other; (2) the acquisition of certain aspects of language before others; (3) the (subconscious) determination of the point at which language acquisition efforts should cease.

Here we could propose that subgroup "A" members are likely to operate the filter maximally such that processing of incoming standard dialect data is inhibited, whereas subgroup "B" members are likely to filter minimally, thereby facilitating standard dialect input. However, in the theoretical framework presented above, "A" and "B" individuals have been considered as archetypes: least and most likely, respectively, to achieve standard dialect proficiency. However, it would not be unreasonable to suppose that, in most groups, the greatest proportion of individuals would fall somewhere between these polarities. This body of "intermediates" can be thought of as comprising those individuals who cannot easily answer "true" or "false" (see Fig. 1) to Propositions 1 and 2. In other words, they cannot subscribe wholeheartedly to a strong or a weak sense of ethnic or class membership, are unsure about the possibility of changes in group status, and feel that responsibility for their group's inadequate conditions is borne partly by the ingroup and partly by the middle class and its institutions (including the school). While Propositions 3 to 5 may be thought to provide little more than situational and personal support for making class or ethnic identification salient for group members, they may also have more direct influence upon the linguistic actions of the "intermediates". These individuals' perceptions of ethnolinguistic vitalities, group boundaries and multiple group memberships may well determine the extent and manner of the operation of the socio-effective filter and, therefore, the degree of proficiency attained in the standard dialect. Ball *et al.* (in press) have incorporated such "intermediates" into the inter-group model of second language acquisition, through the application of the mathematical "catastrophe" theory (Thom, 1975; Zeeman, 1976). Space precludes a discussion of this elaboration of the inter-group model, but those who are interested in the theoretical underpinnings discussed in the present chapter will be able to translate this new perspective into the standard-non-standard context quite easily. However, before allowing ourselves the further luxury of translations from the second-language literature (see Beebe and Giles, in press), there are more immediate priorities. We should develop adequate methods for testing the viability of the constructs already introduced and for assessing the predictive value of the processes posited. From the previous discussion arise many empirical issues regarding the language of children from lower socioeconomic-status backgrounds. These include the following:

(a) To what extent do these children subscribe to a sense of local, ethnic or class belongingness, and what contributions do these and other group memberships make to their personal and social identities at different ages?

(b) To what extent are dialect, and the specific features of it, salient and valued dimensions of class, local and ethnic identity, in relation to other, non-linguistic, characteristics of group membership?

(c) Under what conditions do children define classroom situations as essentially inter-group in nature, and what are the subjective components of such construals? How, if at all, do teachers' language, actions and pedagogical strategies contribute to the perceived inter-group situation?

(d) What are children's attributions of their socioeconomic status position, how do they see the vitality of it, and what cognitive alternatives do they see open to them educationally?

(e) To what extent can children, in reality, be adequately represented in terms of subgroups "A" and "B"; are these predictive of the types of motivation proposed by the inter-group model?

It is obvious from the tenor of this section that we believe traditional research into the relationships among language, class and education has only scratched the surface. Moreover, we require the type of conceptual framework proposed by Ryan *et al.* (1982) to make comparative statements about different educational problems in different speech communities and societies. Hence, we are extremely reluctant to list priorities now, on the basis of what are insufficient and sometimes non-existent data. This is, of course, of little comfort to children who come from lower-class backgrounds, and who speak a non-standard dialect (or to their teachers). What we can propose must therefore be very modest. However, we make no apologies for this especially since, in the current economic/political climate, many researchers are induced to become prematurely applied and policy-orientated.

Pragmatic considerations

As mentioned in the previous sections, the traditional policy of the school was most often to require adaptation on the part of the pupils. Armed with an unshakeable sense of the correctness of their own (i.e. middle-class) speech norms, teachers typically had little hesitation in correcting pupils who spoke "slovenly" or "illogical" English. While this policy is understandable, it doubtless created many difficulties for children to whom it was applied. For example, many teachers of non-standard-speaking children in many parts of the world have noted the sullen and non-verbal nature of these children in class. This is sometimes due to cultural differences with regard to such matters as behaviour in front of authority figures (Abrahams, 1976), or public behaviour in front of peers (Philips, 1972). As well, however, there is reason to believe that teachers have, in large measure, created non-verbal children through early and excessive "correction" policies; the children, unwilling to undergo the inevitable, simply cease to participate in classroom activites. Labov, in a well-known article (1973), demonstrates how reticent and non-verbal black children can be suddenly transformed into the verbally adept individuals we now associate with the orally rich black culture, by the removal of white, middle-class examiners. In so doing, Labov counters the claims of Bereiter and Engelmann (1966) who had maintained that, for black children, language may not be of vital importance and may, in some cases, even be dispensable. Similarly, Shuy (1971) has noted that no non-verbal child that he has encountered has remained so in a non-intimidating context (see also Bernstein, 1973).

On this basis alone we might ask if something could be done at school to remove the possibility of children becoming uncommunicative in the classroom – children who are clearly not at all so in the playground, or at home. It is evident that a minimum requirement here is for teachers, and the school system generally, to be tolerant (and not begrudgingly so) of dialectal variation, and not to brand it as anything inferior. Given current social psychological and linguistic data, we can now provide teachers with the evidence that this, in fact, is the most reasonable thing to do. Dialects and accents are possessions one shares with those who are psychologically similar (see Bishop, 1979; Delia, 1972; Sebastian, Ryand and Corso, in press) and with whom one identifies. They are, as we outlined in the previous section, clearly linked to a child's conception of group membership and self-respect. Children will therefore not wish to converge towards another speech variety unless they want to alter their identity in some way. If teachers reject children's dialects they are also rejecting *them*. Teachers should be made more aware that negative evaluations of non-standard dialects are culture-bound, and that the unfavourable stereotypes are un-doubtedly more *group*-biased than language-biased (St. Clair, 1982; Trudgill and Giles, 1977). To change a child's accent consistently and consciously means that the teacher must pay more attention than normal to *how* some-thing is said, and less to *what* is said. The psychological costs here may be too great, and may even hinder educational progress. It is true that how one says something can sometimes be just as important as what is said, but one should not be pressed for one aspect at the expense of the other. Given this proposed tolerance towards variation in children's oral language, we might expect (based upon what we have discussed here) that children would come towards bidialectalism of their own accord. This seems to some a rather passive approach; Ammon (1977) has said that those who advocate educa-tional tolerance of non-standard dialects, and who further imply that children should gradually learn a standard variety, have offered no practical advice as to how the transition from non-standard to standard can be achieved. Passive approaches have the affect, Ammon claims, of restricting meaningful social mobility. These are, of course, useful points. However, since more active approaches often have the effect of stigmatizing non-standard dialects in ways which are now considered by linguists to be based upon faulty ideas about language varieties, an apparently more passive stance may not be as undesirable as Ammon suggests. For we should remember here that the passivity is really on the part of the teachers, not the pupils: i.e. the children may adopt another variety, and this is an active process. The question is really whether teachers, by adopting a more active strategy for promoting the standard variety, will help children or hinder them. On balance, it would seem that children do not respond well to approaches (however benevolently inspired) which, in essence, suggest to them that their maternal dialect is in some way flawed (see Edwards, 1979a for fuller discussion here). The general practice advocated here, then, could be termed one of linguistic addition rather than one of replacement, where any addition proceeds from a desire of the non-standard speaker and not from direct suggestion by teachers or others. This practice would lead to the expansion of a child's linguistic repertoire, thereby creating bidialectalism. It is a further question as to whether or not bidialectalism can be maintained permanently. Some have suggested that bidialectalism is one step on the road to eradication of the maternal variety (e.g. Moses *et al.*, 1976) but much depends here upon the context. Just as it is possible for bilingualism to be stable or transitory, so bidialectalism can exist in either mode. In any event, the extent to which facility in a second language or dialect leads to eventual linguistic or dialectal assimilation depends largely upon societal variables which extend far beyond the school.

The approach advocated in the previous paragraph has, in particular, seemed too *laissez-faire* to those concerned with reading, a central element in any discussion of educational practice. Some have called for texts written in non-standard dialect, for example (see Baratz, 1970), to ease the lot of the non-standard-speaking child. There are several reasons, however, why this policy seems ill-advised. First, as we have noted, dialect differences are not usually so marked as to make standard English comprehension a real problem for children. Since reading involves decoding to meaning and not to sound (Edwards, 1981a, 1981b), we might agree with Torrey (1973, p. 68) who points out that, with regard to Black English:

> The difference in phonology between standard English and black English is not directly relevant to reading. All children who learn to read English have to break a fairly complex code of sound-spelling relationships. The fact that the correspondences are different for speakers of Afro-American does not in itself prove that they are more difficult than for standard speakers.

We could generalize to all dialects where there is reason to think that the "gears and axles" are essentially similar. Other varieties, including perhaps West Indian English in Britain, may require other approaches; it is interesting to note here, however, that some (e.g. Bailey, 1966) have argued that West Indian English is sufficiently divergent from the standard to be deemed a separate language.

Second, the effort and expense entailed in production of many different non-standard texts, and the difficulties involved in effecting a transition to standard English texts (something which supporters of non-standard texts agree is necessary), rather indicate that this is an inappropriate course to take without much further evidence of real and substantial dialect interference. Third, we would recall here the desires of many parents who would not wish to see non-standard texts used in schools, for the reason that they would perpetuate their children's disadvantage. While linguists might argue that this view is correct, but for the wrong reason, it is clear that parental attitudes must not be ignored. Thus, with reading as with oral language, the reasonable policy seems to be one of enlightened tolerance. Teachers could well allow children, when reading out loud, to render the meaning of standard English texts in their own dialect. This would coincide with the view of reading as decoding in meaning; it is only after the meaning has been assimilated that the child then produces something (i.e. this part of reading aloud is an encoding process).

With regard to written language, instruction in the standard form seems less controversial since all children, regardless of dialect, must learn to translate ideas into writing. It has been argued elsewhere (Edwards, 1979a) that a more or less formal equation of written English with standard English would not likely be destructive of psychological identity (cf. Scollon and Scollon, 1979).

General tolerance of dialectal variation does not seem, perhaps, much to come to. However, any more formal approach (language drills in standard English, formal guidance on "correctness" by the teacher) is not likely to be successful and may in fact widen the gap between the non-standard speaker and the school. We must allow children who have competence (passive, at least) in the standard to choose for themselves linguistically (with an abundance of models around them, of course, chief of which is the standard English-speaking teacher).

This in turn implies that changes in schools may involve teachers more than children: that is, with reference to the two broad possibilities noted earlier (in the section on school life), we are clearly coming out in favour of the one which requires schools to adapt to pupils, rather than vice versa. At the same time, however, we are also saying that this adaptation does not, and should not, inevitably involve formal changes in curriculum, or in texts, or in language forms used by teachers. Rather, it involves a more thorough-going tolerance, which in itself is no small matter. The general point here is that, given a tolerant atmosphere which is accepting of dialectal variations and which understands them for what they are (non-standard rather than substandard), children will define themselves linguistically vis-à-vis the mainstream varieties as seems most appropriate. In addition (with the help of parents perhaps), educators may consider ways in which the variety of linguistic experiences children from different backgrounds bring with them into the classroom may be used as a resource when planning curricula.

Finally, classroom interaction between teacher and pupil is of great potential importance for inter-group definition. Both teacher and pupil will likely use the other's speech style in making group categorizations which lead to expectations concerning the other's abilities, temperaments, etc. The more that pupils strongly identify with some social category, the more likely it is that they will differentiate themselves linguistically from others who represent different group values. This may be particularly so when these others are perceived as representatives of a group which, to the children, symbolizes an illegitimate and oppressive force which has deprived them of socioeconomic and political rights. Hence, some children find teachers' speech styles alien, and come to resent the social gulf which these styles reflect. Thus, they may find teachers' voices "snobbish", "posh" etc., and they may react accordingly. Indeed, "downward convergence" (Giles and Powesland, 1975) on the part of the teacher trying to bridge this gulf may be seen as false or even insulting if it is seen to be patronizing (Edwards, 1979a; Giles and Smith, 1979; Platt and Weber, in press; Shuy, 1977). The implication here is that barriers between teachers and pupils must be reduced if successful education is to occur.

It is crucial, here, that children see the wisdom of identifying more with their classmates as a group, than with only a small faction, selected because they belong to the same ethnic or class category. At the same time, this should not mean the dissolution or devaluation of such categories in the classroom; rather, the sense of the class as an important collectivity which can be identified with in its own right should become more salient. As well, a useful strategy would be to emphasize that teacher and pupils belong to the same social group, for educational purposes, in the school context (see Brown and Turner, 1981; Sherif, 1967; Turner, 1981). Such a collectivity could then take its place among other relevant groups and could assist, through inter-group comparison, in the development of more accurate, favourable, and therefore healthy social identities.

We hope that our use of the educational context has been informative for important aspects of a more general sociolinguistics. Certainly, there are issues with which we have not been able to deal here: bilingual education, for example, suggests itself as an important instance of schools' adaptation to pupils of non-mainstream linguistic backgrouds (see Edwards 1977, 1980, 1981c, in press). However, much of what *has* been treated here has a wider relevance. The issues of language and dialect contact, the prescriptivist ideas of middle-class institutions, the linguistic evidence bearing upon dialect validity, and the persistence of non-standard varieties: these are all matters which can be usefully examined, from a social psychological perspective, within the educational setting, while also having a much broader significance.

References

Aboud, F. E., Clément, R. and Taylor, D. M. (1974). Evaluational reactions to discrepancies between social classes and language. *Sociometry*, **37**, 239–250.

Abrahams, R. D. (1976). "Talking Black". Newbury House, Rowley, Mass.

Ammon, U. (1977). School problems of regional dialect speakers: Ideology and reality. Results and methods of empirical investigations in Southern Germany. *Journal of Pragmatics*, **1**, 47–68.

Ashworth, M. (1975). "Immigrant Children and Canadian Schools", McClelland and Stewart, Toronto.

Bailey, B. L. (1966). "Jamaican Creole Syntax", Cambridge University Press, London.

Ball, P., Byrne, J., Giles, H., Berechree, P., Griffiths, J., Macdonald, H. and McKendrick, I. (1982). The retroactive speech halo effect: Some Australian data. *Language and Communication*, **2**, in press.

Ball, P. and Giles, H. (1982). Do I choose to master your language? *Polycom*, **30**, (in press).

Ball, P., Giles, H. and Hewstone, M. (in press). Second language acquisition: The intergroup theory with catastrophic dimensions. *In* "The Social Dimension: European Developments in Social Psychology" (H. Tajfel, ed.), Cambridge University Press, Cambridge.

Baratz, J. (1970). Teaching reading in an urban Negro school system. *In* "Lanugage and Poverty", (F. Williams, ed.), Markham, Chicago.

Barth, F. (1969). "Ethnic Groups and Boundaries: The Social Organization of Culture Difference", Little, Brown and Company, Boston.

Beebe, L. M. (in press). Risk-taking and the language learner. *In* "Classroom Language Acquisition and Use: New Perspectives", (H. Seliger and Michael Long, eds), Newbury House, Rowley, Mass.

Beebe, L. M. and Giles, H. (in press). Speech Accommodation Theories: A discussion in terms of second language acquisition. *International Journal of the Sociology of Language*.

Bereiter, C. and Engelmann, S. (1966). "Teaching Disadvantaged Children in the Pre-school", Prentice-Hall, Englewood Cliffs, N.J.

Berko-Gleason, J. (1980). The acquisition of social speech: Routines and politeness formulas. *In* "Language: Social Psychological Perspectives", (H. Giles, W. P. Robinson and P. M. Smith, eds), Pergamon, Oxford.

Bernstein, B. (1972). Social class, linguistic and socialization. *In*, "Language and Social Context", (P. Giglioli, ed.), Penguin, Harmondsworth.

Bernstein, B. (1973). A brief account of the theory of codes. *In* "Social Relationships and Language", (V. Lee, ed.), Open University Press, Milton Keynes.

Bernstein, B. and Henderson, D. (1969). Social class differences in the relevance of language to socialization. *Sociology*, **3**, 1–20.

Bishops, G. D. (1979). Perceived similarity in interracial attitudes and behaviours: The effects of belief and dialect style. *Journal of Applied Social Psychology*, **9**, 446–465.

Bourhis, R. Y. (1982). Language policies and language attitudes: Le monde de la Francophonie. *In* "Attitudes Towards Language Variation: Social and Applied Contexts", (E. B. Ryan and H. Giles, eds), Edward Arnold, London.

Bourhis, R. Y. and Genesee, F. (1980). Evaluative reactions to code switching strategies in Montreal. *In* "Language: Social Psychological Perspectives", (H. Giles, W. P. Robinson and P. M. Smith, eds), Pergamon, Oxford.

Bourhis, R. Y. and Giles, H. (1976). The language of cooperation in Wales: A field study. *Language Sciences*, **42**, 13–16.

Bourhis, R. Y., Giles, H. and Rosenthal, D. (1981). Notes on the construction of a "subjective vitality questionnaire". *Journal of Multilingual and Multicultural Development*, **2**, 145–155.

Bradac, J. J. (1982). A rose by another name: Attitudinal conseuqnces of lexical variation. *In* "Attitudes Towards Language Variation: Social and Applied Contexts", (E. B. Ryan and H. Giles, eds), Edward Arnold, London.

Brody, E. B. (1968). "Minority Group Adolescents in the United States", Williams and Witkins, Baltimore.

Brown, R. (1965). "Social Psychology", Collier Macmillan, London.

Brown, R. J. and Turner, J. (1981). Interpersonal and intergroup behaviour, *In* "Intergroup Behaviour", (J. C. Turner and H. Giles, eds), Blackwell, Oxford.

Bruner, J. (1981). The social context of language acquisition. *Language and Communication*, **1**, 155–178.

Carranza, M. A. (1982). Attitudinal research on Hispanic language varieties. *In* "Attitudes Towards Language Variation: Social and Applied Contexts", (E. B. Ryand and H. Giles, eds), Edward Arnold, London.

Carranza, M. A. and Ryan, E. B. (1975). Evaluative reactions of bilingual Anglo and Mexican American adolescents toward speakers of English and Spanish. *International Journal of the Sociology of Language*, 6, 83–104.

Choy, S. and Dodd, D. (1976). Standard-English-speaking and non-standard Hawaiian-English-speaking children: Comprehension of both dialects and teachers' evaluations. *Journal of Educational Psychology*, 68, 184–193.

Clément, R. (1980). Ethnicity, contact and communicative competence in a second language. *In* "Language: Social Psychological Perspectives", (H. Giles, W. P. Robinson and P. M. Smith, eds), Pergamon, Oxford.

Cook-Gumperz, J. (1973). "Social Control and Socialization: A Study of Class Differences in the Language of Maternal Control", Routledge & Kegan Paul, London.

Covington, A. (1976). Black people and Black English: Attitudes and deeducation in a biased macroculture. *In* "Black English: A Seminar", (D. Harrison and T. Trabasso, eds), Erlbaum, Hillsdale, N.J.

Danet, B. (1980). Language in the courtroom. *In* "Language: Social Psychological Perspectives", (H. Giles, W. P. Robinson and P. M. Smith, eds), Pergamon, Oxford.

Day, R. R. (1982). Children's attitudes towards language. *In* "Attitudes Toward Language Variation: Social and Applied Contexts", (E. B. Ryan and H. Giles, eds), Edward Arnold, London.

Delia, J. G. (1972). Dialects and the effects of stereotypes on interpersonal attraction and cognitive processes in impression formation. *Quarterly Journal of Speech*, 58, 285–297.

Denison, N. (1977). Language death or language suicide? *International Journal of the Sociology of Language*, 12, 13–22.

Deschamps, J-C. (1977). "L'Attribution et la Catégorisation Sociale", Peter Lang, Berne.

Dion, K. L., Earn, B. M. and Yee, P. H. N. (1978). The experience of being a victim of prejudice: An experimental approach. *International Journal of Psychology*, 13, 197–214.

Drake, G. (1980). The social role of slang. *In* "Language: Social Psychological Perspectives", (H. Giles, W. P. Robinson and P. M. Smith, eds), Pergamon, Oxford.

Dulay, H. and Burt, M. (1978). From research to method in bilingual education. *In* "International Dimensions of Bilingual Education: Georgetown University Roundtable on Languages and Linguistics, 1978", (J. E. Alatis, ed.), Georgetown University Press, Washington, DC.

Dusek, J. (1975). Do teachers bias children's learning? *Review of Educational Research*, 45, 661–684.

Dweck, C. S. (1975). The role of expectation and attribution in the alleviation of learned helplessness. *Journal of Personality and Social Psychology*, 31, 674–685.

Edwards, A. D. (1976). Social class and linguistic choice. *Sociology*, 10, 101–110.

Edwards, J. R. (1977). Ethnic identity and bilingual education. *In* "Language, Ethnicity and Intergroup Relations", (H. Giles, ed.), Academic Press, London and New York.

Edwards, J. R. (1979a). "Language and Disadvantage", Edward Arnold, London.

Edwards, J. R. (1979b). Judgements and confidence in reactions to disadvantaged speech. *In* "Language and Social Psychology", (H. Giles and R. N. St. Clair, eds), Blackwell, Oxford.

Edwards, J. R. (1980). Critics and criticisms of bilingual education. *Modern Language Journal*, **64**, 409–415.

Edwards, J. R. (1981a). Psychological and linguistic aspects of minority education. *In* "World Yearbook of Education 1981: Education of Minorities", (J. Megarry, S. Nisbet and E. Hoyle, eds), Kogan Page, London.

Edwards, J. R. (1981b). "The Social Psychology of Reading", Institute of Modern Languages, Silver Spring, Maryland.

Edwards, J. R. (1981c). The context of bilingual education. *Journal of Multilingual and Multicultural Development*, **2**, 25–44.

Edwards, J. R. (1982). Language attitudes and their implications among English speakers. *In* "Attitudes Towards Language Variation: Social and Applied Contexts", (E. B. Ryan and H. Giles, eds), Edward Arnold, London.

Edwards, J. R. (in press). Bilingual education revisited: A reply to Donahue. *Journal of Multilingual and Multicultural Development*.

Edwards, V. K. (1979). "The West Indian Language Issue in British Schools", Routledge & Kegan Paul, London.

Elias, N. (1978). "The Civilizing Process", Urizen, New York.

Eltis, K. (1980). Pupils' speech style and teacher reaction: Implications from some Australian data. *English in Australia*, **51**, 27–35.

Fishbein, M. (1980). A theory of reasoned action: Some applications and implications. *Nebraska Symposium on Motivation*, **28**, 1–25.

Fishman, J. A. (1977). Language and ethnicity. *In* "Language, Ethnicity and Intergroup Relations", (H. Giles, ed.), Academic Press, London and New York.

Fuchs, E. (1973). How teachers learn to help children fail. *In* "Tinker, Tailor . . . The Myth of Cultural Deprivation", (N. Keddie, ed.), Penguin, Harmondsworth.

Gardner, R. C. (1979). Social psychological aspects of second language acquisition. *In* "Language and Social Psychology", (H. Giles and R. N. St. Clair, eds), Blackwell, Oxford.

Gardner, R. C. (1982). Language attitudes and language learning. *In* "Attitudes Toward Language Variation: Social and Applied Contexts", (E. B. Ryan and H. Giles, eds), Edward Arnold, London.

Giles, H. (1977). "Language, Ethnicity and Intergroup Relations", Academic Press, London and New York.

Giles, H. (1978). Linguistic differentiation between ethnic groups. *In* "Differentiation Between Social Groups", (H. Tajfel, ed.), Academic Press, London and New York.

Giles, H. (1979). Ethnicity markers in speech. *In* "Social Markers in Speech", (K. R. Scherer and H. Giles, eds), Cambridge University Press, Cambridge.

Giles, H., Baker, S. and Fielding, G. (1975). Communication length as a behavioural index of accent prejudice. *International Journal of the Sociology of Language*, **6**, 73–81.

Giles, H. and Bourhis, R. Y. (1976a). Black speakers with white speech – a real problem? *In* "Proceedings of the Fourth AILA Congress, Volume 1", (G. Nickel, ed.), Hochschul Verlag, Stuttgart.

Giles, H. and Bourhis, R. Y. (1976b). Methodological issues in dialect perception: Some social psychological perspectives. *Anthropological Linguistics*, **18**, 294–304.

Giles, H., Bourhis, R. Y. and Taylor, D. M. (1977). Towards a theory of language in ethnic group relations. *In* "Language, Ethnicity and Intergroup Relations". (H. Giles, ed.), Academic Press, London and New York.

Giles, H. and Byrne, J. L. (1982). An intergroup approach to second language acquisition. *Journal of Multilingual and Multicultural Development*, **3**, 17–40.

Giles, H. and Edwards, J. R. (1983). Language attitudes in multicultural settings. Special Issue of the *Journal of Multilingual and Multicultural Development*, **4**.

Giles, H. and Farrar, K. (1979). Some behavioural consequences of speech and dress styles. *British Journal of Social and Clinical Psychology*, **18**, 209–210.

Giles, H. and Johnson, P. (1981). The role of language in ethnic group relations. *In* "Intergroup Behaviour", (J. C. Turner and H. Giles, eds), Blackwell, Oxford.

Giles, H. and Marsh, P. (1979). Perceived masculinity and accented speech. *Language Sciences*, **1**, 301–315.

Giles, H. and Powesland, P. F. (1975), "Speech Style and Social Evaluation", Academic Press, London and New York.

Giles H., Robinson, W. P. and Smith, P. M. (1980). "Language: Social Psychological Perspectives", Pergamon, Oxford.

Giles, H. and Saint-Jacques, B. (1979). "Language and Ethnic Relations", Pergamon, Oxford.

Giles, H. and Smith, P. M. (1979). Accommodation theory: Optimal levels of convergence. *In* "Language and Social Psychology", (H. Giles and R. N. St Clair, eds), Blackwell, Oxford.

Giles, H., Smith, P. M., Ford, B., Condor, S. and Thakerar, J. N. (1980). Speech styles and the fluctuating salience of sex. *Language Sciences*, **2**, 260–282.

Gleitman, L. and Gleitman, H. (1970). "Phrase and Paraphrase", Norton, New York.

Guimond, S. and Simard, L. M. (1979). Perception et interpretation des inégalités economiques entre Francophones et Anglophones au Québec. Paper presented to the 40th. Congress of the Canadian Psychological Society, Quebec City, June.

Gumperz, J. J. and Hernandez-Chavez, E. (1972). Bilingualism, bidialectalism and classroom interaction. *In* "Functions of Language in the Classroom", (C. Cazden, V. John and D. Hymes, eds), Teachers College Press, New York.

Hamers, J. F. and Blanc, M. (1982). Towards a social psychological model of bilingual development. *Journal of Language and Social Psychology*, **1**, (in press).

Hamilton, D. L. (1979). A cognitive-attributional analysis of stereotyping. *In* "Advances in Experimental Social Psychology, Volume 12", (L. Berkowitz, ed.), Academic Press, New York and London.

Harari, O. and Covington, M. V. (1981). Reactions to achievement behaviour from a teacher and student perspective: A developmental analysis. *American Educational Reserach Journal*, (in press).

Harris, R. McL. (1979). Fever of ethnicity: The sociological and educational significance of the concept. *In* "Mosaic or Melting Pot", (P. R. de Lacy and M. E. Poole, eds), Harcourt Brace, Jovanovich, Sydney.

Hess, R. and Shipman, V. (1965). Early experience and the socialization of cognitive modes in children. *Child Development*, **36**, 869–886.

Hess, R. and Shipman, V. (1968a). Maternal attitudes towards the school and the role of the pupil: Some social class comparisons. *In* "Developing Programs for the Educationally Disadvantaged", (A. Passow, ed.), Teachers College Press, New York.

Hess, R. and Shipman, V. (1968b). Maternal influences upon early learning: The cognitive environments of urban pre-school children. *In* "Early Education", (R. Hess and R. Bear, eds), Aldine, Chicago.

Hewstone, M. and Jaspars, J. (1982a). Intergroup relations and attribution processes. *In* "Social Identity and Intergroup Behaviour", (H. Tajfel, ed.), Cambridge University Press, Cambridge.

Hewstone, M. and Jaspars, J. (1982b). Explanations for racial discrimination: The effect of group discussion on intergroup attributions. *European Journal of Social Psychology*, **12**, 1–16.

Hudson, R. (1980). "Sociolinguistics", Cambridge University Press, Cambridge.

Jaspars, J. and Hewstone, M. (in press), Cross-cultural interaction, social attribution and intergroup relations. *In* "Cultures in contact: Studies in Cross-Cultural Interaction", (S. Bochner, ed.), Pergamon, Oxford.

Kalin, R. (1982). The social significance of speech in medical, legal and occupational settings. *In* "Attitudes Toward Language Variation: Social and Applied Contexts", (E. B. Ryan and H. Giles, eds), Edward Arnold, London.

Kelley, H. H. (1967). Attribution theory in social psychology. *Nebraska Symposium on Motivation*, **15**, 192–238.

Khlief, B. (1979). Insiders, outsiders and renegades: Towards a classification of ethnolinguistic labels. *In* "Language and Ethnic Relations", (H. Giles and B. Saint-Jacques, eds), Pergamon, Oxford.

Kochman, T. (1976). Perceptions along the power axis; A cognitive residue of interracial encounters. *Anthropological Linguistics*, **18**, 261–273.

Kochman, T. (1981). "Black and White Styles in Conflict", Chicago University Press, Chicago.

Kramarae, C. (1981). "Women and men speaking", Newbury House, Rowley, Mass.

Labov, W. (1966). "The Social Stratification of English in New York City", Center for Applied Linguistics, Washington, DC.

Labov, W. (1973). The logical of nonstandard English. *In* "Tinker, Tailor . . . The Myth of Cultural Deprivation", (N. Keddie, ed.), Penguin, Harmondsworth.

Labov, W. (1976). "Lafiguage in the Inner City", University of Pennsylvania Press, Philadelphia.

Lambert, W. E. (1967). A social psychology of bilingualism. *Journal of Social Issues*, **23**, 91–109.

Lambert, W. E. (1974). Culture and language as factors in learning and education. *In* "Cultural Factors in Learning", (F. Aboud and R. D. Meade, eds), Western Washington State College Press, Bellingham.

Lambert, W. E., Hodgson, R., Gardner, R. C. and Fillenbaum, S. (1960). Evaluational reactions to spoken languages. *Journal of Abnormal and Social Psychology*, **60**, 44–51.

Lenneberg, E. (1967). "Biological Foundations of Language", Wiley, New York.

Lind, E. A. and O'Barr, W. M. (1979). The social significance of speech in the courtroom. *In* "Language and Social Psychology", (H. Giles and R. N. St. Clair, eds), Blackwell, Oxford.

Louden, D. M. (1978). Self-esteem and locus of control in minority group adolescents. *Ethnic and Racial Studies*, **1**, 196–217.

Love, N. (1981). Making sense of Chomsky's revolution. *Language and Communication*, **1**, 275–287.

Lyman, S. M. and Douglass, W. A. (1973). Ethnicity: Strategies of collective and individual impression management. *Social Research*, **40**, 344–365.

Marwit, S. (1977). Black and white children's use of standard English at 7, 9 and 12 years of age. *Developmental Psychology*, **13**, 81–82.
Marwit, S. and Marwit, K. (1976). Black children's use of nonstandard grammar: Two years later. *Developmental Psychology*, **12**, 33–38.
Marwit, S., Marwit, K. and Boswell, J. (1972). Negro children's use of nonstandard grammar. *Journal of Educational Psychology*, **63**, 218–223.
McKirnan, K. J. and Hamayan E. V. (1980). Language norms and perceptions of ethnolinguistic group diversity. *In* "Language: Social Psychological Perspectives", (H. Giles, W. P. Robinson and P. M. Smith, eds), Pergamon, Oxford.
Milner, D. (1981). Racial prejudice. *In* "Intergroup Behaviour", (J. C. Turner and H. Giles, eds), Blackwell, Oxford.
Moses, R. A., Daniels, H. A. and Grundlach, R. A. (1976). Teachers' language attidues and bidialectalism. *International Journal of the Sociology of Language*, **8**, 77–91.
Nicholls, J. G. (1979). The development of perception of own attainment and causal attributions for success and failure in reading. *Journal of Educational Psychology*, **74**, 94–99.
Ovando, C. (1978). Male and female Latino college aspirations: The implications for pluralistic education. *Educational Research Quarterly*, **2**, 106–122.
Pendleton, D., Brouwer, H. and Jaspars, J. (1982). Communication difficulties: The doctor's perspective. *Journal of Language and Social Psychology*, Vol. ?
Pettigrew, T. F. (1979). The ultimate attribution error: Extending Allport's cognitive analysis of prejudice. *Personality and Social Psychology Bulletin*, **5**, 461–476.
Philips, S. (1972). Acquisition of roles for appropriate speech usage. *In* "Language and cultural diversity in American education", (R. Abrahams and R. Troike, eds), Prentice-Hall, Englewood Cliffs, N.J.
Piestrup, A. M. (1973). Black dialect interference and accommodation of reading instruction in first grade, *Monographs of the Language Behaviour Research Laboratory*, University of California, Berkeley.
Platt, J. and Weber, H. (in press). Speech convergence miscarried: An investigation into inappropriate accommodation strategies. *International Journal of the Sociology of Language*.
Ramey, C. and Campbell, F. (1977). Prevention of developmental retardation in high risk children. *In* "Research to practice in mental retardation: Care and intervention, Volume 1" (P. Mittler, ed.), University Park Press, Baltimore.
Ramey, C. and Campbell, F. (1979). Compensatory education for disadvantaged children. *School Review*, **87**, 171–189.
Rist, R. (1970). Student social class and teacher expectations: The self-fulfilling prophecy in ghetto education. *Harvard Educational Review*, **40**, 411–451.
Robinson, W. P. (1978). "Language Management in Education: The Australian Context", Allen and Unwin, Sydney.
Robinson, W. P. (1979). Speech markers and socioeconomic status. *In* "Social Markers in Speech", (K. R. Scherer and H. Giles, eds), Cambridge University Press, Cambridge.
Robinson, W. P. (1980). Language management, socio-economic status and educational progress. *In* "Language and Language Disorders in Childhood", (L. A. Hersov and M. Berger, eds), Pergamon, Oxford.
Robinson, W. P. (1981a). "Communication in Development", Academic Press, London and New York.
Robinson, W. P. (1981b). Mothers' answers to children's questions: From socio-

economic status to individual differences. *In* "Communication in Development", (W. P. Robinson, ed.), Academic Press, London and New York.

Robinson, W. P. and Rackstraw, S. J. (1972). "A Question of Answers, Two Volumes", Routledge & Kegan Paul, London.

Rosenfeld, H. (1978). Conversational control function of nonverbal behaviour. *In* "Nonverbal Behaviour and Communication", (A. W. Siegman and S. Feldstein, eds), Erlbaum, Hillsdale, N.J.

Rothenthal, R. and Jacobson, L. (1968). "Pygmalion in the Classroom", Holt, Rinehart and Winston, New York.

Ryan, E. B. (1979). Why do low-prestige language varieties persist? *In* "Language and Social Psychology", (H. Giles and R. N. St. Clair, eds), Blackwell, Oxford.

Ryan, E. B. (1981). Language planning from an attitudinal perspective. Paper presented at the International Conference on Language Problems and Public Policy, Cancun, Mexico, December.

Ryan, E. B. and Carranza, M. A. (1977). Ingroup and outgroup reactions to Mexican American language varieties. *In* "Language, Ethnicity and Intergroup Relations", (H. Giles, ed.), Academic Press, London and New York.

Ryan, E. B. and Giles, H. (1982). "Attitudes Toward Language Variation: Social and Applied Contexts", Edward Arnold, London.

Ryan, E. B., Giles, H. and Sebastian, R. J. (1982). An integrative perspective for the study of attitudes toward language variation. *In* "Attitudes Toward Language Variation: Social and Applied Contexts", (E. B. Ryan and H. Giles, eds), Edward Arnold, London.

Salamone, F. A. and Swanson, C. H. (1979). Identity and ethnicity: Ethnic groups and interactions in a multi-ethnic society. *Ethnic Groups*, **2**, 167–183.

Sapir, E. (1949). "Culture, Language and Personality", University of California Press, Berkeley.

Scherer, K. R. (1980). Personality, emotion, psychopathology and speech. *In* "Social Markers in Speech", (K. R. Scherer and H. Giles, eds), Cambridge University Press, Cambridge.

Scollon, R. and Scollon, S. B. K. (1979). Literacy as inter-ethnic communication: An Athabaskan case. *Sociolinguistic Working Papers*, **59**.

Sebastian, R. J. and Ryan, E. B. (in press). The effects of speech cues on social evaluation and behaviour. *In* "Recent Advances in Language, Communication and Social Psychology", (H. Giles and R. N. St. Clair, eds), Erlbaum, Hillsdale, N.J.

Sebastian, R. J., Ryan, E. B. and Corso, L. (in press). Social judgement of speakers with differing degrees of accent. *Social Behaviour and Personality*.

Seligman, C., Tucker, G. R. and Lambert, W. E. (1972). The effects of speech style and other attributes on teachers' attitudes toward pupils. *Language in Society*, **1**, 131–142.

Sherif, M. (1967). "Group Conflict and Co-operation", Routledge & Kegan Paul, London.

Shuy, R. (1971). Sociolinguistic strategies for studying urban speech. *Bulletin of the School of Education (Indiana University)*, **47**, 1–25.

Shuy, R. (1977). Problems of communication in the cross-cultural medical interview. *ITL*, **35**.

Smith, P. M., Giles, H. and Hewstone, M. (1982). Speech variation and social situations. *In* "Sociogenesis of Language and Human Conduct", (B. Bain, ed.), Plenum, New York.

Snyder, M. (1980). Seek, and ye shall find: Testing hypotheses about other people. *In* "Social Cognition: The Ontario Symposium", (E. T. Higgins *et al.*, eds), Erlbaum, Hillsdale, N.J.

St. Clair, R. N. (1982). From social history to language attitudes. *In* "Attitudes Towards Language Variation: Social and Applied Contexts", (E. B. Ryan and H. Giles, eds), Edward Arnold, London.

Stephenson, G. M. (1982). Intergroup bargaining and negotiation. *In* "Intergroup Behaviour", (J. C. Turner and H. Giles, eds), Blackwell, Oxford.

Stipeck, D. and Nelson, K. (1980). Communication efficiency of middle- and lower-SES dyads. *Human Communications Research*, **6**, 168–177.

Street, R. L. and Hopper, R. (1982). A model of speech style evaluation. *In* "Attitudes Toward Language Variation: Social and Applied Contexts", (E. B. Ryan and H. Giles, eds), Edward Arnold, London.

Tajfel, H. (1978). "Differentiation Between Social Groups", Academic Press, London and New York.

Tajfel, H. and Turner, J. C. (1979). An integrative theory of intergroup conflict. *In* "The Social Psychology of Intergroup Relations", (W. G. Austin and S. Worchel, eds), Brooks/Cole, Monterey.

Taylor, D. M. and Simard, L. (1981). "Les Relations Intergroupes au Québec et la Loi 101". Gouvernement du Québec: Office de la langue française.

Thakerar, J. N. and Giles, H. (1981). They are – so they speak: Noncontent speech stereotypes. *Language and Communication*, **1**, 251–256.

Thakerar, J. N., Giles, H. and Cheshire, J. (1982). Psychological and linguistic parameters of speech accommodation theory. *In* "Advances in the Social Psychology of Language", (C. Fraser and K. R. Scherer, eds), Cambridge University Press, Cambridge.

Thom, R. (1975). "Structural Stability and Morphogenesis", Benjamin, Reading, Mass.

Torrey, J. (1973). Illiteracy in the ghetto. *In* "Tinker, Tailor . . . The Myth of Cultural Deprivation", (N. Keddie, ed.), Penguin, Harmondsworth.

Tough, J. (1977). "Talking and Learning", Ward Lock, London.

Trudgill, P. (1972). Sex, covert prestige and linguistic change in the urban British English of Norwich. *Language in Society*, **1**, 179–195.

Trudgill, P. (1974). "The Social Differentiation of English in Norwich", Cambridge University Press, London.

Trudgill, P. (1975). "Accent, Dialect and the School", Edward Arnold, London.

Trudgill, P. and Giles, H. (1977). Sociolinguistics and linguistic value judgements: correctness, adequacy and aesthetics. *In* "The Functions of Language and Literature Studies", (F. Coppierters and D. Goyvaerts, eds), Story-Scientia, Ghent.

Turner, J. C. (1981). The experimental social psychology of intergroup behaviour. *In* "Intergroup Behaviour", (J. C. Turner and H. Giles, eds), Blackwell, Oxford.

Ullrich, H. E. (1971). Linguistic aspects of antiquity: A dialect study. *Anthropological Linguistics*, **13**, 106–113.

Vaughan, G. M. (1978). Social categorization and inter-group behaviour in children. *In* "Differentiation Between Social Groups", (H. Tajfel, ed.), Acadmic Press, London and New York.

Wells, G. (1981). "Learning through Interaction: The Study of Language Development", Cambridge University Press, Cambridge.

Wells, G. and Robinson, W. P. (1982). The role of adult speech in language development. *In* "Advances in the Social Psychology of Language", (ed.?), Cambridge Univeristy Press, Cambridge.

Wiggen, G. (1978). The use of dialects in the initial teaching of the written language: The Norwegian case. Paper presented at *AILA* conference, Montreal.

Williams, F. (1976). "Explorations of the Linguistic Attitudes of Teachers", Newbury House, Rowley, Mass.

Williams, F., Whitehead, J. L. and Miller, L. M. (1971). Ethnic stereotyping and judgements of children's speech. *Speech Monographs*, **38**, 166–170.

Williams, F., Whitehead, J. L. and Miller, L. M. (1972). Relations between attitudes and teacher expectancy. *American Educational Research Journal*, **9**, 263–277.

Worchel, S. and Norvell, N. (1980). Effect of previous environmental conditions during cooperation on intergroup attraction. *Journal of Personality and Social Psychology*, **38**, 764–772.

Zeeman, E. C. (1976). Catastrophe theory. *Scientific American*, **234**, 65–83.

Note

We are most grateful to W. Peter Robinson and Miles Hewstone for their comments and contributions to an earlier draft of this chapter.

7

Applied sociology of language: vernacular languages and education

A. G. H. Walker

The average English person in the average English town will grow up with English as the language of their home and of their education. Only rarely will he or she come into serious contact with a foreign language. In other words most English people spend their lives in a state of monolingualism. However, such monolingualism is a minority phenomenon in terms of the total world population; bi- or multilingualism is found in most countries in the world. There are an estimated 394 languages in Nigeria (Hansford, 1976) and 760 languages in Papua New Guinea (Wurm, 1979). This does not mean that all speakers of these languages are multilingual, but it is probable that such a concentrated variety of languages in a relatively small area will lead to multilingualism, especially with increased mobility. Similarly, Fishman and Hofmann (1966) estimate that in America in 1960 there were some 18 352 351 speakers of the 23 major non-English mother-tongue groups and Spolsky (1972) considers there were a futher 40 or 50 smaller languages or language groups. In England it is estimated that in 1978 in London alone there were over 100 languages spoken by school-age children.[1]

In the monolingual setting, the concept of "vernacular language" is not too difficult to define, nor is there such a wide variety of sociolinguistic problems connected with education. In the bi- or multilingual setting, however, "vernacular language" is a more nebulous concept, and the sociolinguistic problems connected with its representation in education more numerous.

APPLIED SOCIOLINGUISTICS
ISBN: 0-12-701220-6

Thus, in the wide field of education in bi- or multilingual societies socio-linguistics has an important role to play, first of all in the identification and comprehension of problems, and secondly in the solving of these problems.

In this chapter I shall briefly discuss the concept of "vernacular language", describe various reasons why vernacular language is necessary in education and then illustrate some of the problems and possible solutions to be found in this context. As my own particular area of research is North Frisia (NF) in West Germany, where at the time of writing Frisian is being taught in 12 schools, many examples are taken from here.

What is a "vernacular language"

A vernacular language might be defined as the indigenous language used as the primary means of socialization within the family or tribal unit within a certain area.[2] In a monolingual setting such a definition is not problematical, whereas it can pose some problems in a multilingual context. What, for example, is the vernacular language in the quinquelingual villages of Rodenäs and Neukirchen in NF where Frisian, Jutish and Low German can all be considered indigenous in contrast to the High German and Danish standard languages also spoken here (Larsen, 1983; Spenter, 1976; Walker, 1980a)? All these languages can be used within the family unit, as each language can be used for addressing specific members of the family group. Thus, for example, a boy may address his father in Jutish, his mother in Frisian and his brother-in-law, who comes from the same village, in Low German. As all languages are in daily use in the family and in the sur-rounding neighbourhood, and as it is not possible to ascribe each language an exclusive set of domains generally valid for the two villages, they must presumably all be considered vernacular languages of more or less equal standing. However, although the Frisian case may be of some theoretical interest, I should like to adhere to the above definition of vernacular language and contrast this concept with those of the (1) regional language, (2) official language, (3) national language, and (4) international language.

Regional language

UNESCO (1968, p. 689) gives the following definition for a regional language: "A language which is used as a medium of communication between peoples living within a certain area who have different mother tongues". Thus, for example, NF had Low German as its regional language as speakers of mutually unintelligible Frisian dialects had to revert to it for communication. Today High German has largely taken over this role.

A regional language is practically synonymous with a *lingua franca*, the main difference being perhaps that the latter is not so geographically restricted as the former. The four languages Swahili, Hausa, Arabic and Mandingo are, for example, all African *linguae francae*, all of which encompass at least six different African states.

Official language

An official language is one designated by governmental decree to be the official means of communication of the given state in government, administration, law, education and general public life. Kloss (1968) distinguishes between *endoglossic* and *exoglossic* official languages, whereby an endoglossic official language is one indigenous to the state, e.g. English in England, French in France, whereas an exoglossic one is imported, e.g. English in Kenya, Ghana, Sierra Leone, or French in Zaire, and Portuguese in Mozambique. Tanzania has both an endoglossic (Swahili) as well as an exoglossic (English) official language.

National language

Several writers have discussed the concept of national language (Fishman, 1968a; Le Page, 1964; Nida and Wonderly, 1971) but I should like here to follow Heine (1979) where he differentiates three types of national language:
(1) The *de jure* national language. In this case the national language has been officially chosen by governmental decree. Thus, for example, Tanzania elected Swahili its national language in 1961. Namibia has three national languages: Afrikaans, English and German, and Nigeria has nine. It is interesting that of the 46 African states only 22 have an "official" national language.
(2) The *de facto* national language. This "unofficial" national language must fulfill two of the following criteria:
 (a) it must be used as a spoken medium throughout the nation and be spoken by more than half the population;
 (b) the language must symbolize national unity or identity;
 (c) the language must be considered as a means of expressing national culture and the national way of life.
 An example of the *de facto* national language would be the Wolof language in Senegal.
(3) The *de jure* and *de facto* national language. Examples of an "official" national language with a firm numerical base are Swahili in Tanzania, Somali in Somalia and Arabic in Algeria.

International language

An international language is one used over wide parts of the world for inter-territorial communication.

In each state of the world one or more languages are spoken, each of which corresponds to one or more of the categories outlined above. In Britain, for example, English is a vernacular (together with Scots Gaelic and Welsh) and a *lingua franca*, as well as the official and national language of Great Britain. In West Germany, East and North Frisian are purely vernaculars, Low German both a vernacular and a regional language, and High German a vernacular, *lingua franca* and the official national language of the Federal Republic. In Nigeria English is the official language, there are nine national languages: Hausa, Yoruba, Igbo, Ful, Kanuri, Efik, Edo, Idoma and Ijo. Hausa, Yoruba and Igbo are *linguae francae* and there are an estimated 394 vernaculars. Cameroon, Liberia and Mozambique are examples of countries with no national language.

Having briefly discussed different types of language, I should now like to differentiate three language groups, i.e. groups of speakers all using the vernacular, from which I shall be taking my examples. These are: (1) indigenous linguistic minorities, (2) speakers in developing countries, and (3) immigrants.

Indigenous linguistic minorities

In Western Europe alone there are some 50 minority languages (Stephens, 1978) and in North America there was an estimated 147 American Indian languages in 1941 (Ohannessian, 1972). A linguistic minority can perhaps be defined as a group of people who, within the family or tribal unit and in their everyday lives, predominantly speak a language which differs from the language spoken by the majority of the population in that particular country. Linguistic minorities can range in size from, for example, the estimated 2000 speakers of East Frisian (Saterlandic) (Fort, 1980; Sjölin, 1969) to the 10–12 million speakers of Occitan (Haarmann, 1975).

Developing countries

A developing country is one which is generally considered to be not as highly developed technologically or economically as for example the United States or the countries of Western Europe. In a great number of developing countries an international language, often the language of the colonialists, has been used as the official language and language of education. However, following independence, there have often been attempts to introduce the vernacular into more societal domains including education.

Immigrants

An immigrant is a person who has moved into a different country from the one he was born in. Immigrants are a somewhat different case to the two language groups already mentioned as they are not indigenous and have usually entered the country they now live in of their own volition. However, they often form a linguistic minority, using a language which is indigenous elsewhere and which is not spoken by the majority of the population in their present country of abode. As a lot of the problems encountered by immigrants are similar to those of other linguistic minorities, I have included them here.

Why vernacular language in education?

Following the short description of the types of language and language groups relevant to this paper, I shall now consider the reasons why vernacular education is desirable.

The social factor

When a child goes to school for the first time, it is usually the first major change in his life. The relative freedom of home life where he can run around, make noise and where he is usually one of a few children under his mother's eye, is exchanged for the relatively disciplined atmosphere of school where he has to sit still, is but one of a larger group in the classroom and where he has to do as he is told (UNESCO, 1968). It is an even greater change if the child completely leaves home to go to boarding school as often happened with the Apaches in America (Liebe-Harkort, 1980). In order to facilitate the structural change in the child's daily life, the language used at the new school should be the same as the one used at home so that he is not confronted with a completely new linguistic as well as social situation.

A further aspect is the communication between the child's two worlds of home and school. If the same language is used for both, the child can relate his school experiences at home and *vice versa*, and comprehension is assured. If, however, the child uses a second language at school which is incomprehensible to the parents, they will experience difficulties in understanding their child's school life and in helping his education (UNESCO, 1968), and this could lead to estrangement.

In order to avoid the possible conflicts arising from primary socialization at home in L1 and secondary socialization at school in L2, parents sometimes retain their mother tongue for communication between themselves but prefer to teach their children L2. Similarly, when parents use L1 with their first child but then notice that the child is having difficulties with L2 at school, they sometimes change to L2 for their second and later children. These two examples are often the cause for language shift in minority languages. However, as the parents in such a situation often only have imperfect knowledge of the dominant language L2, the children inherit the mistakes made by their parents. If these mistakes become firmly imbedded in the child's language performance, the teacher has the greatest difficulties in ironing them out again. One classic example is the distinction in High German between *mich* and *mir*. This is not known in Frisian or Low German and consequently children of Low German and/or Frisian parents may well confuse the usage of the two forms. Thus one often hears such constructions as: *Was hast du für mir?* As a result teachers often maintain that parents should teach their children their L1 and leave the teaching of the dominant language L2 to those trained for it.

Ethnicity

One possible definition of ethnicity is "a sense of group identity deriving from real or perceived common bonds such as language, race or religion" (Isajiw, 1974, quoted after Edwards, 1977, p. 254). Nationalism can be considered an extension of ethnicity, as the belief that nations possess certain characteristics which differentiate them from other nations is associated with the desire to promote the strength and ambitions of the nation one belongs to. Language is an important part of group identity, as it provides a link with the past, and a distinctive feature differentiating one group from those around it. Thus the Republic of Ireland states in Article 8 of its Constitution that "The Irish language as the national language is the first official language". This is because, as stated in paragraph 6 of the white paper *The Restoration of the Irish Language* (1965, p. 6).

> The Irish language is the most distinctive sign of our nationality. Our present position as an independent State derives in large measure from the idealism evoked by the Irish language movement.

The Irish language is then considered a major unifying and consolidating factor in the Irish nation. As a consequence it became national policy to introduce Irish into the curriculum of all primary schools in Eire. Irish is, however, an example of a language being used in schools to promote the feeling of national identity even though the language is not native to the majority of the population.

A more genuine mother-tongue education can be found in the teaching of Eskimo children in Alaska. Trifonovitch discovered (1976) that one important by-product of the bilingual education programme in Alaska, which had introduced the tuition of Eskimo children in their mother tongue, was an increasing awareness of their cultural and ethnic identity. In contrast to this, the monolingual English education of Apache children in North America was leading to suicides among the children (Paulston, 1980) or a complete rejection of American culture (Liebe-Harkort, 1980) as their own ethnic identity was being negated.

The child's cognitive development

Wells (1981) argues that the nature of interaction between a child and his parents and teachers is important for the literacy and scholastic development of a child. If a child is unable to communicate adequately with his teachers because of being taught in L2, this will stultify his linguistic development. Furthermore, if the area of intellectual activity at school is in a language which is not readily comprehensible to the child's parents, this will also restrict the possibilities of intellectual stimulus in the interaction between the child and his parents. Intellectual stimulation is, however, necessary as it develops the child's ability to make meaning explicit in a context-reduced situation, which in turn is a prerequisite for scholastic achievement.

Swain (1983) points out that the skills most basic to academic progress and achievement, such as the ability to master speech as a symbolic system, to generalize and abstract, are most easily learnt in L1. As these skills are cross-lingual, they can easily be applied to L2 as well. Thus it is easier to learn to read in L1 and then to apply this skill to L2 than to learn to read *and* learn L2 simultaneously. Once the reading skill is automated through L1, more attention can be paid to the acquisition of L2.

Macnamara (1967) considers that education through a weaker language has negative consequences for a child's academic progress, which Cummins (1976) in turn interprets in terms of a threshhold of linguistic competence which has to be attained if a child is to have any benefit from education in a certain language. For a child to be able to cope with two languages, he needs a proper education in L1, as experiments, for example in the French immersion programmes in Canada, show that children having difficulty with L2 leap forward once L1 is properly taught. If education is to be partly in L2, this can only be in a bilingual situation where the child has achieved the necessary threshholds in both languages. Bilingualism itself is also considered positive as it seems to accelerate the development of a child's verbal and non-verbal abilities and there is a positive association between bilingualism, cognitive flexibility and divergent thinking.

The preservation of a language

One aspect of linguistic imperialism has been the systematic attempt to eradicate minority languages within the sphere of a nation's or state's power. Thus Gregor (1980, p. 340) can quote the French Minister of Education who stated in 1925 that "For the unity of France the Breton language must die". *The Times* can also be quoted for its disparaging attitude towards Welsh when it says in 1866 that "the Welsh language is . . . the curse of Wales . . . its prevelance and the ignorance of the English language have excluded the Welsh people from the civilisation of their English neighbours" (quoted after Stephens, 1978, p. 159). Part of this policy of eradication was the exclusive use of the dominant language in education, although this was often coupled with the genuine belief that education in a minority language was detrimental to a child's development. Thus Billigmeier (1979, p. 338) quotes a teacher from Trin (Switzerland) who writes:

> The school inspector, . . ., would not let an inspection conclude without emphasizing to the teachers, to the school board, and to the students that Romansh was an impediment to instruction and that it must be eliminated as quickly as possible.

This policy, often reinforced by punishing children caught speaking the minority language at school, unfortunately proved quite successful with a number of minority languages, and one can conclude that the lack of education in a minority language is one major factor for its demise. For this reason vernacular education is deemed a major goal in most language movements.

The reasons for the importance of vernacular education within a language movement are: (1) vernacular education will instill children with a sense of pride in their native tongue and culture which counteract the sense of inferiority long connected with minority languages (cf. Ethnicity above); the vernacular language can then be raised to the level of a prestige language such as for example Manx on the Isle of Man (Gregor, 1980); (2) vernacular education serves to develop a child's command of the language in an attempt to make it a viable medium in the modern world; (3) vernacular education will enable those children living in an area with a linguistic minority, but who themselves have no command of the minority language, to learn it. This would facilitate integration into the linguistic community and hopefully prevent ostracization or language shift.

The official view

On the question of vernacular education, it is pleasing to note that politicians and linguists are now obviously in agreement. The *Recommendation 928* (1981) *on the educational and cultural problems of minority languages and dialects in Europe* from the thirty-third ordinary session of the Parliamentary Assembly of the Council of Europe gives a good example:

> The Assembly, . . . Considering that the following principles should form the basis for the scientific, human and cultural treatment of each language: . . . – the right of children to their own language and culture, . . . Recommends that the Committee of Ministers consider whether it would be possible for governments of member states to implement the following measures in whatever manner most appropriate: . . . b. With regard to the human aspect, the gradual adoption of children's mother tongues for their education . . . c. With regard to the cultural aspect, respect and official support for the local use of standardised minority languages, and for their current use in higher education . . . in so far as this approach is favoured by the communities which speak them; . . .

The implementation of vernacular education

The problems arising in the context of the implementation of vernacular education fall into three main fields of enquiry: (1) the society in which the language is found (societal problems); (2) the language itself (linguistic problems); and (3) the school in which the language is taught (problems pertaining to the school).

Societal problems

One prerequisite for the implementation of a policy of vernacular education is the analysis of the linguistic community concerned, in order to avoid unfavourable reactions on the part of the populace. Stewart (1968, p. 532) points out that:

> Where reactions of this [unexpected] type have caught language planners un- awares, it has not necessarily been because they were totally unpredictable, but rather because not enough information was sought in advance about the ways in which languages may interact with other aspects of society.

Thus, although it may be possible to enumerate a number of factors common to different sorts of linguistic community (Ferguson, 1966; Gumperz, 1968; Kloss, 1966, 1968; Rustow, 1968; Stewart, 1962), nevertheless each linguistic community will have a configuration of factors unique to itself, and it is this

configuration which the linguist has to discover. (The validity of this statement does admittedly depend upon the degree of abstraction one is working
with. It will, however, hold for the field-worker we are concerned with here
who is daily confronted with tangible problems on the micro-level).

A second prerequisite is to decide what the aims of the vernacular
education policy are in each particular instance (cf. Karam, 1974). There
may be a policy of language revival where a language which had become
extinct has been reintroduced as a spoken medium such as Hebrew (Fellman,
1973), Manx or Cornish (Gregor, 1980; Stephens, 1978); a policy of language
maintenance as in the case of linguistic minorities where the language is in
decline, such as Welsh (Khleif, 1980) and Frisian (Boelens, 1976; Walker,
1980a); a policy confronted with divided language loyalties as in the case of
two parallel language systems in a country like Norway (Haugen, 1966); a
policy connected with large-scale language reform as in Turkey (Gallagher,
1971); a policy of language expansion introducing vernacular education into
an area where previously a colonial language had been the medium of
instruction. Here one would further differentiate between a vernacular
which is supposed to be developed simultaneously as the national language
as in Malaysia (Omar, 1976), and a vernacular which is purely a regional
language as in Zambia (Ohannessian, 1978a).

In the analysis of a language community the linguist would have to
consider the following factors (Spolsky et al., 1976):

The social structure of the area
In many areas where one finds a declining minority language, one of the
principal reasons for its decline is a change in the social structure. This can
have direct consequences for the schools in the area. As linguistic minority
areas are often rural and attractive holiday spots, e.g. Wales, Scotland,
Brittany, North and West Frisia, this leads to tourism. As the rural areas are
often economically underdeveloped the tourism brings a welcome influx of
jobs and wealth and many inhabitants become dependent upon tourism for
their living. However, the tourists introduce the dominant language into the
community and strengthen its position there. In addition, a larger labour
force is often needed for the "season" than can be culled from the area itself,
which again means introducing speakers of the dominant language into the
community. In both instances mixed marriages are often the result whereby
the' member of the linguistic minority usually gives up his or her mother
tongue in favour of the dominant language.

Tourism also has the effect of raising the price of houses and land so that
members of the indigenous population can no longer afford to live there and
are forced to move. On the island of Sylt in NF, the schools have great
difficulty in finding teachers, as potential candidates cannot afford to live on

the island in the manner to which they are accustomed. As a result of the very high cost of living on Sylt, a large part of the labour force has to commute from the mainland each day. In a similar case in Wales some Welsh people have taken to burning down holiday homes belonging to English people as a protest against the influence of the English language in the Welsh-speaking area and the consequences of English tourists on the property market.

Another consequence of the economic underdevelopment of the minority language areas is the shortage of jobs available for young people, especially qualified young people, so that many are forced to emigrate. However, in an attempt to solve this problem, governments sometimes try to develop areas that are economically weak by introducing industry. This may bring more prosperity into the area but tends to have a disastrous effect on the minority language. Kramer (1978) describes the beginning of the new era some 28 years ago, when the East Frisian language really went into decline, as coming with the advent of the 'Emsland plan' which included the building of roads and the settling of industry in the area. In Eire the government tried to settle industry in the Gaeltacht, but discovered that the local populace had little interest in working in factories and that the trained and qualified staff needed to run a factory had largely to be imported. This meant another English incursion into the Irish-speaking area (Gregor, 1980). Similarly, in NF, there are large units of the German Air Force and of the "Bundesgrenzschutz" (border police) which on the one hand bring employment for the local populace but on the other hand change the ethnic composition of the area so that many children going to school in NF are now neither linguistically nor ethnically Frisian.

Ethnicity and attitudes
It was noted earlier that language is an important part of a person's or a linguistic community's ethnic identity. However, as Edwards points out (1977), one has to differentiate between the communicative and the non-communicative aspects of language. Although many in Eire see "the value of Irish as a symbol of national or ethnic identity, or as a symbol of cultural distinctiveness" (Committee on Irish Language Attitudes Research, 1975), and although 76 per cent questioned by the Irish Marketing Surveys approved of Irish being taught in national primary schools (Macnamara, 1971), there was nevertheless a large amount of hostility towards the Irish Language Education Programme set up by the Government. In other words, people in Eire were prepared to accept the symbolic value of Irish but not the attempted coercion by the Government in order to reinstate Irish as the main medium of instruction in schools and as the main medium of communication in the country. As a consequence, certain measures taken by the

Government, such as the obligatory examination in Irish for candidates for the Civil Service, have since had to be revised.

In contrast to Eire, Wales and West Frisia provide examples where the language plays an important role in a person's identity. Here, the proof of ethnicity is not only the language as such but also the ability to speak the language. This, however, applies mainly to members of the language movements, and in Wales the members of the *Welsh Language Society* had to convince the public that giving Welsh a place in the school curriculum would not lead to a decline in standards attained in English before they could introduce a programme of Welsh education (Williams, 1973). According to Chapman *et al.* (1977) there are now three groups of people in Wales who consider themselves Welsh: (1) fluent speakers of Welsh, (2) learners of Welsh, and (3) those who consider Welsh a waste of time but who still show their "Welshness" by the linguistic distinctive feature of a Welsh accent in English. In fact all three groups reject standard RP English. Thus, in the third case, the Welsh accent can be considered the equivalent of the Welsh vernacular. It is interesting to note that in all three examples there is a reaction against one form or other of government coercion. In Eire the Government tried to impose Irish on the populace and met with a hostile reception, whereas in Wales and West Frisia the central Government (London and Den Haag) tried in one form or other to suppress the minority languages.

Ethnicity is one of the greatest problems facing plurilingual and pluriethnic societies. If a pluriethnic nation decides to give preeminence to one particular language (and therefore also to the ethnic group it represents) by making it the national language, this will probably cause bitter resentment amongst the other ethnic groups. In Nigeria, for example, the naming of one of the indigenous languages as the national language to the exclusion of the others would probably lead to civil war. Similarly the name of the language can have the same effect, as witnessed in Malaysia. Following independence in 1957 the national language was called "Bahasa Melayu". This, however, caused much unrest among the Tamil and Chinese sections of the population as they interpreted the name as meaning the language of the Malays. Following a severe racial clash in 1969 the Government changed the name to Bahasa Malaysia, which meant "the language of Malaysia". This name seems to be acceptable to all ethnic groups and problems of ethnicity should not now disrupt the education programme the Government has embarked upon, which envisages "one type of education for all, which uses Bahasa Malaysia as medium of instruction right up to the university level" (Omar, 1976, p. 5).

An integral part of ethnicity is the question of attitudes. Each group or community has certain attitudes towards itself and towards the other groups around it. These attitudes usually offset one group from the others and are evaluative, e.g. our group A is better than group B which in turn is better than group C. The attitude can apply to the group as such, but also to certain features of the group such as language. A negative attitude towards a group will probably include the group's language, but a negative attitude towards a language need not include the group which speaks it. In Schleswig-Holstein, for example, many people consider Danish an "ugly" language, principally because of its glottal stop (stød), but are very fond of Denmark and the Danes. The attitude one has towards one's own group can be influenced by the attitude another group has towards it, especially in the asymmetric relationship of a minority group *versus* a majority group. Thus, if the majority group considers the minority group inferior, it is possible that the members of the minority group will accept this opinion and take it as their own. The attitude a person has towards his own group is, however, important, as it may influence his desire to retain or reject those features which determine his membership of the group (Giles *et al.*, 1977), which in turn will be of relevance for education, as it may affect a parent's willing-ness to allow his child to participate in vernacular education and/or a child's willingness to study (in) the vernacular.

The black population in North America, the Commonwealth immigrants in Britain and the immigrants from Turkey, Yugoslavia etc. (*Gastarbeiter*) in West Germany tend to be considered socially inferior. Thus, in Germany Turks are often addressed with the intimate but in this context socially degrading *du*. As these groups are considered socially inferior, so are their languages and their accents. In England, for example, this often results in making the Indian and Pakistani English accents the butt of jokes (cf. Chapman *et al.*, 1977 for a discussion of this phenomenon with reference to Welsh). We find a similar case with indigenous linguistic minorities. As minority languages are often found in economically underdeveloped regions, the group speaking the language is often relatively poor and holds a low social standing. Gregor (1980, p. 294f) quotes for example *An t-Ultach* (The Ulsterman) of June 1951 which had stated:

> For some, Irish is synonymous with poverty and social inferiority. . . . Young people think it is a sign of social inferiority if their parents speak Irish, especially in the presence of a stranger.

Such attitudes to language are also found in pluriethnic and plurilingual societies. Heine (1979) reports for Africa that vernacular languages are often considered symbols of the somewhat limited horizon of the tradi-tional tribal way of life and as such do not have much prestige. The *linguae francae* such as Swahili are preferred as they represent the free modern way of life and offer better job opportunities and social recognition. Similarly, in Ghana many people see English (the official language) as the key to the new material civilization. In this they find active support from the politicians who consider the vernacular languages to have a negative influence on the nation's future, and who prefer English to promote national unity, the suppression of tribalism, rapid industrialization and accelerated economic development (Ohannessian, 1978b). Another reason why politicians and officialdom in developing countries tend to have a negative attitude towards vernaculars is their desire to retain the *status quo* for socio-economic reasons. Many senior officials have attained their posts through, among other things, a good command of the official language when their country was a colony of a foreign power. Because of their expertise in this language they can command a certain elitist position in society. If, however, the former colonial language is reduced in status to that of the vernacular, it is possible that the officials will lose at least part of their own status and priviliges as they would then practically be on a par with all other vernacular speakers. In this instance the officials wish their additional linguistic competence to be rewarded, although it does not necessarily mean that they simultaneoulsy reject the vernacular.

In another example, the lack of material benefits the vernacular brings makes the vernacular unpopular so that children or students see little point in learning or using it. In Āndhara Pradesh, a state in Southern India, Telugu was introduced as the official language in 1966. Telugu proved very unpopular as a medium with the students and parents as there was no policy for preferential treatment for Telugu-medium students and because employers such as banks and businesses still carried out their work in English and preferred English-medium students (Krishnamurti, 1978). This is in contrast to NF, where it seems that a command of Frisian may soon prove economically useful. There is at the time of writing a greater supply of teachers in Germany than the schools can employ, and it is probable that teachers speaking Frisian will be given preferential treatment in NF. Such measures should enhance the language's prestige.

Socio-economic considerations may persuade a person to abandon his ethnic group and its language. Edwards (1977) mentions two examples where members of an ethnic group have considered it to their advantage to identify more strongly with a different ethnic group.

In Montreal, in which the majority of the citizens are French–Canadian, big business has traditionally been an English-speaking domain . . . French speakers clearly had to become bilingual in order to ascend the economic ladder. Such a situation has given rise to the phenomenon of French-speaking Montrealers attempting to identify more strongly with English Canadians than with members of their own group. (1977, p. 257).

The second example relates to the immigrants in the "melting pot" of the United States where there was a

> process of Americanization by which ethnic groups of every origin submerged the characteristics of these origins, were assimilated into the mainstream of American society, and reappeared after a generation or so as more or less homogenous Americans . . . [Thus] the evident rewards that full participation in American life offered, have been the causes of the apparently rapid 'de-ethnicizing' of immigrants. (1977, p. 261).

Both these examples show a group wishing to assimilate into another group which sometimes results in parents refusing to send their children to schools set up for their ethnic language group. In NF we have a similar example, but there a further factor must be taken into consideration. On the mainland of NF the Frisians can be roughly divided into two groups: the Frisians oriented mainly towards Germany and the Frisians oriented mainly towards Denmark. The majority of the Frisians are not very politically minded but, if forced to make a decision, would consider themselves more members of the first group because they are not members of the second group. Thus we have here the phenomenon of the "minority within the minority". The Frisians as such are a minority within the German majority, but they in turn can be sub-divided into the German Frisian majority and the Danish Frisian minority. It is, however, the Danish Frisian minority which is most active in the promotion of the Frisian tongue. Because in this area to be called a "Dane" has certain negative connotations, this has the effect of inhibiting a number of potential activities, as people would often rather acquiesce to German than support Frisian for fear of being considered a Dane.

The negation of one's ethnicity is often the result of the desire to be assimilated into the mainstream of the society one is living in. However, once one has been assimilated to a certain degree and has achieved a certain standing in society, one can then afford to return to one's true ethnic heritage. This explains why leaders of language and "cultural revival" groups are often politicians or academics. The question, however, is whether these leaders actually do articulate the true needs and desires of the group they claim to represent, and also to what extent the average member of the ethnic group can identify with them. To what extent, for example, will the average working man accept the credibility of the person who advocates that everyone should speak the minority language with their children and that it should be taught in schools, when he himself speaks the dominant language with his family as a result of the previous assimilation process? Similarly, as Tholund (1980) asks, is the resurgence of ladies' native costumes in NF really a sign of the awakening of the Frisian identity or rather an excuse for politicians to show their "love" for the country and to have a couple of beautifully clad fair maidens to accompany them on festive occasions? It is difficult to assess the true effect of such people and such manifestations of "culture" in an ethnic group. On the one hand they tend not to represent the true needs and desires of the average member of the group, but on the other hand they do lend the language and culture more prestige by their personal dedication to it.

In a discussion of attitudes one can differentiate not only various types of society but also the sexes. Labov (1966) notes that women in a minority group tend to be more language conscious and prefer the dominant language. Girls may then be more resistant to being taught the vernacular at school than boys. However, in a different situation girls may be the principal bearers of the vernacular. On the island of Föhr, for example, where the menfolk used to go to sea for a good part of the year, they became multilingual. The women who stayed at home retained their Frisian and ensured the continuity of the Frisian community and language. It is possible that the boys here preferred to learn High and Low German in expectation of their own travels in contrast to the girls who saw their futures in the narrow confines of the village. Similarly Liebe-Harkort (1980) reports the differences in attitudes between Navajo boys and girls. As Navajo men tend to do traditional outdoor jobs and Navajo women do subordinate work in offices and hospitals, girls are more proud of their English and use it more whereas boys tend to regard a compliment on their English as an insult.

Demographic factors
The number of speakers of a language can be of importance for educational planning, as economic factors may forbid the inclusion of too small a language in the school curriculum, and speakers of this language would then be forced to use a second language. However, establishing the true number of speakers of a language can be problematical as (1) the concept "speaking a language" would need an exact definition, and (2) a method would have to be evolved for eliciting accurate information corresponding to the working definition. Censuses are not always reliable. In Ireland and Wales, for example, they do not differentiate between those who have Irish or Welsh as their mother tongue and those who have acquired the language later in life, e.g. at school or in evening classes (Price, 1973). Similarly, the Lapps living in the coastal districts of Northern Norway refused to admit their true identity in a census, as Lapp is considered a negative identity in Norway (Aarseth, 1969). However, even a linguist conducting a personal interview is not free from error, as the interviewees will often give the answer expected or hoped from them rather than the true answer. In the case of speakers of a language with low prestige there will be a tendency to negate one's language competence, and in the case of a minority language

where the interviewer is obviously a supporter of the language, there will be a tendency to overestimate one's linguistic ability. One possible method of checking the true linguistic competence of an interviewee is to converse in the given language. If the interviewer switches codes, however, it is possible that the interviewee will not be able to follow suit if he has the linguistic rule 'one person one language'. (I have experienced this in my field work in NF.)

Linguistic relationship
In a bilingual community (in the sense that two languages are used in the community, while not all members of the community are necessarily proficient in both) with two completely unrelated languages, such as the Eskimos in Alaska (Yup'ik and English) or the Apaches in North America (Apache and English) it will probably be more difficult for the children to comprehend and acquire the second language than in a community like West Frisia, where West Frisian and Dutch are closely related West Germanic tongues. On the other hand, the incidence of interference will probably be more marked between two related and similar languages than between two unrelated ones.

Similar to the linguistic relationship of the languages in question is the relationship between cultural concepts embodied in the two languages. Finnish and Swedish, although genetically completely unrelated, will have more European concepts common to both than English and Eskimo (Mackey, 1978).

The functions of each language
An analysis of the functions each language has in the community, whereby a function can perhaps be defined as the set of speech acts ascribed to a language in the community (Johnson, 1977), is important, as a language which has hitherto been restricted primarily to the domains of the home and the hearth will face different problems when introduced into education than an officially recognized language already in wide use. (The term "language function" has been used in a variety of ways; see for example (*after* Johnson, 1977); Barker, 1947; Fillmore, 1973; Fishman, 1971; Le Page, 1964; Nida and Wonderly, 1971; Okonwo, 1975; Stewart, 1968; Weinreich, 1953). Whiteley (1969) gives a brief description of the language functions in the multilingual state Tanzania. Swahili is the national language and is used in the National Assembly, the Party, the Trade Unions, the lower courts, regional administration, primary education and in certain areas of the Civil Service. English is used in inter-territorial affairs, higher education, the High Court and certain technical fields of government, e.g. medicine. The home language is probably the vernacular if both parents are from the same language community. If the parents come from different language communities, then

probably Swahili will dominate. However, speakers of Haya, Nyakyusa, Chaga and Gogo have a certain sense of language loyalty and would probably rather retain the vernacular than use the *lingua franca* Swahili. If the parents have enjoyed a certain education and have been to secondary school, they will probably include English in the languages used at home.

Linguistic problems

Two main problems can be differentiated with reference to the vernacular language itself. These are the language's range of functions and the linguistic norm.

The language's range of functions

It was mentioned earlier that an analysis of the functions of the languages used in the community was important. If, as is often the case, the vernacular is restricted in its functions, the number of styles will also be restricted, perhaps to the extent of mono-stylism as witnessed in Brittany, where young Bretons only have a command of the casual style. Formal situations are usually coped with in French (Dressler and Wodak-Leodolter, 1977). However, as the spectrum of education must go beyond the purely casual level, the problem arises how further levels of style can be introduced. There is a similar problem with respect to the vocabulary if the language is used only in certain domains. If, as in the case of Welsh, the language is spoken primarily in the home in a rural area, the vocabulary will be rich in terms for the domestic and agricultural domains, but lacking in technical, commercial and other such "sophisticated" teminology (Jones, 1973). Here the vocabulary must be extended (cf. Modernization).

The linguistic norm

For languages lacking a standardized norm, Kloss (1969) has described one aspect of language planning as "corpus planning". This can, in agreement with Ferguson (1968), be subdivided into three sections: (1) the creation of a written form (graphization), (2) the choice of a standard form (standardization), and (3) the modernization of the language (modernization).

Graphization.   The question of the making of alphabets has long been the subject of debate, and Berry (1968) posits certain scientific principles and social factors which must be taken into account in order to create a successful alphabet. He states that "an alphabet is successful in so far and only in so far as it is scientifically and socially acceptable." (1968, p. 737). In a later article

(1977) he shifts the emphasis slightly from the scientific aspect and stresses the social aspect more. Fishman (1977) points out that a language community in a bi- or multilingual situation may be guided by two opposing forces when forming their attitudes to a possible orthography, as they may desire their orthography to be similar or dissimilar to those of the languages around them.

It is said of the West Frisians that, if anyone attacks their language, they will man the barricades, but even on the barricades they will continue their squabbles about the orthography (Jörgensen, 1979). The same applies to the North Frisians. The present North Frisian orthographic system states that all long vowels shall be written with a double vowel, e.g. *naame* [naːmə] "to take", and short vowels with a single vowel, e.g. *ham* [ham] "him". No consonants can be doubled. This is in contrast to the German orthographic system where short vowels are indicated by a doubling of the following consonant, e.g. *Butter, Hölle*, and long vowels are followed by a single consonant or a length symbol such as *h* in *Mehl* or *e* as in *Sieg*. Århammar (1976) considers that this radical deviation from the dominant language's norm is to emphasize Frisian's independent identity. This orthographic principle has been widely accepted although one symbol has caused some trouble. As the mainland dialects are characterized by an abundance of vowel phonemes, the symbol *å* was introduced in the phonemes /å/ and /åå/ to differentiate them from the phonemes /oo/ = [oː] and /oo/ = [ɔː], the latter two phonemes being examples of the desired principle of one phoneme one grapheme not being fulfilled as each phoneme is written oo. As, however, Danish also uses the symbol *å* as in *Århus*, some Frisians rejected the orthography as they considered it too Danish. A further more serious argument, however, evolved around the discussion whether or not nouns should be written with a capital letter as in German. One argument forwarded was that all children are used to the German orthography and that it must be pedagogically sensible to use the same principles in Frisian i.e. the orthographic principles a child is used to in his literacy L1 should be transferred to his literacy L2. The counter argument was that all other languages in Europe use small letters for nouns, such as English, which the children also learn at school. This "pedagogical" argument was in fact a political one, as the German-oriented Frisians saw the noun with the capital letter as their last bastion of German identity in the Frisian orthography. Thus dissimilarity from German is sought by that group striving for a degree of Frisian autonomy and similarity is desired by that group which wishes to see Frisian firmly clutched to the bosom of the German state. At present a certain form of anarchy reigns as each group publishes its works according to its own principles.

Standardization.   Feguson (1968, p. 31) sees language standardization as

> the process of one variety of a language becoming widely accepted throughout
> the speech community as a supradialectal norm – the 'best' form of the language
> – rated above regional and social dialects, although these may be felt appropriate
> in some domains.

Standardization is necessary if a language is to be included in the school
curriculum as a subject or a medium. If, however, the language is an as yet
uncoded or insufficiently coded vernacular, there are various factors which
may influence the choice of one variant as a norm. Fishman (1968c, p. 10f),
for example, lists the following considerations:

> number of speakers, . . . past association with a Great Tradition, current
> association with major social trends . . ., greater purity in the sense of fewer
> influences from varieties or languages considered undesirable or, conversely,
> greater similarity to other highly regarded varieties or languages, and, finally, a
> middle-ground position *vis-à-vis* overly pure and overly indistinguishable
> varieties.

I should, however, like to discuss the question of the norm by considering
three axes. These are the temporal, the areal and the societal axes.

(1) The temporal axis. Language is permanently changing, which perhaps
helps explain why each generation complains that the following generation
no longer speaks the language properly. However, change can have different consequences for different languages. English has, for example,
relatively recently gained the words *streaker* and *punk* and is in the process
of losing the pronouns *thee* and *thou*. These changes will, however, have
little effect on the English language community. English, as result of these
changes, is in no way endangered. It is a different case, however, for a
linguistic minority, where changes may be interpreted as symptoms of
language decline. Haugen (1980) has coined the concept of *the cycle of
language shift* whereby a monolingual community gradually introduces L2,
the dominant language. For a period of time there is a lot of interference in
L2 from L1. After a while there comes a diglossic situation. Following this
the interference stems from the dominant language L2 and is found in the
minority language L1. Finally monolingualism is reintroduced following the
extinction of L1.

In the declining East Sutherland Scots Gaelic dialect showing interference
from the dominant L2 English, Dorian (1977, p. 23)

> discovered considerable differences in the Gaelic of the oldest available fluent
> speakers and the youngest, the Gaelic of the latter showing reduction and loss in
> certain areas in comparison with the former.

Walker (1977) found in three generations of trilingual Frisian-Low German-High German speakers (where both Frisian and Low German are L1 in Haugen's cycle, 1980), that the forms of address had changed in Frisian and Low German from the binary system of second person singular (familiar) and third person singular (respect) to the equivalent of the High German system with *du* and *Se* in Low German, and to an insecure system in Frisian where the High German system had been partly adopted, but where also part of the old Frisian system with the third person singular had been retained. These two examples indicate that a declining language shows (1) a reduction in forms, and (2) a change in various sub-systems which then adopt the dominant language form. As a result of this it is difficult to establish exactly what the norm is. In traditional dialectology the field workers have always preferred the oldest inhabitants of a village as informants as they "reflect the speech of a bygone era" (Chambers and Trudgill, 1980, p. 35) and are generally considered to speak the "best" dialect. This could also be used as the criterion for selecting the norm, especially if the older generation grew up monolingual. However, a grammar based on the dialect variant represented by the older generation may well be severely criticized by the younger generation of speakers and school children who would not wish to accept that variant as a norm. In NF we then hear such comments as: "That's alright for old grannies and philologists, but no-one speaks like that now." If, however, the norm is based on the speech of the younger generation, in all probability various forms unique to the minority language and which helped differentiate it from the dominant language would be lost. Thus the question arises whether one wishes to retain or reintroduce the old pre-language-contact grammar, or work with a grammar which can be interpreted as showing all the symptoms of a declining language. As it were, puristic prescriptivism *versus* pure descriptivism.

(2) The areal axis. Most languages of the world display a variety of dialects. With those languages with a standardized norm, there often arises a case of bidialectal diglossia whereby the "local" dialect is, for example, used at home and the "standard" dialect i.e. the standardized form of the language, is spoken at school. There are problems here (cf. Trudgill, 1975) but the teacher does at least know what standard he or she is supposed to be teaching. With a non-standardized language showing great dialectal variation, the fundamental problem of the norm is most acute. One may find that the speakers of a non-standardized language consider the language inferior to the standardized dominant language, but that within the non-standardized language each speaker considers his dialect to be the only correct norm, making him reject the choice of any other norm. For NF, for example, Wilts (1979, p. 198) writes:

Der einzelne nordfriesische Dialekt darf sich auf Grund seiner subjektiv empfundenen Überlegenheit über die friesischen Nachbardialekte bereits als Vertreter des Nordfriesischen *par excellence* fühlen.

As a consequence it is possible that a dialect speaker will reject books, dictionaries etc. which are not written in his norm. A multidialectal dictionary as a compromise would probably only result in confusing the reader. If, however, one dialect *is* chosen as the norm this may lead to the speakers of the other dialects considering their dialect incorrect and inferior which, in the case of a declining language, might make them refuse to speak it and revert to the dominant language.

When constructing a norm for a language consisting of a variety of dialects, a factor which has to be taken into consideration is the mutal intelligibility of the dialects. Statements on this subject can, however, be misleading as they may be subjective and subject to a certain ideology. Thus, an objective linguist considers some North Frisian dialects to be so dissimilar that mutal comprehension is practically impossible (Hofmann, 1956), whereas certain eminent members of the language movement see no reason why intra-dialectal comprehension should be difficult. It is, however, difficult to find objective criteria for comprehensibility. Linguistic similarity does not suffice, as socio-psychological factors such as prestige may render two objectively similar languages incomprehensible. In Nigeria, speakers of the Kalabari dialect of the Ijo language are relatively prosperous and consider the other dialect groups such as Nembe to be backward. The latter have no difficulty in understanding Kalabari, whereas the Kalabari maintain they are unable to understand the Nembe. This is an example of non-reciprocal comprehension. Similarly, socio-political factors may be at work, as exemplified in the Urhobo language in Southern Nigeria, where speakers of the Isoko dialect group maintain they cannot understand the other dialects of the language. This is accredited to the Isoko group's desire for autonomy (Heine, 1979).

There are also more objective factors which can render dialects incomprehensible. The Lapp language is spoken over an area which encompasses four different countries. There are seven main dialects, some of which are mutually incomprehensible, so that a Lapp from Finnmark cannot understand one from Trøndelag (Norway). One of the reasons for this is that different languages are used as sources of loan words. As Finnish and Norwegian belong to two completely different language families (Finno-Ugrian and Germanic), any loan words taken from them can only widen the already existent gap between the two Lapp dialects (Aarseth, 1969).

In NF a certain amount of tolerance is exercised in the orthography designed for the mainland dialect of the Bökingharde in NF around the

Risum Moor, as words are written and accepted using forms from both the main sub-dialects (East and West Mooring). Admittedly there are only minor differences between the two dialects, but nevertheless people do recognize a given form as belonging to a certain village. If, however, one goes seven kilometers to the south or ten kilometers to the north, one encounters two completely different dialects which adhere to the same orthographic principles outlined above (p. 177), but which demand that the lexicographical realization of the individual words should conform to their dialect and not to the norm established for the Mooring dialects. This is quite understandable, as various features with a high frequency rate differ quite strongly as, for example (after Walker, 1980c):

	East Mooring	Fahretoft (south)	Emmelsbüll (north)
Old	ō > ö (fötj)	ou (fout)	öi (föitj) *foot*
Frisian	ē > ä (brädj)	äi (bräid)	äi (bräid) *bride*
	ā > üü (üülj)	ù (ùl)	ù (ùl) *old*

For these dialects a different orthography has to be used.

The diversity of dialects has sometimes led to a compromise whereby books etc. are published in a number of dialects. In Eire, three dialects are used (Connacht, Munster and Ulster) and in NF sometimes six. In Eire, speakers from each dialect take it in turn to read the news bulletin in the radio (Stephens, 1978).

(3) The societal axis. In a language consisting of a multiplicity of dialects, history would appear to show that the dialect of the elitist group in the society usually develops as the standard language. Present-day standard English, for example, originates from the language spoken at the Royal Court in London in the fourteenth century. This may cause a conflict between various criteria, as an elitist dialect is not necessarily numerically the strongest, the one most free of external influence, or the most developed. The choice of the norm depends upon the question of priorities and the degree to which the elitist group is capable of influencing the relevant authorities.

Language planning can suffer set-backs if language planners are insufficiently trained or if inadequate field-work or sociolinguistic survey-work is carried out beforehand. Ohannessian (1978a), for example, complains that the members of the committees set up to standardize the seven officially taught languages in Zambia had, with few exceptions, no training in Bantu linguistics, Zambian languages or language pedagogy. As there is often an insufficient number of qualified indigenous linguists in a developing country to establish a system of language planning, experts are frequently called in

from outside. These, however, usually lack the intimate knowledge necessary to appreciate the subtleties of the society they are working in, and as a
result produce a language form which is considered by the indigenous
population to be lifeless and stilted, as in the case of Swahili in 1934
(Whiteley, 1969). Furthermore, certain parts of the population may feel
offended, as in the case of Malawi, where a group of impartial linguistic
experts created the language "Union Nyanja" as a synthesis of two main
dialects. Despite the neutrality of the language planners, members of each
dialect group rejected the new creation as each group saw too many features
of the other language in it and not enough of their own (Heine, 1979).

As a result of various problems that have arisen in language planning,
Mülhäusler *et al.* (1979) suggest that the best method would be to observe
how communication works between various language varieties, where the
difficulties arise which need standardization, and to note what degree of
variation is tolerated without impairing communication. As an example of
tolerated variation in an otherwise very norm-conscious society, Tauli
(1968, p. 154) quotes a count published in 1936 which established that

> the first 300 pages of the German Duden dictionary comprised over 1,100
> substantives with variant inflectional forms, as *des Aales/Aals, die Karnevale/
> Karnevals,* over 600 orthographic variants, e.g. *Grafik/Graphik*, over 100 words
> with gender variants, e.g. *der/die/das Klafter,* hundreds of verb form variants,
> e.g. *du fragst/frägst, ich angele/angle.*

Modernization. Ferguson (1968, p. 32) considers the modernization of a
language as being "the process of its becoming the equal of other developed
languages as a medium of communication; . . ." and sees "the expansion of
the lexicon" as an important aspect in this process. With respect to the
expansion of the lexicon it would appear that one positive aspect of language
decline is that it sometimes encourages laymen to write dictionaries in order
to preserve the diminishing vocabulary and in a valiant effort to produce
new terms for the modern world. There is perhaps the belief that a dictionary
is a language's redemption. Bendsen (1860), for example writes with respect
to North Frisian:

> Da nun diese, gewiss uralte, Sprache mit jeder Generation von allen Seiten
> durch die dänische und plattdeutsche immer mehr beschränkt wird, und ihrem
> allmähligen Aussterben entgegengeht, so habe ich mich der, wahrlich nicht
> leichten, Mühe unterzogen, sie durch gegenwärtige Arbeit von ihrem gänzlichen
> Untergange bei der Mit- und Nachwelt zu retten.

However, despite the trouble that laymen put themselves to, their lexical
creations are often not accepted by the language community. This could also

happen to an official lexicographical institution, though in this case there may well be a tendency to feel that a dictionary produced by trained academics carries an aura of infallibility, although this will depend on the general esteem accorded academics in the society concerned. In the case of the North Frisian dictionary for which a university department was especially created in 1950, the informants are very reluctant to question the lemmata, even though in some instances they may be contrary to their native-speaker intuition. Admittedly most of the words listed are the result of field work, or have been culled from books written over the past three centuries, but many words are included which must have been attempts by earlier lexicographers to modernize their language and which in all probability were never fully accepted by the language community. However, a word which can be proved to have been recorded a long time ago tends to be rather uncritically regarded as correct, although this in no way means that the word will then be used.

In many countries, institutions have been set up to standardize and modernize a language, such as the Icelandic Language Commission founded in 1964. This institution tries to modernize Icelandic by reviving old Icelandic words which appeared in the sagas rather than accepting loan words. They have two five-minute broadcasts a week on the radio and have succeeded in making the population take an interest in their language. Examples of revived words with a new semantic content are: *simi* (telephone) which is the old word for "wire" or "thread", *þjálfa* (to train) which meant "to work hard". A lot of new creations are composita using two Icelandic words, such as *flug-maður* (pilot) coming from *flug* (flight) and *maður* (person, or *gervi-tungl* (satellite) coming from *gervi* (artificial) and *tungl* (moon) (Jónsson, 1979). Such a policy is possible in such a small and compact community as Iceland, especially as the language here is an integral part of the Icelander's identity. In other communities a better policy might, according to Wilts (1983), be to observe the forms created by the speakers themselves rather than try to impose forms upon them.

Problems pertaining to the school

The problems affecting vernacular education and pertaining to the school can also be discussed under various headings.

The school in the community
As there is considerable interaction between the school and the community, the role of the school in the community will play a decisive part in the success or failure of education in general and vernacular education in particular. Burns (1965) considers a school's responsibilities to be social, moral and

pedagogic, and the success of an educational programme to be dependent upon the school's ability to enter into the life of the community and identify itself with the community's needs. The Eskimo programme in Alaska is a positive example of this, where the children are highly motivated because of high community involvement in the project (Trifonovitch, 1976). When, however, the community is dissatisfied with the school, a programme can be jeopardized as witnessed in NF where one reason for the parents in Risum-Lindholm rejecting Frisian tuition was that they thought the school was not educating their children properly (Walker, 1980b).

Various factors may determine the relationship between the school and the community. Spolsky et al. (1976, p. 239), for example, consider the authorities responsible for the school policy and the framework they work in to be important. They suggest three types of authorities:

> the superintendent of a school district, his specialist advisors and the principals of the schools in the district; . . . the top educational bureaucrats in a nation, . . . [and] group representatives of the community that a particular school serves.

A further factor may be the proximity of the school to the community. If there are village schools or similar, these will probably be integrated into the village community and the teachers will play a part in community life. If, on the other hand, the children are obliged to go to large centralized schools or boarding schools, there is little connection with the community, and one possible consequence is that the parents take little interest in their children's education. Burns (1965) reports that one factor leading to outbreaks of indiscipline at some boarding schools (which generally constituted the secondary schools) in Rhodesia (1962), Swaziland (1960), Uganda (1959) and Zambia (1960) was the lack of personal ties between the school and the community. He also considers it unfortunate that the parents were not unduly perturbed when their children were expelled as a result.

The centralized school is also affected by the problem of logistics. If a central school has a large catchment area, this can involve a lot of travelling for pupils, which in turn may impair their ability to concentrate during the lessons and also renders the school time-table less flexible for additional tuition. In the Chinle Public School District (a Navajo Reservation), for example, there are nine schools for 4559 children within an area of 7200 square miles, which results in four-hour bus runs for some of the children (Liebe-Harkort, 1980). Mackay (1969) similarly reports that the children in the Scottish Highlands often have to leave home at 8 am and do not return until 6 pm.

Perhaps one of the main problems facing the centralized school, though, is the plurilingual intake of a large catchment area. This can have a negative effect on a minority language such as Scots Gaelic, which was mostly used in village schools in the Highlands. When, however, these were closed and the children sent to a large central school, they were found to adopt the dominant English language (Mackay, 1969). Gaelic could no longer be fostered here as it was in the small village school. There is sometimes, however, the possibility for a minority language community to open its own school, although this is very dependent upon the good will of the majority. In Finland, for example, 18 children are needed to open an elementary school for a language community (Ahlskog, 1969). Once a small school like this has been opened, it is possible that it will gain more pupils than originally planned, as other people decide to send their children there for a variety of reasons, e.g. less stress, better teacher–pupil ratio, different methods and principles of education. This could prove beneficial for the vernacular concerned, though on the other hand parents might sometimes be tempted to send their lesser gifted children there for the above mentioned reasons, thus giving the school more quantity but less quality.

A school may enhance its standing in the community by itself becoming an employer in a possibly underdeveloped area. Spolsky *et al.* (1976) reported that as a result of the introduction of Navajo into the school curriculum for the 53 000 Navajo pupils, a further 1000 Navajo speaking teachers were required, which naturally brought more funds and employment into the Navajo community.

The educational programme

If vernacular education is to be given in school, it will usually be part of a bi- or multilingual programme unless, of course, the vernacular is English or similar (cf. p. 162). The actual design of the programme will depend upon the educational policy being pursued (cf. p. 168). In a developing country in a plurilingual setting, a decision will first have to be made as to which language is to be considered the vernacular for educational purposes, and then as to which languages shall also be included in the school curriculum. Ferguson states (Ferguson *et al.*, 1977, quoted after Paulston, 1980, p. 1f) two of the implicit goals of bilingual education are: "To unify a multilingual community" and "To enable people to communicate with the outside world." Thus a regional and/or national language could be introduced in a developing country as an attempt at unification, and at a later date the official language (usually a world language) to facilitate communication with the outside world. Another goal is seen in the desire "To assimilate individuals or groups into the mainstream of society." This is usually again in the interests of unity and is often practised with respect to immigrants and linguistic minorities. Edwards (1977) argues that many of the bilingual projects in America are designed to facilitate the transition to the dominant language for the immigrants. Two further goals are "To preserve ethnic or religious ties" and "To give equal status to languages of unequal prominence in the society". These goals are relevant for linguistic minorities, firstly as bilingual education could re-educate children in their parents' language once they have completed the language shift away from their ancestral tongue to the dominant language. This is the case on the mainland of NF, where Frisian has to be taught to a certain degree as a foreign language. The second reason is that if a minority language is given equal prominence, it will be less stigmatized, so that language shift can perhaps be halted, if not reversed. This, it might be argued, is the case on the island of Föhr in NF. The particular goal will determine whether a policy of transfer is adopted, whereby the vernacular is later abandoned for the dominant language as in the process of acculturation, or a policy of maintenance, whereby the vernacular is maintained next to the second language (Mackey, 1978).

There are a number of other factors influencing the design of a bilingual programme which can be discussed individually:

The linguistic competence of the children involved. The monolingual Navajo or Eskimo child would need a different programme from his bilingual cousin who, perhaps due to the proximity of an English-speaking town or television station or because of some English-speaking neighbours in the village already has a certain competence in English (Trifonovitch, 1976). However, even though in the latter instance a certain knowledge of the dominant language might be present, would it be sufficient for use as a medium in education? Paulston (1980, quoting Gaardner n.d.) refers to the concept of "folk bilingualism" which refers to bilinguals who are members of an underprivileged section of society and whose bilingualism arises through confrontation with the dominant language. This confrontation does not necessarily lead to a sufficient command of the dominant language for use as a medium of instruction.

The status of bilingual education. Bilingual education must take cognisance of its special status and not just teach two languages parallel to but independent of each other. The minority child with some competence in the dominant language can by no means be taught the dominant language in the same way as a native-speaker. One unfortunate phenomenon observed in Schleswig-Holstein is that there are no text-books describing High German grammar as contrasted with Low German and/or Frisian. Thus points of interference are not rectified and the child is punished without knowing why. There are, however, contrastive grammars in other parts of Low German speaking Germany, e.g. Niebaum (1977).

The applicability of immersion education.   One very successful bilingual programme is the immersion education practised in Canada, and Swain (1980) suggests that it might be applicable in other situations. In this programme, a group of children homogenous in its complete lack of knowledge of L2 is taught L2 as a medium by a bilingual teacher. The teacher understands the children's utterances in L1 but replies in L2. Thus the children first of all learn to comprehend L2. L1 is, however, later also incorporated into the programme, and both languages thereafter serve as languages of instruction throughout schooling. Swain does, however, point out that certain criteria have to be present if such a programme is to be successful. In the Canadian programme the parents belonged to the linguistic majority and wanted their children to learn French, on the condition that their ability in their native English was not impaired. In the case of a vernacular low in prestige, such a programme would probably lead to rapid assimilation, or, in Lambert's words (1975), to "subtractive bilingualism" where competence is gained in L2 to the detriment of L1. Thus Swain concludes that such a programme could be successful in some instances, but not in all.

When should which language be introduced?   There are two possible ways of answering this question, firstly with respect to simple expedience, and secondly with respect to a child's learning ability.

In some developing countries the observation has been made that there has been a shift since independence "in the direction of the Europeanization of the media of instruction with a concommittant neglect of the teaching of African languages" (Bokamba and Tlou, 1977, p. 38). In the independent francophone and lusophone African states, education is carried out purely in the earlier colonial languages, and in the one-time British and Belgian colonies there is a trend back to the colonial language. Where vernacular languages are taught, the colonial language is usually introduced in the third or fourth grade. The arguments for this are practical, e.g. national unity, national progress, and efficiency. The latter case encompasses such considerations as the low degree of standardization and modernization of African languages, the lack of teaching materials, the lack of teachers trained in or competent in the vernacular, the lack of syllabuses drawn up in the vernacular. In some countries like Ghana, the vernacular is taught only in the first years of primary school, until the children have sufficient knowledge of English to be able to continue their schooling in this language. At secondary school level in most countries, pupils need a command of a world language, as all advanced technical literature is written in them, and in Zambia the Zambian languages do not qualify for university entrance (Ohannessian, 1978c). Tanzania is an interesting exception, where it is hoped to introduce Swahili as the medium into the complete educational span (Bokamba and Tlou, 1977).

The question of the theoretically optimal age for starting second language acquisition has not as yet been satisfactorally answered. McLaughlin (1978, p. 131) summarizes research findings with the conclusion that the "optimal time to introduce a child to a second language is at birth". However, if this is not possible, then research would seem to indicate that "a later, rather than an earlier, start in the second language is better". There is one exception to this as young children were found "to be superior in acquiring the sound system of the second language". The main argument for the later introduction of second language teaching is the greater cognitive maturity of the children. Weighed against this, one has the uninhibitedness and spontaneity of the younger child. Genesee (1978) agrees in principle with these arguments, stating that late instruction has the advantage of the learner's greater learning efficiency. However, because of the additional factor of length of exposure to a language he argues that early instruction gives a child extended opportunities for language learning in and outside school. If then the language instruction is continued through the higher grades, which includes the advantage of greater learning efficiency, then early instruction is probably "more conducive to attaining the higher levels of second language proficiency.," (1978, p. 153) However, one must not forget that age alone is not necessarily the decisive factor in determining a child's ability to acquire a second language, as other factors such as motivation and attitudes may play an important role.

Should languages be divided according to subjects or time?
Very often the use of the vernacular is restricted in a bilingual school to such subjects as the vernacular, local history, etc. – essentially subjects belonging to the humanities – whereas science and technical subjects are taught in the medium of a world language, as this has the vocabulary and the literature needed. To give lessons in these subjects in the vernacular presupposes a programme of modernization. If, however, it is possible to teach all subjects in the vernacular, then a division of time may be preferred, e.g. morning tuition in L1 and afternoon tuition in L2, to give the children maximum exposure to both languages.

How many languages can be taught?
In a multilingual setting, children may be forced to learn various languages. In NF, for example, at the Danish minority school in Risum, children are taught Frisian, High German, Danish and English, and they learn Low German in the village. In India children may also be forced to learn up to five languages. Two questions arise here: (1) can the children cope with so many

languages? and (2) does the language element take up too much time in the curriculum? Possibly one would have to differentiate the degree of competence that should be attained in each language, whether listening comprehension, oral, reading or writing competence. This might depend on the function each language is to have in the pupils' lives.

Should vernacular education be obligatory or voluntary?

This applies principally to minority languages being re-introduced into a community. Experience has proved voluntary classes in Frisian in NF to be unsuccessful, because children soon stopped attending the classes after an initial bout of enthusiasm. In one experiment on Sylt, Frisian was used as a medium for teaching voluntary classes of wood-work, chess etc. which proved very successful, as the children could at least understand Frisian, but they too left as soon as they had acquired the manual skill they desired. There is as yet no back-up here. A further point is connected with logistics. If the lesson is voluntary it must be placed in one part of the time-table where non-participants could then go home. However, if the child has a long distance to travel, he must take the school bus along with the non-participants, which effectively bars him from the tuition. Obligatory tuition ensures full participation but can cause a negative reaction on the part of some parents.

The teachers

Two of the main problems facing vernacular education are the lack of suitable teachers and the lack of training. Burns (1965) reports that African countries which had introduced compulsory primary education had to employ large numbers of untrained teachers. Thus in 1961, of the 40 000 primary school teachers in West Nigeria, 26 000 (65 per cent) were untrained. This was due (1) to a lot of qualified teachers going to work in secondary schools, and (2) to the large number of extra pupils following the introduction of compulsory education without a prior teacher-training scheme to provide sufficient teachers. As a result of the lack of training, standards dropped, vernacular languages and the teaching profession lost in status, and wages were reduced. This in turn caused a lot of teachers to leave for more remunerative or less arduous jobs, so that the remaining teachers were basically of two groups: those with a sense of vocation, and those who could not pass exams.

In higher education many teachers are expatriates. In Zambia, for example, about 90 per cent of the teaching force at secondary schools in 1970 were expatriates who all taught in English (Ohannessian, 1978b). Burns (1965) thought this figure applied also to the African universities in 1962, although it was hoped to increase the number of African members of staff.

However, Brann points out[3] that it is practically impossible to gain qualified lecturers for Hausa in Nigeria, as the qualified potential candidates seek better jobs such as in the diplomatic corps. Only when the saturation level has been reached for such positions will there be candidates for university posts.

Teacher-training colleges also have their difficulties. Ohannessian (1978a), for example, sees the following problems in Zambia: the low calibre of the students due to the low status accorded the teaching profession; the lack of training of the lecturers themselves; the small amount of time allotted to the teaching of Zambian languages as such and to the teaching of the pedagogical and didactic principles of vernacular education; the preponderance of English in the courses; the confusion arising because of the seven official languages, as (1) the students have mixed linguistic backgrounds, (2) the lecturers are not competent in all the languages, and (3) the students do not know in which language area they will eventually be employed; the dearth of materials in and on Zambian languages; and the lack of facilities for teaching practice so that sometimes children have to be brought by lorry to the college for the students to practice. This is symptomatic of the problems facing colleges too small to be able to give their students proper training. In interesting contrast to these problems, Omar (1976) emphasizes that in Malaysia the curriculum for the teacher trainee has two parts: language mastery, and the methodology of language teaching. This includes phonetics and phonology, so that the trainee can cope with the great dialectal diversity in Malaysia, and a training in the analysis of grammar leading to a better understanding of the standard language and of the written and oral mistakes made by the pupils. This reflects recognition of the fact that a teacher's competence in a language is not sufficient but that he must also know *about* a language if he is to teach it.

One reason why many young people do not wish to study a vernacular language with a view to teaching is the lack of motivation. Ohannessian (1978a) mentions the lack of advancement opportunities in teaching Zambian vernaculars, the lack of advancement opportunities in other fields because of a knowledge of the languages, the minor role they play in higher education so that no premium is set on excellence, and the small amount of attention given them at the University of Zambia. Perhaps one major reason is the lack of status afforded the teaching profession and/or the vernacular in many countries. Linguistic minorities suffer from similar problems. Minority schools tend to be small, limiting the possibilities of a personal career, and there is often conflict with the majority schools (Ahlskog, 1969). Also, due to the smallness of a minority group, a person may refuse to return to his village as a teacher, as he is afraid of the animosities that might arise if he failed a nephew or niece in an exam. This is one reason why there is still no teacher of Frisian on the island of Amrum. However, motivation is not always lacking, as teachers in West Frisia with a Frisian Teaching Certificate receive an extra bonus in most municipalities, and in the Eskimo programme in Alaska the teachers of Yup'ik are mostly well trained even though they are not officially qualified. They hope, however, to gain a certificate through their work which would endow them with more prestige and probably more money.

Vernacular languages are sometimes considered a "soft option" at school and university because of a lack of status and because there is perhaps not such a literary or philological tradition as in major subjects, meaning that in theory there is less for a student to learn. Therefore the students are often not of the best quality or ones who cannot come to terms with a large department. Conversely though, some students are idealists of very high calibre. However, one wonders what use some of the students will be to the language community as, especially in a linguistic minority, much idealism and personal initiative is required of a teacher. Similarly, if students are studying a language without prior knowledge, it is most unlikely that they will be able to learn the language sufficiently to be able to teach it after four years at university or teacher-training college. However, if these are the only sources to be culled for teachers, little can be done, unless the authorities are understanding enough to allow amateur (i.e. unqualified but pedagogically gifted) native-speakers to teach. In NF the problem of teachers has been partially solved by persuading Frisian speakers already in the profession to teach Frisian as well as their own subjects. The school authorities have also agreed in principle to laymen being allowed to give lessons in their native tongue (Walker and Wilts, 1979), and the field-workers try to gather information in the villages about Frisian children scattered through the various universities of Germany who might be persuaded to return to NF as teachers. Unfortunately, many move to a different part of Germany following marriage. In all three instances, though, the individuals will have had no formal training in Frisian and will require assistance from outside. In recognition of this fact, a teacher's working group is now planned. Formal tuition in Frisian is given at the University of Kiel and the Teacher Training College in Flensburg, and it is hoped that in the near future some students may become qualified.

The teacher actually in school also deserves some discussion. The community's attitude towards a teacher will influence his ability to teach. If, for example, the teacher has only limited knowledge of the vernacular so that the children or the parents can see him making mistakes, or if he speaks a different dialect or is considered a poor pedagogue, perhaps due to a lack of talent or laziness, he will enjoy little respect in class. The teacher's own attitude is important. If he is dedicated, he has more chance of success. If on the other hand he considers the job a burden, allowing other people to prepare his teaching materials for him, his lack of enthusiasm will not escape the children's notice. The teacher's attitude may be influenced by other members of staff, and it is important that they be in agreement, or else the vernacular teacher may give up rather than suffer an unfriendly staff room. Also, if it is known in the community that some members of staff are against vernacular education, this may spark off latent hostility.

The class room
In a plurilingual community one basic problem in the classroom can be the number of languages found there. Ohannessian (1978a) found in a survey in Zambia that the highest number was 17, and only 82 of the 254 classes examined had a "unilingual" class where more than 80 per cent of the children spoke one language. He distinguishes three classroom types: (1) a heavily multilingual class where only a handful are being taught in their mother tongue, (2) a homogenous group where the language being taught is *not* that of the majority group, and (3) a homogenous group where the majority speaks the approved language as the mother tongue. The problems resulting from the multilingualism can be heightened by the mutual un-intelligibility of the various languages, so that a teacher may be forced to interpret the official approved vernacular to the pupils who do not understand it. Luckily, teachers themselves tend to be multilingual in Zambia, with an average of three languages per teacher. However, despite the teacher's own multilingualism, Ohannessian found that only 39 per cent of the 254 teachers interviewed were teaching their mother tongue, 55 per cent the language they were most fluent in, and that 42 per cent were teaching neither. As a result, the teachers were sometimes not teaching the vernacular in the prescribed lessons, but doing something else like mathematics or letting the children read. Furthermore, the teachers were sometimes not familiar with the culture of the children they were teaching, and had to ask for help with riddles, etc.

If, as a result of such indigenous plurilingualism or as a result of social changes in a linguistic minority community, there is bi- or multilingualism in the class, how should the children be taught? In Switzerland an experiment was tried using two schools, one for Romansch children and one for German. This failed, as the parents sent their children to the prestige (German) school rather than the one corresponding to their true linguistic background (Gregor, 1980). If instead of two different schools one has two different classes, this can have the effect of one class feeling socially inferior, as happened in Malaysia where tuition was divided between the native speakers who worked with literature and classical texts, and learners who concentrated on acquiring the language (Omar, 1976). However, experience in NF would seem to indicate that separate classes are best, as otherwise frustration soon overcomes the children competent in the language.

The method of teaching used is also important. If children are to learn a vernacular such as Irish or Frisian, then it must be taught as a living language, and not as a dead language concentrating on verb paradigms etc. otherwise the children will probably leave school without any oral competence. Similarly, tuition should not be purely oral, perhaps because of a fear of the orthography, as reading and writing help imprint the contents of a lesson on a child's brain.

Materials

Burns (1965) notes that education in Africa has often had the effect of alienating the children from their own society, as education was not geared to Africa. He considers that education should bring a synthesis of the old values of the tribe and the new ones of the wage-earning society, and as such must refer to the realities of life in an African community. Thus any materials used in education should be culturally relevant and not be as foreign as circuses, railway-stations and cricket bats to the Scots Gaels on Lewis (Stephens, 1978) or the European and early American settler accounts to the Eskimos in Alaska (Trifonovitch, 1976). The contents and style should also be adapted to the age group. Omar (1976) reports that the book *Sejarah Melayu* was recommended for primary schools as it was supposed to represent the best Malay language. However, it proved unsuitable, as the texts were too heavy and the language dated from the seventeenth century.

One of the characteristics of most vernaculars which are not world languages is a dearth of materials. To remedy this, books etc. are often translated from another language. There is, however, some doubt as to the advisability of this policy. On the one hand children may find it a help to read a book in the vernacular they already know in the original language, e.g. in the case of linguistic minorities; but on the other hand it may undermine their confidence in their own language if they discover that most of the literature is merely translated from other languages. The authenticity of the vernacular must also be lost in translation, as the original was conceived in a different linguistic and cultural background. Perhaps though this is not so important at school level, and again practical considerations may determine the choice, as it seems that translation is easier than the creation of new works. Translation does, however, also pose its problems, as one version may not suffice. One book was adapted, for example, for primary school use on Sylt featuring dunes, beaches, the Sylt flag and the Sylt style of architecture. The book is excellent for Sylt Frisian but has to be completely re-adapted for the mainland as here there are only dikes, a different flag and different architecture. Furthermore, the Sylt Frisian grammar differs somewhat from the mainland Frisian grammar, e.g. two as opposed to three genders, one as opposed to two forms of the definite article. This necessitates a different division of the pages, a re-ordering of the pictures and the drawing of new ones. Considering the amount of work involved with this small project, it might prove simpler to write a completely new text-book.

Who should write the text-books? Few people are prepared to write in a vernacular as (1) there is probably no financial reward, (2) there is the possibility of unfavourable reviews, which in a small community could prove embarrassing, (3) readership is limited, and (4) the editions are small. The ideal writer should have linguistic and educational qualifications, a good knowledge of the area and its educational problems, and some experience in teaching his mother tongue. In the case of a language being reintroduced to children, he would also have to know how to present his mother tongue as a foreign language. This would involve a contrastive analysis of the languages involved (Boon, 1969). The sort of materials required are: (1) primers, (2) readers, (3) informative reading material, and (4) non-informative reading material, such as comics, the latter being important as children learn best to read by reading for entertainment.

One way of solving the problem of materials is for the children to write them themselves in collaboration with the teachers. This is being actively encouraged in the Rough Rock Demonstration School (Liebe-Harkort, 1980) and in the Eskimo programme (Trifonovitch, 1976), as it fosters pupil involvement in and a sense of identity with the school curriculum.

The economics of vernacular education
The theoretical needs of vernacular education are often compromised by the simple expedience of economics. Many developing countries are obliged to introduce a world language as a medium of instruction and use the corresponding text-books, because their own resources are so slender that they cannot afford a programme of text-book translation or teacher-training in the vernacular (Whiteley, 1969). The same applies for linguistic minorities. Each time a book is written for Frisian tuition, for example, the author has to find some generous Frisian association or authority who will supply the funds to have it published. These funds are, however, limited. There is also usually relatively little return on sales, because books in such small editions (e.g. 500 copies) are expensive to produce but cannot be sold at too expensive a price as otherwise the public aimed at will not be able to afford the book. Thus a large percentage of each grant is automatically lost. Because of the cost, printing as such has largely been abandoned in NF, at least for school materials, and the off-set production technique is preferred, or materials are simply produced, xeroxed and thrown away after use. This

does, however, have the disadvantage that no permanent text-book appears.

Despite these problems, Tadadjeu (1977) argues that an efficient cost-benefit analysis of the language programme could minimize costs and maximize benefits, for example by improving cooperation between various countries sharing a common vernacular, thus rendering education possible in most African languages.

A further economic problem is the question of when minority schools are economically viable. This problem tends to become more acute the higher the school level. In a grammar school there will be fewer pupils than in a primary school, whereas there will be a demand for a larger number of teachers covering a variety of subjects if an adequate training is to be guaranteed. Furthermore, if an absolute number is set, how can fluctuations in school numbers be catered for? Ahlskog (1969) reports that in Finland the minimum number for a grammar school was set at 270 but that of the 40 Swedish-language schools only eight had more than 150 pupils.

Tests
If tests are carried out, there is a need to differentiate between why the test is initiated, what is being tested and who is being tested. In the Eskimo programme, tests are carried out monthly to evaluate progress in both English and Yup'ik, to isolate difficult concepts and to identify students' problems and weaknesses (Trifonovitch , 1976). Tadadjeu (1977) lists the skills to be tested as (1) listening comprehension, (2) oral competence, (3) reading, and (4) writing; and Williams (1973) suggests three groups of pupils in Wales each requiring his own type of exam: (1) pupils with Welsh as a foreign tongue, (2) pupils with Welsh in the environment but not in the home, and (3) pupils with Welsh as their mother tongue.

Legislation
Legislation regarding vernacular education usually gives vernacular speakers the right to education in their own language and is certainly commendable. However, legislation alone is not enough, as a method of enforcement is also necessary. Williams (1973, p. 99) reports that the Welsh Board of Education stated that "where Welsh is the mother-tongue of the infants, that language shall be the medium of instruction in the classes". The local education authorities and teachers, however, responded only very sluggishly. Similarly, in West Frisia, where Frisian was introduced as a compulsory subject on first August 1980, the board of each individual school can decide how much attention it pays to the law: whether there is one lesson a week for Frisian or a bilingual programme is introduced (Zondag, 1982).

Institutions

Institutions working with vernacular languages can prove very beneficial, and Omar (1976), for example, considers a central language centre necessary at the University of Malaya to coordinate the courses and the different needs of the various faculties where Bahasa Malaysia is being taught. The *Algemiene Fryske Underrjocht Kommisje* in Leeuwarden (Netherlands) produces excellent materials for Frisian classes in school. However, institutions can also have a negative effect and stultify private enterprise, as laymen and teachers may refuse to show any initiative, arguing that the staff of the institutions are paid to do the work and not the laymen. This has the danger in a minority language movement of reducing the active members to the "professionals" (i.e. those paid to work with the language), and taking away the grass roots essential to a successful movement. Similarly, if the institution is not recognised by the language community, it might do some harm. In NF, for example, there seems to be the feeling that a person wins respect by being proficient in his own profession, e.g. as a teacher, farmer or business man. If he then also works with Frisian, this is applauded and others will follow. A person, however, who earns his money by working with Frisian alone seems not to be considered to be making a useful contribution to society, and thus will not rank very high in the community's esteem.

In this chapter I have tried to illustrate some of the problems facing vernacular education in the context of developing countries, minority languages and immigrants. Sociolinguistic knowledge and expertise are prerequisites for successful programmes of vernacular education. Without them, it is impossible to comprehend and, hopefully, solve the problems involved, ranging as they do in complexity from a simple lack of finance to the intricate social and linguistic patterns found in a pluriethnic and plurilingual society.

Notes

[1] Further research with respect to the number of languages spoken is currently being conducted in selected areas of England by the Linguistic Minorities Project, based at the University of London Institute of Education. Even this project does not, however, expect to arrive at comprehensive figures for the whole country as nothing short of a census questionnaire could produce such statistics. (My thanks to Euan Reid of the Linguistic Minorities Project for this information.)

[2] I diverge from the UNESCO definition of vernacular (1968, p. 689) which states: "A language which is the mother tongue of a group which is socially or politically dominated by another group speaking a different language." A vernacular *may* be a

minority language, but this is not a prerequisite. The Englishman's vernacular is after all a world language.

³ C. M. B. Brann – in the discussion following his lecture at the Sixth AILA Conference in 1981 in Lund.

REFERENCES

Aarseth, B. (1969). The Situation of the Lapps, especially in Norway. *In* "Lingual Minorities in Europe." (E. Holmestad and A. Lade, eds), pp. 73–85. Det Norske Samlaget, Oslo.

Ahlskog, S. H. (1969). Educational Problems in Finland. *In* "Lingual Minorities in Europe." (E. Holmestad and A. Lade, eds), pp. 73–85. Det Norske Samlaget, Oslo.

Århammar, N. (1976). Historisch-soziolinguistische Aspekte der nordfriesischen, Mehrsprachigkeit. *Nordfriesisches Jahrbuch, NF* 12, 55–76.

Barker, G. C. (1947). Social Functions of Language in a Mexican-American Community. *Acta Americana* 5, 185–202.

Bendsen, B. (1860). "Die Nordfriesische Sprache nach der Moringer Mundart". E. J. Brill, Leiden. Reprint Sändig, Walluf, 1973.

Berry, J. (1968). The Making of Alphabets. *In* "Readings in the Sociology of Language". (J. Fishman, ed.), pp. 737–753. Mouton, The Hague.

Berry, J. (1977). 'The Making of Alphabets' Revisited. *In* "Advances in the Creation and Revision of Writing Systems". (J. Fishman, ed.), pp. 3–16. (Contributions to the Sociology of Language 8). Mouton, The Hague.

Billigmeier, R. H. (1979). "A Crisis in Swiss Pluralism". (Contributions to the Sociology of Language 26). Mouton, The Hague.

Boelens, Kr. (1976). "Friesisch und Niederländisch. Zweisprachiger Grundschulunterricht in den Niederlanden." Ministerium für Unterricht und Wissenschaft, Den Haag.

Bokamba, E. G. and Tlou, J. S. (1977). The Consequences of the Language Policies of African States vis-à-vis Education. *In* "Language and Linguistic Problems in Africa". (P. Kotey and H. Der-Houssikian, eds), pp. 35–53. Hornbeam Press, South Carolina.

Boon, I. (1969). Problems of Text-books for lingual minorities. *In* "Lingual Minorities in Europe." (E. Holmestad and A. Lade, eds), pp. 169–175. Det Norske Samlaget, Oslo.

Burns, D. G. (1965). "African Education: an Introductory Survey of Education in Commonwealth Countries." Oxford University Press, London.

Chambers, J. K. and Trudgill, P. (1980). "Dialectology". Cambridge University Press, Cambridge.

Chapman, A. J., Smith, J. R. and Foot, H. C. (1977). Language, Humour and Intergroup Relations. *In* "Language, Ethnicity and Intergroup Relations". (H. Giles, ed.), pp. 137–169. Academic Press, London.

Committee on Irish Language Attitudes Research (1975). "Report submitted to the Minister for the Gaeltacht". Government Stationery Office, Dublin.

Cummins, J. (1976). The Influence of Bilingualism on Cognitive Growth: A Synthesis of Research Findings and Explanatory Hypotheses. *Working Papers on Bilingualism* 9, 1–43.

Dorian, N. (1973). Grammatical Change in a dying Dialect. *Language* **49**, 413–438.

Dorian, N. (1977). The Problem of the Semi-Speaker in Language Death. *In* "Language Death" (W. Dressler and R. Wodak-Leodolter, eds), pp. 23–32. (International Journal of the Sociology of Language 12). Mouton, The Hague.

Dressler, W. and Wodak-Leodolter, R. (1977). Language Preservation and Language Death in Brittany. *In* "Language Death". (W. Dressler and R. Wodak-Leodolter, eds), pp. 33–44, (International Journal of the Sociology of Language, **12**) Mouton, The Hague.

Edwards, J. R. (1977). Ethnic Identity and Bilingual Education. *In* "Language, Ethnicity and Intergroup Relations" (H. Giles, ed.), pp. 253–282. Academic Press, London.

Fellman, J. (1973). "The Revival of a Classical Tongue" (Contributions to the Sociology of Language 6). Mouton, The Hague.

Ferguson, C. A. (1968). Language Development. *In* "Language Problems of Developing Nations" (J. Fishman, C. Ferguson and J. Das Gupta, eds), pp. 27–35. John Wiley, New York.

Ferguson, C. A., Houghton, C. and Wells, M. (1977). Bilingual Education: An International Perspective. *In* "Frontiers of Bilingual Education" (B. Spolsky and R. Cooper, eds). Newbury House, Rowley, Massachusetts.

Fillmore, C. A. (1973). A Grammarian looks to Linguistics. *Georgetown University Monograph Series on Languages and Linguistics* **25**, 273–287.

Fishman, J. A. (ed.) (1966). "Language Loyalty in the United States". Mouton, The Hague.

Fishman, J. A. (1968a). Nationality-Nationalism and Nation-Nationalism. *In* "Language Problems of Developing Nations" (J. Fishman, C. Ferguson and J. Das Gupta, eds), pp. 39–51. John Wiley, New York.

Fishman, J. A. (ed.) (1968b). "Readings in the Sociology of Language". Mouton, The Hague.

Fishman, J. A. (1968c). Sociolinguistics and the Language Problems of the Developing Countries. *In* "Language Problems of Developing Nations" (J. Fisman, C. Ferguson and J. Das Gupta, eds), pp. 3–16. John Wiley, New York.

Fishman, J. A. (1971). The Sociology of Language. *In* "Advances in the Sociology of Language I" (J. Fishman, ed.), pp. 217–404. Mouton, The Hague.

Fishman, J. A. (ed.) (1974). "Advances in Language Planning" (Contributions to the Sociology of Language 5). Mouton, The Hague.

Fishman, J. A. (ed.) (1977). "Advances in the Creation and Revision of Writing Systems" (Contributions to the Sociology of Lanuage 8). Mouton, The Hague.

Fishman, J. A. and Hofman, J. E. (1966). Mother Tongue and Nativity in the American Population. *In* "Language Loyalty in the United States" (J. Fishman, ed.), pp. 34–50. Mouton, The Hague.

Fishman, J. A., Ferguson, C. A. and Das Gupta, J. (eds) (1968). "Language Problems of Developing Nations". John Wiley, New York.

Fort, M. C. (1980). "Saterfriesisches Wörterbuch mit einer grammatischen Übersicht". Helmut Buske, Hamburg.

Gaarder, B. (n.d.) "Political Perspectives on Bilingual Education". Ms.

Gallagher, C. F. (1971). Language Reform and Social Modernization in Turkey. *In* "Can Language be Planned?" (J. Rubin and B. Jernudd, eds), pp. 159–178. East–West Centre Press, Honolulu.

Genesee, F. (1978). Is there an Optimal Age for Starting Second Language Instruction? *McGill Journal of Education*, **XII, 2,** 145–154.

Giles, H., Bourhis, R. Y. and Taylor, D. M. (1977). Towards a Theory of Language in Ethnic Group Relations. *In* "Language, Ethnicity and Intergroup Relations" (H. Giles, ed.), pp. 307–348. Academic Press, London.

Gregor, D. B. (1980). "Celtic: A Comparative Study". Oleander Press, Cambridge/New York.

Groustra, G. R. (1976). Was geschieht in Seelterlound? *Nordfriesland*, **35/36**, 180–182.

Gumperz, J. J. (1968). Types of Linguistic Communities. *In* "Readings in the Sociology of Language" (J. Fishman, ed.), pp. 460–472. Mouton, The Hague.

Haarmann, H. (1975). "Soziologie und Politik der Sprachen Europas". Deutscher Taschenbuch Verlag, München.

Hansford, K., Bendor-Samuel, J. and Stanford, R. (1976). "An Index of Nigerian Languages" (Studies in Nigerian Languages 5). Summer Institute of Linguistics, Accra.

Haugen, E. (1966). "Language Conflict and Language Planning: The Case of Modern Norwegian". Harvard University Press, Cambridge, Massachusetts.

Haugen, E. (1980). Language Problems and Language Planning: The Scandinavian Model. *In* "Languages in Contact and Conflict" (P. Nelde, ed), pp. 151–157. Zeitschrift für Dialektologie und Linguistik, Beihefte 32. Franz Steiner, Wiesbaden.

Heine, B. (1979). "Sprache, Gesellschaft und Kommunikation in Afrika" (Afrika Studien 103). Weltforum, München.

Hofmann, D. (1956). Probleme der nordfriesischen Dialektforschung. *Zeitschrift für Mundartforschung* **XXIV**, 78–112.

Isajiw, W. W. (1974). Definitions of Ethnicity. *Ethnicity* **1**, 111–124.

Johnson, B. C. (1977). Language Functions in Africa: A Typological View. *In* "Language and Linguistic Problems in Africa" (P. Kotey and H. Der-Houssikian, eds), pp. 54–67. Hornbeam Press, South Carolina.

Jones, M. (1973). The Present Condition of the Welsh Language. *In* "The Welsh Language Today" (M. Stephens, ed.), pp. 110–126. Gomer Press, Llandysul.

Jónsson, J. H. (1979). Zur Sprachpflege im heutigen Island. *In* "Friesisch heute" (A. Walker and O. Wilts, eds), pp. 43–45. Schriftenreihe der Akademie Sankelmark NF 45/46, Sankelmark.

Jörgensen, V. T. (1979). Tu di nordfrasche Schriwwise. *In* "Friesisch heute" (A. Walker and O. Wilts, eds), pp. 102–115. Schriftenreihe der Akademie Sankelmark NF 45/46, Sankelmark.

Karam, F. X. (1974). Toward a Definition of Language Planning. *In* "Advances in Language Planning" (J. Fishman, ed.), pp. 103–112. (Contributions to the Sociology of Language 5) Mouton, The Hague.

Khleif, B. B. (1980). "Language, Ethnicity and Education in Wales" (Contributions to the Sociology of Language 28). Mouton, The Hague.

Kloss, H. (1966). Types of Multilingual Communities: A Discussion of Ten Variables. *Sociological Inquiry* **36**, 135–145.

Kloss, H. (1968). Notes concerning a Language-Nation Typology. *In* "Language Problems of Developing Nations" (J. Fishman, C. Ferguson and J. Das Gupta, eds), pp. 69–85. John Wiley, New York.

Kramer, P. (1978). Wät int Seelterlound geschjut. *Nordfriesland* **45/46**, 45–47.

Krishnamurti, Bh. (1978). Language Planning and Development: The Case of Telugu. *Contributions to Asian Studies* **XI**, 37–56.

Labov, W. (1966). "The Social Stratification of English in New York City". Center for Applied Linguistics, Washington DC.

Lambert, W. E. (1975). Culture and Language as Factors in Learning and Education. *In* "Education of Immigrant Students" (W. Aaron, ed.), pp. 55–83. Ontario Institute for Studies in Education, Toronto.

Larsen, N.-E. (1983). "Statistical Investigations of Language Death in a North Frisian Community". (In press).

LePage, R. B. (1964). "The National Language Question". Oxford Univserity Press, London.

Liebe-Harkort, M.-L. (1980). Factors Influencing the Survival of Minority Languages: A Catalogue and its Application to the Situation of the Apachean Languages. *SAIS. Arbeitsberichte aus dem Seminar für Allgemeine und Indogermanische Sprachwissenschaft, Christian-Albrechts-Universität Kiel* 2, 67–125.

Mackay, D. J. (1969). Educational Problems in Scotland. *In* "Lingual Minorities in Europe" (E. Holmestad and A. Lade, eds), pp. 142–145. Det Norske Samlaget, Oslo.

Mackey, W. F. (1978). A Typology of Bilingual Education. *In* "Bilingual Education" (H. LaFontaine, B. Persky and L. Golubchick, eds), pp. 192–203. Avery Publishing Group, New Jersey.

Macnamara, J. (1966). "Bilingualism and Primary Education". University Press, Edinburgh.

Macnamara, J. (1967). The Effects of Instruction in a Weaker Language. *J. Soc. Issues* **XXIII**, 2, 121–135.

Macnamara, J. (1971). Successes and Failures in the Movement for the Restoration of Irish. *In* "Can Language be Planned?" (J. Rubin and B. Jernudd, eds), pp. 65–94. East–West Centre Press, Honolulu.

McLaughlin, B. (1978). "Second-Language Acquisition in Childhood". Lawrence Erlbaum Associates, New Jersey.

Mühlhäusler, P., Wurm, S. A. and Dutton, T. E. (1979). Language Planning and New Guinea Pidgin. *In* "New Guinea and Neighbouring Areas: A Sociolinguistic Laboratory" (S. Wurm, ed.), pp. 263–276. (Contributions to the Sociology of Language 24). Mouton, The Hague.

Nida, E. A. and Wonderly, W. M. (1971). Communication Rules of Languages in Multilingual Societies. *In* "Language Use and Social Change" (W. Whiteley, ed.), pp. 57–74. Oxford University Press, London.

Niebaum, H. (1977). "Westfälisch" (Dialekt/Hochsprache Kontrastiv, Sprachhefte für den Deutschunterricht 5) Schwann, Düsseldorf.

Ohannessian, S. (1972). The Language Problems of American Indian Children. *In* "The Language Education of Minority Children" (B. Spolsky, ed.), pp. 13–24. Newbury House, Rowley, Massachusetts.

Ohannessian, S. (1978a). The Teaching of Zambian Languages and the Preparation of Teachers for Language Teaching in Primary Schools. *In* "Language in Zambia." (S. Ohannessian and M. Kashoki, eds), pp. 292–328. International African Institute, London.

Ohannessian, S. (1978b). English and Zambian Languages in Secondary Schools. *In* "Language in Zambia" (S. Ohannessian and M. Kashoki, eds), pp. 355–375. International African Institute, London.

Ohannessian, S. (1978c). Zambian Languages in Secondary Schools: Attitudes of Teachers in Training. *In* "Language in Zambia" (S. Ohannessian and M. Kashoki, eds), pp. 376–397. International African Institute, London.

Okonkwo, C. J. E. (1975). A Function-oriented Model of Initial Language Planning in Sub-Saharan Africa. *Ohio State University Working Papers in Linguistics* **19**, 37–52.

Omar, A. H. (1976). "The Teaching of Bahasa Malaysia in the Context of National Language Planning". Kuala Lumpur, Malaysia.

Paulston, C. B. (1980). "Bilingual Education: Theories and Issues". Newbury House, Rowley, Massachusetts.

Price, G. (1973). Minority Languages in Western Europe. In "The Welsh Language Today" (M. Stephens, ed.), pp. i–17. Gomer Press, Llandysul.

The Restoration of the Irish Language (1965). Stationery Office, Dublin.

Rustow, D. A. (1968). Language, Modernization and Nationhood – an Attempt at Typology. In "Language Problems of Developing Nations" (J. Fishman, C. Ferguson and J. Das Gupta, eds), pp. 87–105. John Wiley, New York.

Sjoberg, A. (1966). Socio-Cultural and Linguistic Factors in the Development of Writing Systems for Preliterate Peoples. In "Sociolinguistics" (W. Bright, ed.), pp. 260–276. Mouton, The Hague.

Sjölin, B. (1969). "Einführung in das Friesische". Sammlung Metzler, Stuttgart.

Spenter, A. (1977). Zur Mehrsprachigkeit in der Gemeinde Rodenäs. Nordfriesisches Jahrbuch NF 13, 167–177.

Spolsky, B. (1972). The Language Education of Minority Children. In "The Language Education of Minority Children" (B. Spolsky, ed.), pp. 1–10. Newbury House, Rowley, Massachusetts.

Spolsky, B., Green, J. B. and Read, J. (1976). A Model for the Description, Analysis and perhaps Evaluation of Bilingual Education. In "Language in Sociology" (A. Verdoodt and R. Kjolseth, eds), pp. 233–263. Institut de Linguistique de Louvain, Louvain.

Stephens, M. (1978²). "Linguistic Minorities in Western Europe." Gomer Press, Dyfed.

Stewart, W. A. (1962). An Outline of Linguistic Typology for Describing Multi-Lingualism. In "Study of the Role of Second Languages." (Ed. F. Rice), pp. 15–25. Centre of Applied Linguistics of the Modern Language Association of America, Washington DC.

Stewart, W. A. (1968). A Sociolinguistic Typology for Describing national Multi-lingualism. In "Readings in the Sociology of Language." (Ed. J. Fishman), pp. 530–545. Mouton, The Hague.

Swain, M. (1980). "Immersion Education: Applicability for Non-vernacular Teaching to Vernacular Speakers." Paper presented at the Symposium on Standard Language/Vernacular Relations and Bilingual Education; Racine, Wisconsin.

Swain, M. (1983). "Bilingual Education for Majority and Minority Language Children." (In press).

Tadadjeu, M. (1977). Cost-Benefit Analysis and Language Education Planning in Sub-Saharan Africa. In "Language and Linguistic Problems in Africa" (P. Kotey and H. Der-Houssikion, eds), pp. 3–34. Hornbeam Press, South Carolina.

Tauli, V. (1968). "Introduction to a Theory of Language Planning". Acta Universitatis Upsaliensis 6, Uppsala.

Tholund, J. (1980). Quo vadis, Sylt? Quo vadis, Nordfriesland? Nordfriesland 56, 121–126.

Trifonovitch, G. J. (1976). "A Brief Evaluation of the Primary Eskimo Program". Bureau of Indian Affairs, Bethel, Alaska.

Trudgill, P. (1975). "Accent, Dialect and the School". Explorations in Language Study. Arnold, London.

UNESCO (1968). The use of Vernacular Languages in Education: The Report of the

UNESCO Meeting of Specialists, 1951. *In* "Readings in the Sociology of Language" (J. Fishman, ed.), pp. 688–716. Mouton, The Hague.

Walker, A. G. H. (1977). Sprachwandel in Nordfriesland. *Jahrbuch des Vereins für niederdeutsche Sprachforschung* **100**, 86–107.

Walker, A. G. H. (1980a). North Frisia and Linguistics. *Nottingham Linguistic Circular* **9/1**, 18–42.

Walker, A. G. H. (1980b). Some Factors Concerning the Decline of the North Frisian Tongue. *In* "Languages in Contact and Conflict" (P. Nelde, ed.), pp. 453–460. Zeitschrift für Dialektologie und Linguistik, Beihefte 32. Franz Steiner, Wiesbaden.

Walker, A. G. H. (1980c). "Die nordfriesische Mundart der Bökingharde. Zu einer strukturell-dialektologischen Definition der Begriffe 'Haupt-', 'Unter-' und 'Dorfmundart'". Zeitschrift für Dialektologie und Linguistik, Beihefte 33. Franz Steiner, Wiesbaden.

Walker, A. G. H. and Wilts, O. (eds) (1979). "Friesisch heute". Schriftenreihe der Akademie Sankelmark NF 45/46, Sankelmark.

Weinreich, U. (1953). "Languages in Contact". Publications of the Linguistic Circle of New York.

Wells, G. (1981). "Learning through Interaction: The Study of Language Development". Cambridge University Press, Cambridge.

Whiteley, W. H. (1969). "Swahili, the Rise of a National Language". Methuen, London.

Williams, J. L. (1973). The Welsh Language in Education. *In* "The Welsh Language Today" (M. Stephens, ed.), pp. 92–109. Gomer Press, Llandysul.

Wilts, O. (1979). Lexikographie zwischen Sprachwissenschaft und Sprachpflege. *Us Wurk*, **28**, (Scripta Frisica, Tinkbondel foar Arne Spenter), 197–206.

Wilts, O. (1983). Sprachplanerische Aspekte der nordfriesischen Lexikographie. *In* "Friserstudier III". (N. Danielsen, E. Hansen, H. F. Nielsen, H. Bekker-Nielsen, eds), pp. 9–24. Odense Universitetsforlag Odense.

Wurm, S. A. (1979). The Language Situation in the New Guinea Area. *In* "New Guinea and Neighbouring Areas: A Sociolinguistic Laboratory" (S. Wurm, ed.), pp. 3–10. (Contributions to the Sociology of Language 24). Mouton, The Hague.

Zondag, K. (ed.) (1982). "Bilingual Education in Friesland". T. Wever, Franeker.

8

Applied discourse analysis and educational linguistics

Michael Stubbs

Introduction

This chapter is about some aspects of educational linguistics, and the most
basic question to be discussed is: what should teachers and students know
about language? I will attempt to give one possible answer to the question
posed in the following quote from Halliday (1978, p. 207):

> I am often asked by teachers if it is possible to give a succinct account of the
> essential nature of language in terms that are truly relevant to the educational
> process. It is not easy to do this, because it means departing very radically from
> the images of language that are presented in our schoolbooks and in the
> classroom . . . We have to build up an image of language which enables us to look
> at how people actually do communicate with each other . . .

My general argument will be that a model of language relevant to educational purposes should focus on language in use in connected discourse. I
will review some general issues concerning the relation between linguistics
and teacher-training, and then discuss two very different in-service teacher-
training courses which I have prepared, discussing the theoretical rationale
behind the courses, which lies in recent work on discourse analysis. Finally, I
will review some applications of discourse analysis in teaching both the
mother tongue and foreign languages.

APPLIED SOCIOLINGUISTICS
ISBN: 0-12-701220-6

In considering discourse analysis and education, there are two logically possible areas of application. One could (1) study the discourse of teaching itself, as part of a study of institutional language. Alternatively, one could (2) teach about discourse and communication, as part of the content of a foreign language or mother tongue syllabus. There are two main topics for (1), a study of classroom discourse. One is spoken classroom interaction between teacher and students, and this has been a major research area in the social sciences since the late 1960s. The other is the study of the discourse organisation of written teaching texts, primarily "textbooks" and related material. Education in Western schools and higher education is, in these senses, predominantly verbal and textual (cf. Van Dijk, 1981, p. 2), and a study of teaching itself therefore demands a study of its written and spoken discourse. Possibility (2), teaching about discourse and communication, could also have two rather different emphases. The main aim might be to increase students' communicative competence, by giving them more ability in a wider range of discourse types, and therefore increasing the functional potential of students' language (cf. Halliday, 1978, p. 57). Alternatively, one could teach directly the theory of discourse analysis, as part of a course on language or linguistics. Teaching about language in the education system usually means teaching about either grammar or literature, with only un-systematic discussion of the wide variety of non-literary discourse.

This framework of possible applications of discourse analysis underlies this chapter, although not all four areas are equally discussed. The frame-work is similar to one proposed by Van Dijk (1981), in a very useful survey article on discourse studies and education. Van Dijk admits however that his article is entirely speculative and programmatic: I will try here also to give more concrete examples.

I will not attempt to give a comprehensive overview of the applications of discourse analysis. It would not be practicable to attempt a survey of such a recent and open-ended field, which draws on several different academic traditions including linguistics, cognitive psychology, sociology and artificial intelligence. It is probably more useful to try and tackle a few more specific questions with reference to particular examples. In educational linguistics, this means discussing particular syllabus proposals and teaching strategies. Amongst other possible applications of discourse analysis which I will not be able to discuss here are: a view of psychotherapy as conversation (e.g. Labov and Fanshel, 1977); an approach to developing the communicative com-petence of mentally retarded patients (e.g. Price-Williams and Sabsay, 1979); training doctors, either native or foreign speakers, to interact more efficiently with patients (e.g. Candlin, Bruton, Leather and Woods, 1977); and social skills training (e.g. Hargie, Dickson and Saunders, 1981), in-cluding the vast literature on effective communication in business and management. The applied study of discourse in these and other areas is, however, concerned with training professionals of different kinds to understand better the rules and conventions underlying spoken and written discourse. Again, it may be more useful to avoid bland overviews, and to develop most of my points specifically with reference to teachers, making points relevant to other professional groups by implication. I have preferred therefore to be mildly original rather than to attempt a comprehensive survey, and my bibliographic references are intended as representative but in no way exhaustive.

Milroy (in this volume) provides one general alternative approach to a socially responsible applied discourse analysis, in her discussion of the theoretical and practical issues raised by communicative problems. In particular, she discusses the kind of cross-dialectal communicative problems which are likely to have serious social consequences when professionals and clients from different social groups and with different dialects meet in school classrooms, doctors' surgeries, courtrooms and other comparable settings. For case studies which analyse the discourse in such settings, and discuss such cross-dialectal communicative problems, see Harris (1980) on magistrates' courts and Malcolm (1979) on school classrooms.

Definitions and terminology

There is considerable variation in the use of the term *discourse analysis*, so I had better insert a brief note on what I mean by it. First, I do not intend to draw any important distinction between *text* and *discourse*. As these terms are normally used, they often imply only a difference in emphasis, but nothing of theoretical importance need hang on the distinction. A distinction is sometimes implied between written text and spoken discourse. Alternatively, discourse refers to interactive language *versus* text as non-interactive monologue, whether spoken or written. For example, one can talk of the text of a speech. Another distinction is that discourse implies length whereas a text may be very short. Halliday and Hasan (1976) define a text as a semantic unit and point out that complete texts include *Exit* and *No smoking*. Some scholars have used the two terms to label theoretically important distinctions, but since I will not be concerned with those distinctions here, I will ignore them.

Similarly, I will favour the term *discourse analysis* over other terms for reasons of convenience rather than theory. The term *text analysis* would do equally well except that it usually implies a particular European tradition of text linguistics. The term *conversational analysis* might also serve, except that it almost always implies work which derives from ethnomethodology. It is also too narrow in that it implies a restriction to conversation, and the exclusion of more formal discourse, although there are problems in the analysis of discourse which are common to formal and informal, written and spoken laguage – for example, the analysis of lexical and grammatical cohesion.

By *discourse analysis* I mean therefore the linguistic or sociolinguistic analysis of naturally occurring discourse or text, spoken or written. This does not deny the validity of other approaches: a full understanding of discourse is necessarily interdisciplinary. It merely restricts my topic here to manageable limits. (This definition of discourse analysis is developed at length by Stubbs, 1983b).

Discourse analysis in teacher education

Linguistics in teacher-training: some general points

The main question to be discussed in this chapter is: what kind of understanding of language is relevant in teaching the mother tongue or foreign languages, or in teaching in general? Which linguistic concepts should be presented to teachers and how? What therefore is the relation between linguistics and teacher-training? Language is complex, so some simplification in the presentation is inevitable; but how can the simplification be managed without distorting the material or patronising the audience? These questions are not often discussed explicitly by linguistics, although it is only professional linguists who have the necessary knowledge and full-time commitment to linguistics which would allow them to select what is relevant to teachers, or to any other professionals. Educationalists could not be expected to do this for the simple reason that there is so much in contemporary linguistics which is of no direct relevance to education. It is arguably a social responsibility of linguists as a profession to present to non-linguists in an accessible way the aspects of knowledge about language which are of important practical value.

The complexity, breadth and specialization of contemporary linguistics has itself meant that educationalists have often rejected linguistics *in toto*. Not being able to see the wood for the trees, they have jumped to the conclusion that linguistics comprises jargon and formalism, and discusses only a model of language which is of no use to teachers and pupils, since it avoids real language behaviour. Descriptions such as linguistics is "scientific", "mathematical" or "abstract" are often used to refer in a slightly confused way to such feelings. There is no point in ignoring the problem that linguistics is now as much as a turn-off for many teachers as grammar used to be. This may be a superficial reaction, but it must be countered: there is no point in talking if no-one wants to listen. It follows that questions of presentation are crucial.

There is often a suspicion in teacher education of anything that practising teachers might not understand immediately, and linguistics has a reputation for conceptual difficulty. Many teachers have an image of themselves as practical and down-to-earth folk, having to cope with everyday life at the chalk-face, in the blackboard jungle, and as taking a sensible standing against the impractical theorising of linguists, sociologists and psychologists of education, and all the rest,

> those sinister figures in the wings, faintly contemptuous, armed with the para-phernalia of expertise and tapping ominously their research findings. (Rosen, 1978)

There is doubtless much justification in such a sceptical attitude towards theory, and it has to be taken into account in preparing training courses. If the clients are not interested, they will not learn anything. And they are often justifiably sceptical after past promises and disappointments. Teachers are under constant pressure from new ideas and information, not only from linguistics, but also from psychology, sociology and other disciplines, and under constant pressure to respond to what often turn out to be short-lived fashions.

However, the view that teacher-training must have the practical short-term goal of making them better teachers in the classroom tomorrow may be short-sighted and dangerous. It is short-sighted since there are other, longer-term, and possibly more interesting and ambitious goals. And it is dangerous since it implies that teachers have no need for, or are incapable of continuing their own general education or engaging in their own scholarly study about their subject or about their own professional behaviour. Teachers *are* scholars. However, some recent educational thinking has retreated into well meaning but ultimately sentimental concern with children, sometimes disguised as a practical stance against abstract theorising. This has sometimes led to teacher training courses which flirt with the peripheral aspects of academic disciplines. It must be admitted, for example, that some courses focus almost exclusively on psycholinguistic and sociolinguistic aspects of language, but avoid any detailed analysis of language itself. Carter (1980, p. 228) has likened this to the absurdity of a mathematics course which avoids doing too much mathematics. However, it has to be demonstrated that training can provide interesting intellectual challenges, of inherent interest to teachers as educated people. Also it must be admitted that a real problem with teaching linguistics is that it requires a very considerable initial investment by students before they begin to see the general value of what they are doing, and can use their understanding to prepare their own teaching materials. Studying linguistics is like going on a blind date.

A danger of an overly practical, short-term view is that without principles teachers are condemned to follow techniques superficially, without being able to adapt them for their own particular circumstances. They may take particular examples as orthodoxy, mistaking them for unchangeable prescriptions, and be unable to invent new examples. Finally, of course, an insistence on a practical approach may conceal a basic misunderstanding, if it is taken to imply that teaching can be theory-free. All teaching takes place on the basis of some theory (whether Piagetian, audio-lingual, or whatever, or simply classroom folklore), and this should be made explicit. As I have begun to indicate, discourse analysis can itself begin to analyse the assumptions underlying classroom dialogue and written texts.

There are further problems related to how abstract and analytic teaching about language and linguistics should be. It is plausible that a functional view of language in use will be of more direct relevance to teaching practice than a purely abstract view of language as system and structure. A view of language in use also starts from everyone's everyday experience of language. However, it is difficult to introduce samples of real language in use, without immediatley decontextualizing and trivializing them. It has often been pointed out that the search for authenticity in language teaching materials is an illusory one. If an authentic text (that is, a text originally written for some real purpose, without the linguist's intervention and not specially prepared as teaching material) is taken out of its context, and used for something else (teaching), it is thereby made inauthentic. However, this is simply to note that all teaching implies some contrivance, which may be more or less extreme.

A more basic problem may be that, even if it is accepted that a functional orientation is of more interest to teachers, this functional view may appear hopelessly vague if there is no formal analytic model to support it. If one starts with functions, one often never gets (back) to forms. To argue in a Hallidayan fashion, for example, that language is as it is formally, because of the functions it serves, assumes a sophisticated prior understanding of forms: of concepts such as rank-scale, and the mapping of one layer of structure onto another. More generally, one might argue that the valuable thing which is to be gained from a study of linguistics is not the details of particular formal arguments, but the style of argument itself: the nature of the data used, the attention to evidence of different kinds, the concept of a counterexample to a clearly formulated statement, and so on. However, this kind of argumentation can only be properly demonstrated on detailed examples, and has been fully developed only in descriptions of phonological and syntactic forms. Again, at least some analytic work seems necessary.

It is important, in summary, to distinguish between language in education and linguistics in education: they are potentially very different. (cf. the papers in Carter 1982, which make this distinction very clearly.)

Although these questions of selection for pedagogic purposes are not often explicitly discussed in print by linguists, they are probably constantly discussed in the course of meetings over syllabuses and examinations, and they have to be faced in one way or another by any linguist who has to select some topics in his subject in preparing a lecture course or writing a text book. Probably all teachers have to adopt a policy of diminishing deception: starting with plausible but strictly speaking unsound and oversimplified arguments, to get students used to the style of argument and the basic subject matter. This starting matter is then gradually refined and replaced by something better. Different teachers will take different decisions on how much initial distortion is defensible. However, some is inevitable, and if anyone feels unhappy with the situation, it can be pointed out that the process of diminishing deception is in any case what happens in anyone's intellectual development, and what happens at a much slower pace in the whole history of intellectual progress. As Feyerabend (1979, p. 156) has pointed out, an argument does not necessarily reveal the true beliefs of the arguer. One may, for example, adopt and express arguments which one believes to be false, in order to persuade an audience. This is a common pedagogic tactic, since false arguments may have to be followed through to their logical conclusion, before being revealed as false.

Although all teachers are familiar to some extent with such decisions, their interest here is that they constitute a possible definition of applied linguistics: the selection or development of theories for different purposes. However, the view that applied linguists interpret and mediate linguistics for practitioners is only one possibility. There has been considerable debate recently over whether applied linguistics is (1) a body of linguistic knowledge which is applied to practical problems (i.e. linguistics applied), or (2) a quasi-independent body of knowledge and specially developed theories (i.e applied linguistics). For example, Widdowson (1977, 1980a, 1980b) provides a series of arguments which represent his own changing views about the degree to which applied linguistics should develop its own theories independent of theoretical linguistics. He argues in later papers (e.g. 1980a) that models developed by theoretical and applied linguistics are incompatible, since there is a radical difference between analysts' and users' models of language, and applied linguistics has to take account of the latter.

One also has to be careful about the general rationale which is proposed for linguistics in teacher-training, or indeed more generally. It is often argued that language is peculiarly central in human society, that humans are *homo loquens*, that human society would be impossible without language, that a detailed understanding of language can tell us how the human mind works, and so on. In studying language therefore, students learn about essential and defining characteristics of their psychological and social environments. These arguments may all be true, and they are convincing rationales for studying linguistics. However, they do not clearly distinguish linguistics from other traditional academic disciplines, including biology, physics, geography, history or mathematics. All these disciplines and others tell us about the relationship between human beings and their environment. They also have much to teach students about valid forms of argument, different ways of evaluating data and evidence, and so on. And, in any case, the relationship between an abstract knowledge of language (or any other subject) and behaviour is indirect.

There are, then, several general problems concerning the presentation of linguistics to educationalists, and by implication to other professionals. These problems are inseparable from the more specific problem of formulating "a succinct account of the essential nature of language in terms that are truly relevant to the educational process" (Halliday, 1978).

Other problems do arise, however, from the admittedly special relationship between speakers and their native language. Everyone has a native language, and this is a great advantage in such teaching, since this implicit linguistic competence provides an enormous resource to draw on in teaching an explicit and conscious knowledge of language. However, it is also a disadvantage, since language is so notoriously open to misunderstanding and myth. Language is so central to everyone's life that it is surrounded with mystique. It is difficult to see any need for explanation at all. It either all seems natural and is taken for granted without the need for explanation being seen at all. Or speakers assume that just being a native speaker makes them experts, especially if they have been further sensitised by some language study, for example a training in literary criticism or learning a foreign language. Carter (1981) therefore argues that teacher-training must explicitly tackle misunderstandings about linguistics as the systematic study of language, since the attitude of mind required in linguistics is often believed to be contrary to the sensitivity required in literary study. It is almost certain, for example, that any course will have to tackle the common prejudice against formalism, idealization and explicitness, held by many students with literary training. Linguists are regularly accused of wanting to have things neater than they are, and of idealizing away just what is interesting about instances of language in use. Since linguists themselves differ in their view of how much idealization is permissible or useful, this provides a major source of confusion for students. So any course therefore starts from a certain necessary demystification: some students find it exhilarating to have their assumptions challenged; others find it uncomfortable and destructive.

To discuss here any further the issues involved in the dissemination of information about language and linguistics would take me too far from my main theme, so I will make just a few concluding comments central to any application of sociolinguistics. Information is never neutral: it is always transmitted in the face of prevailing expectations, preconceptions and entrenched professional interests. Any serious discussion of such problems would have to examine the way in which such prevailing views are supported and legitimated by institutions. In Britain, this would involve, for example, a study of the role of NATE (National Association for the Teaching of English) and its journal *English in Education* in forming the ideas of teachers, teacher-advisers and other educationalists. Or see Gordon (1980) or Stubbs (1980, Chapter 7) for discussions of the way in which Bernstein's ideas have often been distorted and simplified in their transmission to teachers and their subsequent application. To take a more general example: sociolinguistics is the study of language variation. It argues, contrary to much recent theoretical linguistics, that language is inherently hetero-geneous. When they have written on educational issues, sociolinguists have therefore tended to stress the value of diversity, and have seen bidialecal-ism, bilingualism and biliteracy as positive resources which teachers can use and encourage. By and large, however, the educational system, and govern-ment itself, has seen such diversity as a problem. For such reasons and others, applied sociolinguistics cannot avoid consideration of the practical sociology of knowledge.

Discourse analysis and foreign language teaching

It has often been argued by both linguists and teachers that theoretical linguistics has little or nothing to offer the practice of language teaching. For example, one extreme statement is by Sampson (1980, p. 10):

> I do not believe that linguistics has any contribution to make to the teaching of English or the standard European languages.

Sampson admits that linguistics may contribute to the teaching of exotic languages, but only insofar as it provides descriptions which are not other-wise available of such languages. Sampson's statement clearly recalls, in an even more extreme fashion, a famous quote from Chomsky (in Lester, *ed.*, 1970, p. 52). It may be, however, that such beliefs are due to looking for the contribution of linguistics in the wrong place. Sampson's and Chomsky's view appears to be that theoretical descriptions of syntax have nothing to offer the teacher, who has his own more appropriate pedagogic descriptions. However, what I will now argue more directly is that recent work in discourse can be very helpful in constructing an appropriate and coherent pedagogic description of language.

On the face of it, the most obvious application of discourse analysis to foreign language teaching is to help to construct the kind of model dialogue common to so much language teaching material. Role-playing, drama and simulated conversations are one established method in foreign language teaching (e.g. Maley and Duff, 1978). It is therefore plausible that a better understanding of real dialogue should lead to better dialogues for teaching purposes. However, it is obvious that a close transcript of a real conversation is very far from what is normally required for teaching. Any conversation will contain many characteristics which are relevant only to its original context of occurrence. The indexicality of everyday conversation has been the particular study of conversational analysis which derives its theoretical impetus from ethnomethodology (cf. Atkinson, 1981, for a discussion of ethnomethodology and applied linguistics, and the argument that situation and notional syllabuses are both rather crude attempts to apply sociological ideas.) If real conversations are used as the basis for pedagogic material, they will have to be carefully adapted to be at the right level of generalization. Davies (1978) compares in detail differences between an audio-recording of a real family breakfast and a foreign language textbook representation. He discusses the several different kinds of idealization required if one is to be turned into the other (cf. also Burton, 1980, for a detailed comparison of real discourse and simulated dialogue in playscripts.)

Another problem is that both teachers and students are, in general, ignorant of the structure and functions of conversations: discourse has simply not been studied in the educational system in the way that grammar has been for hundreds of years. Roulet (1981) therefore argues that foreign language teaching must be supported by mother tongue teaching, in which conversational analysis based on authentic documents is taught. Such suggestions are made within the more general context of suggested rapprochements between foreign language and mother tongue teaching which are currently (in the early 1980s) being debated.

If one is thinking of the direct applications of discourse analysis to language teaching, then this could mean also several other things. In general it suggests teaching language as communication (cf. Widdowson, 1978; Brumfit and Johnson, eds, 1979), and communicative syllabuses rather than grammatical syllabuses (cf. Munby, 1978). Teaching English for science and technology (EST) or for other academic purposes (EAP) or more generally teaching English for special purposes (ESP) imply teaching communicative competence, since the aim is generally to teach adults a foreign language for some specific, real, possibly quite restricted purpose, not for the artificial purpose of passing an examination. Applied linguistics has to recognise that language is studied for different reasons. Often the study of language is instrumental: not an end in itself, but a means to an end. The concept of notional or functional syllabuses is closely related here (Wilkins, 1976; Van Ek, 1975): that is, the view that the syllabus can be constructed round a list of speech acts, communicative and semantic categories, rather than the traditional grammatical organisation of most syllabuses. Whilst a communicative syllabus would necessarily be partly functional, it has been pointed out however, that a notional syllabus may be a list of isolated functional categories, and not take fully into account the sequential organisation of connected discourse (Widdowson, 1979b). In fact this important criticism has been levelled against speech act theory itself: that it studies isolated acts, although often the illocutionary force of an utterance can only be interpreted from knowledge of its place in a discourse sequence.

More narrowly still, applied discourse analysis might imply teaching something which has been neglected in the past, but about which we now have information due to recent research. For example, Brazil et al. (1980) propose teaching discourse intonation. Or one can teach directly other interactional skills, such as teaching students to interrupt politely. In general, discourse analysis is beginning to provide information at the level of contrastive pragmatics. Different speech communities differ in their rules for turn-taking, expression of politeness, amounts of talking, use of ritualistic formulae and the like, and such information is of potential use to the language learner. Textual conventions similarly vary in different languages: written Arabic, for example, makes little if any distinction between sentences and paragraphs, and punctuation conventions therefore differ considerably between Arabic and English. Detailed contrastive analyses of specific speech events have begun to appear: for example, Godard (1977) compares behaviour on the telephone in France and the USA by analysing sequential rules for openings. On the other hand, such work clearly has a long way to go before comprehensive contrastive descriptions are available. It has frequently been pointed out that much of the work on speech act theory and conversational maxims is western European in its assumptions. For example, Ochs Keenan (1976) criticises Grice (1975) on these grounds, showing that not all of Grice's conversational maxims hold in Malagasy.

The papers in Sinclair (ed., 1980) provide other views on applied discourse analysis and foreign language teaching.

There are however alternatives to these kinds of direct application. One alternative is to try to convey to teachers a general view of language which constantly takes into account its use in connected discourse in different social contexts. This is the topic of the next section.

Discourse analysis and training EFL teachers: course description and discussion

The course material described here was part of an intensive eight-week course taught in China. [1] The course material filled about 90 hours of lectures and seminars: 8 weeks of 6 days each and roughly one lecture and one seminar each day. Another one or two hours each day were generally filled with other related topics in modern English language, language teaching methodology, cultural background, films, and so on.

The students were over fifty Chinese lecturers in English at institutes of higher education, including universities and teacher-training colleges. They came from all over China, some from high prestige institutes in Peking and Shanghai, others from small institutes a long distance from main centres. Their command of English varied from near native speaker competence to some students who had almost no useful comprehension of normal spoken English at all. Many had, of course, no opportunity to hear native speakers: none had ever spent any period of time in an English-speaking country; and some had recently been "turned around" from teaching Russian. The break in Sino–Soviet relations came in 1960, and from 1966 to 1972 all universities in China were closed during the Cultural Revolution, and the study of foreign languages was stopped. In general, the students' comprehension of written English was much better, and many of them were in fact teaching intensive or extensive reading. Their knowledge of descriptive linguistics was in general restricted to traditional grammar. Quirk *et al.*'s (1972) grammar was well known, although in many cases students had clearly not understood the linguistic principles on which it is based. The students were also very familiar with the International Phonetic Alphabet and with broad phonemic representations of words, as this is standardly marked in even elementary EFL textbooks in China. The 50 students were divided into three groups on the basis of a cloze passage and a listening comprehension test, plus subsequent minor adjustments to the groups. The course described here was given to the "top" group of 16 students. On the oral testing procedures used by the Foreign Service Institute (Oller, 1979, p. 320) these students would have been at points 3 or 4 on the 5-point scale:

(3) Able to speak the language with sufficient structural accuracy and vocabulary to participate effectively in most formal and informal conversations, on practical, social and professional topics.
(4) Able to use the language fluently and accurately on all levels normally pertinent to professional needs.

The aim of the course was to teach neither EFL nor TEFL, but to teach descriptive linguistics with reference to modern English language and to TEFL. It attempted to provide a coherent approach to describing English which was particularly appropriate to TEFL, with the underlying theoretical coherence coming from work in discourse analysis, text analysis, narrative analysis, cohesion, speech act theory and related areas. In other words, the course was predominantly theoretical, but was theory explicitly geared to teaching practice. This would hopefully: (1) improve the student's own communicative competence in English; and (2) allow them to improve their own teaching and testing techniques, by (3) teaching them about linguistic description. Hopefully this would be of both practical value and also be intellectually interesting. As the course progressed, I realized how important requirement (2) was. Since we knew next to nothing about actual teaching conditions in Chinese higher education, we could not impose actual teaching methods, but only provide the underlying principles in the hope that our students would then be able to adapt our ideas to their own circumstances.

There were several constraints on the course, which may seem extreme, but which doubtless have parallels elsewhere. These must be taken into account, since there is little point in providing students with impractical ideas. First, a communicative approach to foreign language teaching requires, to all intents and purposes, native speaker competence in the teacher. It is worth remembering that the communicative approach was developed very much through courses in ESP where native English speakers were developing basically study skills courses for improving reading ability to handle written academic English (EAP). There are considerable dangers in having non-native speakers produce texts for teaching purposes. For a teacher who has less than native speaker competence, the safest method may well be to base teaching firmly on given texts. Much teaching in China is very traditional and text-based, for this and other reaons. Many of the ideas in the course therefore aimed to provide students with ways of manipulating naturally occurring texts.

At the outset, I had intended a course fairly evenly balanced between spoken and written discourse. However these various practical constraints led to a concentration on written texts with some work on listening comprehension: the less than native competence of the students; the need to start from and develop the traditional text-based methods already used by the students; the lack of books and the need to exploit available texts to the maximum effect; the difficulty of using native models of spoken language; and the fact that many of the students were explictly teaching extensive or intensive reading for EST or EAP. Given the general isolation of the students (and *their* students) from native English speakers, there was in any case no direct motivation for attempting to develop their competence in spoken English. Teaching communicative skills in spoken English was therefore not a direct aim, although during the course they heard a lot of spoken English in lectures, seminars and more informal conversation.

One basic decision was that all materials used should be authentic texts. I have already admitted above that the search for authenticity is illusory, since material is taken out of its original context if it is used for teaching. (Allwright, 1979, proposes one way round this problem, albeit in a very special situation.) Given the students' need to exploit texts to the maximum effect in their own teaching, I relaxed the authenticity criterion to allow the manipulation of texts for teaching purposes. (I give examples below.) Nevertheless, here authentic texts means material originally produced for native speakers, and not produced for teaching and designed for learners. There are several very useful collections of such material from a wide variety of written styles (e.g. Maley and Duff, eds, 1976; Levine, ed., 1971) and collections of short stories (e.g. Cochrane, ed., 1969; Dolley, ed., 1968). This decision leads inevitably to other consequences. It follows that all work was on analysing and interpreting connected text. It also means that no linguistic feature or content will ever be introduced for its own sake. This point applies both to syntax ("Today we learn the passive") and also to function ("Today we do polite requests"). Texts may be selected because of some central or recurrent feature, but that feature will always be con-textualized in other features. The choice of materials also makes it fairly easy to avoid both linguistic correction and linguistic aid (e.g. supplying words) if this is thought desirable. All theory and practice was, therefore, explicitly related to this aim of handling real connected text.

The general model of language underlying the course, and put over more or less explicitly at different stages, was as follows. Learning a language is essentially learning to make correct predictions. As soon as something is said, one can make predictions about what is likely or unlikely to be said next. Expectations may be broken, predictions may be wrong, and people say unexpected things. However, unfulfilled predictions show that there were predictions made, and whatever does occur is interpreted in the light of what was expected. If something is not expected, this surprisal value is part of its meaning. These points can be reformulated in terms of redundancy: if an item is predictable, then this means that it is redundant. Linguists are fully familiar with this information theory approach to language and meaning. And they are fully familiar with the way in which it is equally applicable to all levels of language: phonology, graphology, lexis (e.g. collocations), syntax, semantics and discourse. It is also evident to linguists how this concept may be reformulated into a concept of structure as constraints on linear sequence. In one way or another, all modern linguistics is based on the concept that language is polysystemic: that is, there are always constraints on linear sequence, and different paradigmatic choices are available at different points in the sequence.

From a theoretical point of view, these ideas are very powerful and general, although of course they run into all kinds of difficulties as a theoretical model, and these are well known. However, what we are concerned with here is their appropriateness as a model for understanding foreign language learning, and for producing coherent and interesting language teaching materials. They relate well, for example, to the influential view of reading as a psycholinguistic guessing game (Smith, 1973), with all its implications for teaching reading. Learning a foreign language is seen, therefore, as acquiring preditive competence. Halliday (1978, p. 200) points out that there are certain things which are particularly difficult for a speaker of a foreign language. These include: (1) saying the same thing in different ways; (2) hesitating and saying nothing much; and (3) predicting what the other person is going to say. These aspects of linguistic competence are all closely related; they all have to do with understanding and producing language in discourse under the constraints of real time. They all also concern ways of exploiting the redundancy of natural language in use.

The expectancy model is a good one for foreign learners for very practical reasons. First, when they are listening to spoken language, learners are often worried when they do not understand every word. They miss a word, wonder what it was, and miss the next few words. However, native speakers do not listen to every word: they exploit the redundancy of any piece of language, make predictions and then check their predictions by sampling. It can be good for foreign learners' confidence to be made aware of this. And the principle immediately suggests ways of preparing listening comprehension materials (cf. Brown, 1978, and below on "helping the listener"). Learners have to listen like a native, as Brown puts it. A comparable point holds for reading comprehension where it is sometimes difficult to break learners of the habit of looking up every unfamiliar word in a dictionary. Again this leads to many obvious reading exercises involving guessing word meanings from context and the like (e.g. *see* Clarke and Nation, 1980, for many suggestions). It is worth also pointing out to students, that in order to find the meaning of a word in a dictionary, this assumes that part of the meaning has already been guessed from context. All words are ambiguous in isolation, and dictionary users have to select the relevant dictionary entry. Students can therefore gain a more sophisticated theoretical understanding of both word meaning and of the organisation of dictionaries. The general aim of the model of listening and reading comprehension is to make students independent: of dictionaries, teachers and so on. This might be proposed as the whole aim of education: to make students independent of teachers. This was certainly an important consideration on the present course, where students were used to very formal teacher-centred classes, and lacked any confidence in their own ideas.

Taking now one topic on the course in a little more detail, a major component was classic structural lexical semantics. However, this was taught as a way of analysing texts, and therefore proposed as one kind of discourse analysis. At one level it was presented as a way of teaching directed reading: by forcing students to identify key-words in arguments, and by identifying hyponyms, antonyms and synonyms, to identify the outline of the argument. At a more theoretical level, this led immediately to a discussion of lexical cohesion. This in turn was taught both as a technique of linguistic description, and also as a further method of intensive reading, with particular reference to the stylistic analysis of literary texts. This led further to a redefinition of such lexical relations in terms of relations between sentences: entailment, paraphrase, contradiction, presupposition, and so on – and hence to other ways of analysing the organization of texts. It is also possible to relate structural semantics directly to language teaching strategies. For example, Blum and Levenston (1978) have proposed that there are universals of lexical simplification which include the use of superordinate terms, synonymy, paraphrase and the like, and therefore principled ways of making do with less words: precisely what a language learner often has to do. Hudson (1980, pp. 93–4) also puts forward the suggestion that in hierarchic lexical taxonomies such as sets of terms for plants or animals, there are maximal information levels. To take a simple example, a term such as *mammal* is less useful than *animal* for most everyday purposes, and *collie* will less often be useful than *dog*.

This aspect of the course involved practical work on intensive reading, summarizing, note taking, explaining and reformulating. All such activities involve understanding the semantic structure of texts, both in their local and global organization. As well as these aspects of lexical cohesion and logico-linguistic relations, the theory also covered narrative structure (cf. Labov, 1972b) and speech act theory, as well as communicative competence in general. Such practical activities blur the distinction between EFL and study skills. This means that language is not being taught in an intellectual vacuum, but as a tool. It also blurs the distinction between EFL and mother tongue teaching, since many such analytic activities are also useful with native speakers.

I have room here to give only a few practical examples of the kind of classroom activities which were based on such a view of semantic organisation and discourse predictions.

(1) The technique of cloze passages is well known. Passages are specially prepared by deleting words; students have to make predictions from context and complete the gaps. Such exercises are linguistically

principled, but nevertheless involve artificial preparation of texts. A real alternative which I used was to take a newspaper article in East African English which contained a large number of Swahili loan words, incomprehensible out of context to an English speaker. These loan words provided real lexical gaps for students to translate into English.

(2) A common situation in which hearers have to predict large parts of a conversation occurs when they hear one end of a telephone call. It is usually possible to predict much of what is said at the other end of the line. It is easy to tape record a telephone call, and to delete one speaker's contributions from the transcript to form a discourse cloze passage.

(3) A short story can be divided into sections and fed to students one section at a time. Their task is to predict what will happen next, and to write the continuation of the story. Again, this involves some manipulation of a text, but forces students to make explicit their expectations in a way which is essentially similar to that involved in an intelligent first reading of a literary text. Any such exercises can provide material for subsequent more formal analysis of the students' own predictions. This will inevitably involve comparison between different students' predictions, and between these predictions and the original. This will inevitably lead also to an analysis of the grammatical and lexical cohesion in the passages, of semantic relations such as paraphrase and entailment, as well as of the macrostructure of narratives and other discourse types. (In Stubbs, 1983a, I discuss in more detail some aspects of the semantic organisation of a literary text and give other examples of such classroom activities, suitable for mother tongue teaching in secondary schools.)

It might be argued that the model of language proposed here is not specifically linguistic, and that the concepts of predictability and redundancy are applicable to many aspects of psychological activity (e.g. memory) and social behaviour. Nevertheless they are particularly clear when applied to language, and the theory has been most explicitly developed with reference to linguistic examples. Furthermore, as the concern with autonomous linguistics mellows, it may be useful to start looking for a basis of linguistic organisation in wider psychological and social competence. It is not entirely plausible that linguistic competence is as distinct from other cognitive abilities as some linguists have proposed.

Discourse analysis and analysing classroom language

The view of teaching which has been widely held in the west for centuries is a predominantly verbal one. A teacher does things such as lecturing, explaining, asking questions and telling students to do things. Students have a largely complementary role of listening, understanding, answering and basically responsing to the initiative of the teacher. Many people also hold some version of the view that people learn things by expressing them in their own words. This is why we distrust students' work if it is copied verbatim from a book. And it appears reasonable that "talking through" a problem can often clarify it. A widely held and often taken for granted view of classroom behaviour is therefore based on some version of teacher–student verbal dialogue, with a high value placed on the public, explicit, verbal expression of knowledge. This view of education, with its equation of teaching and talking, is of course, culture-specific. Not all cultures take it for granted that the verbal channel is the primary channel for learning, but believe that learning occurs through silent observation, participation, self-initiated testing, experience, and so on. In addition, the western model of teaching has often been attacked by educational theorists, but it has proved remarkably resistant to such criticism. In a culture such as ours which assumes a close relationship between teaching, learning and talking, an obvious application of discourse analysis is to analyse the teacher–student classroom dialogue itself. This *is* the educational process as it is experienced day by day by most students. It is important that teachers have systematic ways of analysing their own daily professional behaviour; and such reflection on the process of classroom interaction itself is becoming a standard component of teacher-training courses. For example, micro-teaching is now a common teacher-training technique. Such training is also becoming increasingly common for doctors, managers and other professionals.

A very substantial body of work on classroom interation has been published since the late 1960s. There is no room to review this work here, and it is in any case fairly well known. The work varies according to how it draws on linguistic, sociological, anthropological and psychological methods, but broadly speaking there have been three influential kinds of study of classroom language. Type 1 could be called insightful observation. This involves detailed study and commentary on recorded lessons. It is valuable in that it demands close attention to be paid to the details of real language, but is inevitably limited since it is restricted to impressionistic and selective commentary. The best known British work is probably that of Barnes *et al.* (1969). There is no doubt that many teachers find Barnes' work very helpful: it has made them aware of all kinds of things they had never noticed before, and Barnes is a very sensitive observer. This is precisely one of the problems; there is no method or guiding principle for those of us who are not as sensitive and full of insight as Barnes. Such work can be made more principled and theoretically secure by using fieldwork methods developed in sociology and anthropology, and by relating the observational data to an explicit theoretical framework such as symbolic interactionism. Type 2 involves the use of coding schemes: that is, sets of categories designed to code or classify large amounts of language, usually as it happens in real time. This may be valuable in allowing broad trends to become visible and in making gross comparisons between different teachers, different school subjects, even groups of teachers in different countries, and so on. However, it inevitably means that close attention is no longer paid to the actual language used. This approach derives from work done in the 1950s by the American social psychologist Robert Bales. The best known work on classroom language is by Flanders (1970). Such coding schemes are often frequently used in micro-teaching when this is used as a teacher-training technique. Type 3 could simply be called discourse analysis. The aim here is to describe spoken discourse as a linguistic system in its own right: to discover what the units of analysis are, and how these units relate into sequences.

There are various applications of such linguistic analyses of classroom discourse. Several researchers have studied teacher–pupil interaction to investigate whether teachers and pupils understand each other. Willes (1978, 1981, 1983) and Holmes (1983) report on miscommunications between teachers and pupils in infant classrooms in Britain and New Zealand respectively. And Malcolm (1979) reports on communicative interference between teachers and Aboriginal pupils who speak varieties of non-standard English in Western Australia. He also goes further to propose how such sociolinguistic study can lead to action research, involving teachers and Aboriginal classroom aides.

I will not be concerned here further with such direct applications of studies of classroom discourse, but will discuss whether it is possible to combine an increased understanding of teacher–pupil interaction with an increased understanding of language in general. Ideally, a linguistic approach to classroom discourse would: sensitise teachers to the complex but orderly nature of classroom dialogue; improve their teaching via this increased sensitivity; provide them with a firmer theoretical basis for understanding their own professional behaviour in the classroom; and provide them with a theoretically interesting account of an important aspect of language. This is undoubtedly too tall an order to be fulfilled on many teacher-training courses, and in the next section I will discuss what might be possible with reference to part of a second in-service training course which I have prepared.

Discourse analysis and classroom language: course description and discussion

The material which forms the basis of discussion in this section is published as Stubbs and Robinson (1979). This is part of an Open Univeristy course on *Language Development*. Other material on the course covers phonetics and phonology, lexis, syntax, semantics, communication and context, assessing children's language and the language curriculum in schools. The course is designed as a post-experience course for schoolteachers. The course is reviewed by Carter (1980), which is in turn criticized by Czerniewska (1981).

At the beginning of the material on discourse, we express the objectives as follows (Stubbs and Robinson, 1979, p. 9):

> After studying (this part of the course) students should (a) have a broad view of different approaches to analysing classroom language; (b) have had experience in the problem of transcribing natural spoken language from classrooms; (c) be able to describe classroom lessons using one particular system of analysis; (d) understand some general limitations on all systems for describing language behaviour; (e) have several ideas for ways of exploring the language of their own classrooms; (f) have an increased understanding of the study of discourse as a level of linguistics, as are phonology, syntactic study and semantics; (g) have a set of criteria to think about the work they read on classroom language; (h) have a way of talking precisely about their own classroom language, and of studying aspects of it.

In my discussion here, I will concentrate on the objectives which have to do with an appropriate approach to analytic techniques and theory and their relation to practice, which I have commented on above. Note that the objectives do not hold out the promise of improved teaching, and we add also the following caveat (Stubbs and Robinson, 1979, p. 13–14):

> We are concered at every stage with the details of real language in classrooms, and for some readers this may lead to an assumption that such work is directly and obviously relevant to teaching practice. However, while we do see such work as very relevant, such an assumption needs qualification. There is no reason, for example, why increased insight into teacher–pupil discourse should in itself lead to better teaching. It may do or it may not (it depends on the *educational* decisions and action that the teacher takes) . . . Nor is there any special value in the analysis of classroom discourse for its own sake, and it would be wrong of us to promise that there is.

The material summarizes and criticizes different approaches to classroom language: insightful observation and coding schemes (pp. 16–26); defines criteria for linguistic descriptions of discourse: descriptive categories should be finite in number, relatable to data, comprehensive in coverage, and restricted in their possible sequential combinations (pp. 26–31); discusses problems of transcription (pp. 32–3); discusses differences between grammar and discourse (pp. 33–4); discusses the nature of teachers' questions (pp. 34–9); and then presents a summary of Sinclair and Coulthard's (1975) analysis of classroom discourse in enough detail to allow students to analyse their own data (pp. 39–55). This analytic approach is also the subject of an accompanying television programme by Willes.

One major problem concerns the amount of analytic skill which students should have at the end of such a course. As I discussed briefly above, this is a general problem for any course in linguistics. How much should students be expected to be able to apply the description in the narrow sense of applying its categories in a replicable way to data? An emphasis on textual analysis means concentration on one descriptive framework, ignoring or playing down its limitations, and neglecting alternative descriptions. Whereas a lack of detailed description may mean vagueness. With reference to the grammatical sections of the course, Czerniewska (1981, p. 38), one of the Open University staff who prepared the course says

> Our decision . . . was merely to provide students with an awareness of a descriptive approach . . .

However, merely to be aware that pupils' language requires to be seen systematically, for example, is surely not adequate for an in-service course for teachers. Mere consciousness-raising can lead to a course which is "all bricks and no foundations" (Carter, 1980 p. 226).

Another problem is how such a course can be evaluated in general. Czerniewska (1981) accuses Carter (1980) of judging the course by inappropriate criteria, those of academic linguistics, and in commenting (1981, p. 39) on the whole course, says that "the real test is its usefulness to teachers". In fact, she defines (p. 37) an in-service course in an even narrower fashion as "one that will lead to improved classroom practice". The claim that applicability to the classroom teacher in this sense is primary, is a common type of argument, which I have already discussed. This is only one test. Others are accuracy, consistency, clarity, interest, academic and intellectual value. Furthermore, the relation between analysis (e.g. of discourse) and behaviour (e.g. in classroom interaction) will rarely be direct.

The main question is one of the practical educational value of analysis. A major part of the material is concerned with analysing characteristic teacher–pupil exchanges which have a structure initiation-response-feedback (IRF), for example:

Teacher: Now what can you tell me that all reptiles do, all reptiles do it.
Pupil: Lay their eggs on land.
Teacher: Good, lay their eggs on land, lay their eggs on land.

There is a danger that such descriptions may be taken as prescriptions. They might either be taken as a model of good, clear teaching, confusing what is a norm with what ought to be a norm. Or they might be taken as a warning of what should be avoided as restrictive teaching practice. However, the question of whether such exchanges are pedagogically good or bad is a separate question from their analysis. Presumably they are good for some purposes (e.g. checking factual knowledge), but hopelessly restircted for others (e.g. discussing literature). What such analyses can do is to provide a firmer basis for such interpretation and value judgments, by providing a precise way of talking about recurrent patterns in classroom discourse. This is analogous to the role of linguistic description in stylistics. Linguistics can provide more evidence and a firmer basis for a literary interpretation, but the analysis is not an interpretation.

The fact that people make this kind of interpretative leap is itself interesting, however, and suggests another educational use of discourse analysis. It is almost impossible to avoid such value considerations in doing such analyses. Ideological questions are thus opened up by any critical analysis of institutional discourse, whether between teachers and students, magistrates and defendants, doctors and patients, and in general between professionals and their clients. In such areas, discourse analysis can provide ways of studying the language of social power and control, prestige, status and deference, manipulation and misunderstanding, and can provide evidence for discussion of the moral, ethical, social and political questions which arise. This is a modern study of rhetoric.

Related work which manages a skillful integration of descriptive theory, methodology and practical educational concerns is by Willes (1978, 1981, 1983). (Willes, 1978, is part of the set reading for the Open University course.) She has studied the teacher–pupil interaction in reception classes in British infant schools. Her descriptions are based on Sinclair and Coulthard (1975), but the descriptive system is not mechanically applied. It is put to practical exploratory use in an innovative and imaginative way. She uses Sinclair and Coulthard's description of classroom discourse as a theoretical statement about communicative competence in classrooms. She argues that not all classroom discourse fits the IRF pattern which they have identified (a descriptive point); and she investigates the different rates at which pupils learn to conform to this pattern (findings based on the description). But she also discusses the social and educational value of the IRF pattern, and argues that teachers should try to depart from it (a pedagogical point). She also uses the descriptive framework to develop other research methods. For example, some children seldom speak in the classroom, and their communicative competence cannot therefore be directly observed. Willes devised a discourse cloze procedure to test their competence: a story about classrooms with blanks in the teacher–pupil dialogue for the children to fill in. Such an integration of theory, methods and practice is rare, but provides a model study in applied discourse analysis.[2]

Discourse analysis in classroom practice

Introductory points

It is traditional to consider language under separate headings of reading, writing, listening and speaking. There is obviously much to recommend these distinctions, although they are often artificial. For example, there are processes of linguistic comprehension common to both reading and listening, despite the often used divisions of reading comprehension and listening comprehension, and foreign language or mother tongue courses designed to teach one or the other. In addition, the division into two productive and two receptive aspects of competence must clearly not be taken to imply that speaking and writing are active, whereas listening and reading are passive. Listening and reading comprehension clearly involve active processes of prediction, for example. Given these caveats, I will use the traditional distinctions to structure the following sections, although the categories will sometimes overlap. So far, I have discussed discourse analysis in teacher-training. The remainder of the chapter discusses the content of syllabuses for students, whose aim is either to develop students' communicative competence or to teach them about language and linguistic theory.

Helping the reader: literacy and stylistics

It is now commonplace to assume that the written language used in basal readers should be adjusted to the spoken language of learner. Otherwise the beginning reader has to learn a new style or dialect at the same time as learning to read; and it is assumed best to learn one thing at a time. Thus, much scorn has been poured on "primerese" of the type *Run, Spot, run. See Spot run, Jane.* Such primerese does of course make a plausible attempt to control the language presented to the beginner, but the basis of the selection may be wrong. Lexical items are chosen for their regular sound-letter correspondences, shortness, and so on, rather than for their contribution to meaningful connected prose. More recently, it has been argued that an approximation of reading primers to the spoken language of beginners should also involve discourse organization. This is important, given the general failure of attempts to break reading down into discrete subskills, such as vocabulary recognition, identifying key ideas, and so on. Both local and global textual organization appear to contribute to reading comprehension, and to be inseparable.

A useful summary statement of discourse factors to consider in preparing literacy materials is by Longacre (1977). He argues that discourse is the primary unit of linguistic structure, in the sense of being the unit which people are aware of. Examples include functional units at the level of speech acts and speech events: story, explanation, request, giving directions, and so on. If literacy materials are to approximate to the actual usage of spoken language, the choice of discourse genre is crucial. The general argument is that materials should be in line with learners' expectancies. This general approach fits well with Goodman and Smith's model of reading as a psycholinguistic guessing game, although Goodman and Smith have not developed their model at the level of discourse. An active, interpretative search for meaning takes place at all levels of language. (For more general reviews of the contribution of sociolinguistics to literacy teaching see Gudschinsky, 1976; Stubbs, 1980) Much discourse oriented work on the preparation of literacy materials has been carried out by linguists working with the Summer Institute of Linguistics. As a result, there is much work which is based on tagmemic theory, or which is predominantly concerned with Bible translation into exotic languages, or both (e.g. Callow, 1974).

A different academic tradition which has contributed a great deal to the structural analysis of prose passages is psychological work on the cognitive processing of discourse. Both the overall macrostructure of narratives, descriptions, explanations and the like, and also the micropropositional development of texts from sentence to sentence, are seen as cognitive schemas which play an important part in the comprehension and production of texts. Mandler and Johnson (1977) and Van Dijk and Kintsch (1978) provide useful reviews of this work. And examples of applied educational studies are provided by Stein and Glenn (1979) who investigate young children's comprehension of stories, and by Waters (1980) who provides a case study of a single child's written production over a year. Much of this work is within the cognitive psychological approach to studying memory, which is defined as the ability to recall the semantic content of texts. This derives from the classic work of Bartlett (1932) who showed that remembering a story is not mere repetition, but an active process of interpretation and reconstruction based on familiar structures and standard story schemas.

Such work turns out to be very compatible with work which sets out to specify the discourse structure of academic textbooks and articles. Such analysis has often studied science texts, both because they are highly structured in some rather obvious ways, and also because of the importance of such texts to foreign learners of English in EST and EAP courses. The aim of such work is to identify discourse plans such as: problem-solution; assertion-justification; exemplification-clarification-conclusion. (*See* Roe, 1977, Hutchins, 1977, on science books; and Tadros, 1980, for similar work on economics textbooks). Montgomery's (1977) work on the discourse structure of science lectures also contributes to this approach to EAP. Academic lecturing is characteristically a mixed mode: partly spontaneous spoken language, but based on written notes. But Montgomery's work could also be considered under listening comprehension below.

Such work is of theoretical interest to linguists, since it is concerned with the semantic organisation of texts. It has obvious applied interests in helping students to understand academic materials. The basic pedagogical rationale is clear enough. We try at least to teach students explicitly about the organization of written language at the level of graphology: although our teaching may often be inadequate. We do less well at the level of syntax: since there is as yet inadequate description of the differences in grammar between spoken and written English. But systematic teaching about semantic organization (including cohesion and paraphrase) and discourse (e.g. narrative structure) is almost non-existent.

Such work is therefore beginning to have an educational impact. Work is beginning to be done on the way in which pupils in British schools actually use textbooks in classrooms, and this involves both observational studies of school classrooms and also analyses of the textual structure of school textbooks (Lunzer and Gardner, eds, 1978, and subsequent unpublished work at the University of Nottingham). In foreign language teaching, it is now common to have courses designed specifically to promote reading ability in relatively well defined academic areas. Typically, for example, students of chemistry or music might require a reading knowledge of German, students of art might require a reading knowledge of Italian, or students of history or law might require French. There are now several ESP textbooks on the market which aim to develop skills of effective reading in the sense of understanding textual organization and finding sense relations in texts. (*See* Allen and Widdowson, 1974, for a discussion of such material; Widdowson, 1975b, 1979a, for discussion of the underlying discourse theory; and Von Faber and Heid, eds, 1981, for a description and discussion of several specific courses.)

It might be thought that such work on written texts is rather far from the analysis of spoken discourse or conversation, since written texts are not interactive. However, as Sinclair (1981) has pointed out, a written text could in principle consist only of strings of propositions with logical connectors.

Anything else is interactive, including: predictive structures, discourse labelling, cross references, and so on. Any such organizational features serve to present the text interactively, by taking account of the readers' likely knowledge and reactions at different points in the text. Thus, to take a rather obvious example, I began this paragraph by writing "It might be thought that . . .", in order to take into account an objection to my argument which I predicted at this point from some readers.

As far as an educationally relevant model of language is concerned, it is also important that this view of reading, as coping with the textual organization of books and articles in order to read for meaning, is compatible with the increasingly accepted view that we learn to read and write by using language. In real life, discourse always has a reason for being interpreted. With written discourse, these reasons range from passing a pleasant hour with a detective novel to retrieving a specific bit of information in a scientific article or telephone directory. It does not occur to us as fluent adult readers to confuse such different functions of reading. However, there is increasing evidence that many children have problems learning to read because they never understand what reading is for (Stubbs, 1980, p. 98ff.). So, to emphasize the main theme of this article, such a view of reading contributes to a coherent overall view of language. It must be admitted that this view is not yet well defined or very explicit, but it may be explicit and coherent enough for practical eductional purposes.

At a more analytically sophisticated level again, from the students' own point of view, stylistics can be regarded as a training in close reading, and work on discourse has also begun to influence analysis here. Stylistics is usually taken to mean the linguistic analysis of literary texts: a study of how literary effects are created and how readers' intuitive reactions to texts can be explicitly accounted for. In so far as stylistics uses descriptive linguistic techniques to explain literary effects, it is already applied linguistics. There are many problems in such a view of stylistics which attempts to take such a linguistic account of texts as a theoretically adequate account of literary effects. For example, it is arguable that a systematic linguistic analysis will necessarily concentrate on superficial features of linguistic form, that it can only provide comprehensive accounts of short, and possibly minor, texts, and that any analysis only provides the literary critic with more data, but does not in itself lead in any rigorous way to an interpretation. These problems do not directly concern us here. However, as Widdowson (1975a) argues in detail, stylistics can also be useful a teaching strategy. Techniques which force students to pay close attention to linguistic features of texts can provide a way in to understand the organization of complex texts and therefore a help in the interpretation of literature.

Recently many studies have drawn on work in discourse analysis and speech act theory. Pratt (1977) proposes a speech act theory of literature. Searle (1975) discusses the logical status of fictional discourse and what kinds of speech acts literature is performing. Carter (1979) uses discourse concepts in an analysis of Auden's poetry. Stubbs (1983a) uses the concepts of conversational implicature, following Grice (1975) in an interpretation of a Hemingway story. Stylistics and literary criticism in general have often been restricted to prose and poetry, and drama has been neglected. It is dramatic dialogue which provides an obvious area of application of discourse analysis. Burton (1980) provides a detailed study of short plays by Ionesco and Pinter, and a general discussion of the relationship between theatrical dialogue and natural conversation, both using discourse analysis to develop literary theory and also using the insights of dramatists as data for the description of natural discourse. (*See also* Short, 1981.) A related body of work studies narrative structure: this includes work by scholars such as Propp (1928), Todorov (1969), and Genette (1980). Some of this work is predominantly literary criticism; other work on oral narrative is more obviously sociolinguistic (Labov, 1972b). All of this work uses basically linguistic-structural techniques of description to provide a more explicit account of the local and global structure of literary texts. Where literary criticism previously discussed related questions at all, it was often restricted to rather superficial commentary of, for example, differences between spoken and written language (e.g. Page, 1973, on the uses of direct speech in novels).

Helping the writer: written composition

Teachers are often understandably at a loss when require to correct students' written compositions. First, there is often no clear dividing line between coherent and incoherent text, as there typically (or at least often) is between grammatical and ungrammatical sentences. A text in which surface lexical or grammatical cohesion is faulty may often seem unclear or in bad style, rather than obviously "wrong". Second, our intuitions about grammatical well formedness have been sharpened by two thousand years of explicit syntactic study. Comparably explicit work on discourse organisation is only now starting to appear. (For a detailed discussion of how far the concept of well formedness applies to discourse, *see* Stubbs, 1983b, Chapter 5.)

The tradition of teaching written composition is mainly confined to schools in Britain, and almost unknown at university level, although there are occasional courses in report writing for engineers and the like. The American tradition of teaching rhetoric in the form of freshman composition tends to be derided (in Britain) as remedial English, and its often vague aims satirised as "a course in existential awareness and the accurate use of the comma" (Bradbury, 1976, p. 111). This is precisely the kind of observation which has kept linguists away from discourse analysis in the past: the fear that discourse either involves questions of mere surface style; or that discourse is impossible to delimit, and that there is no way to prevent semantics, pragmatics, culture and the world from flooding in. The plot in several campus novels revolves around the frustrations of teaching freshman composition in American colleges (e.g. Bradbury, 1965; Lodge, 1975, not to mention Pirsig, 1974). However, an excellent recent British book on writing to a directive which could be used on such courses is by Nash (1980). He aims to strengthen students' intuitions about structures in discourse, and discusses varieties of rhetorical design and textual cohesion.

There is no doubt that manuals of style such as the famous American high-school text by Strunk and White (1979) discuss important issues of textual organisation. What such manuals often lack is any systematic framework within which to discuss such organisation, and often matters of information structure or cohesion are described vaguely as questions of emphasis, balance, rhythm, monotony or variety, or simply as good or bad style. Similarly, work by British educationalists (e.g. Britton *et al.*, 1975) has usefully discussed the different functions of written language, such as poetic, expressive and transactional. They have also usefully pointed to the unfair demands often placed on school pupils who are expected to produce final draft writing before producing and revising preliminary drafts, arguing for the value of both exploratory talk and exploratory writing. Again, however, such work is often inexplicit in its discussion of form–function relations.

Enkvist (1981) provides a useful summary of some rhetorical application of text linguistics, which is very relevant here, and suggests how the teaching of both mother tongue and foreign languages could benefit from a more explicit discussion of text strategies which is now available. In teaching English as a mother tongue, this could make explicit the ways in which language is adapted to hearers and readers. In EFL, such work could provide an explicit basis for explaining the ways in which information may be concentrated or diluted for different audiences: for example, a discussion of how much redundancy foreign learners require in a text. One way to "dilute" a text is to insert existential structures (Enkvist, 1981, p. 199):

> There were three books on the table. All fell down.
> The three books on the table all fell down.

Such topics have received much explicit discussion in recent work on natural conversation (e.g. Ochs, 1979, on left-dislocation structures in casual conversation versus formal or written language).

At a practical level, Keen (1978) and Gannon and Czerniewska (1980) demonstrate ways in which teachers can analyse the textual cohesion in children's writing, and therefore better assess it and correct it.

Helping the listener: listening comprehension

For obvious reasons, listening comprehension has traditionally been a topic for the foreign language classroom rather than in mother tongue teaching, although it should become clear that some of the points discussed here are relevant to both. It is worthwhile also bearing in mind that the strict foreign language/mother tongue distinction is often much less clear than often appears at first sight, especially in the increasingly multilingual classrooms in Britain and the USA, and with the existence of varieties of language such as creoles which blur the language/dialect distinction. I have also pointed out above that recent courses on ESP blur the distinction between foreign language learning and study skills.

Brown (1977, 1978) has discussed the inadequacy of many EFL tests of listening comprehension, which make demands on learners which are never made on native speakers. Her main general point is that it is inappropriate to judge spoken language by criteria only applicable to written language. For example, a test which requires hearers to extract discrete details of information from casual conversational language rather than the overall significance of the utterance, may be confusing the forms and functions of written and spoken language. Spontaneous speech is not usually used for transmitting detailed information. Where it is, it is usually backed up with written or visual aids, as in much teaching. Or the propositional information occurs in short bursts, as in giving directions in the street, or giving orders in a shop. Alternatively, hearers will probably record at least the gist of what is said in writing, as in giving complex orders to workmen. It is therefore inappropriate to ask questions about the detailed cognitive content of casual conversational language. Brown's work is based on an examination of both the phonological obscurity (including elisions and assimilations) which characterizes most spoken English (Brown, 1977); and also of the differences in discourse organization between written transactional and spoken interactional language. Adult interactional language is characterized by: slow tempo; division into short chunks with a lot of pauses; one-place predicates in which one thing is said about one referent at a time; topic–comment structures; paratactic structures which rarely make explicit logical relations between clauses (cf. Ochs, 1979). In general, these features mean that information is not densely structured. Brown points out that when spoken language is intended to transmit detailed factual information, then special discourse structures have evolved. For example, in a radio news broadcast, a typical structure allows information to be repeated three times. Brief headlines are followed by an expansion of the news items which is followed in turn by a repetition of the main points.

Crystal and Davy (1975) have published transcripts of unedited audio-recorded conversations, representing standard, educated colloquial English usage. They admit, as might be predicted from the arguments which Brown puts forward, that they are "unclear as to how data of this kind can best be used in a teaching situation" (p. x). A paradox is whether informal language can be formally taught or tested. Such conversational English is important as it is different from the language presented to learners in most textbooks. Usually students are exposed to formal varieties, although informal conversation must provide some kind of baseline for a description of English, if only because of its massively common occurrence. Crystal and Davy do not suggest teaching the productive use of such a variety of English; they propose a policy of exposure to increase the receptive skills of discrimination and comprehension. Similarly, Brown (1977, p. 156) does not approve of teaching foreign learners to produce assimilated and elided phonological forms, but only developing students' listening comprehension of such forms.

One of the main teaching points suggested by such work is that there is much more variety in English than is often realized. This is often not realized since spoken language varies much more than written language, but is more difficult to observe. (cf. Stubbs, 1980: Chapters 5 and 6 for a more detailed discussion.) This point is relevant to both foreign language and mother tongue teaching.

Helping the speaker: rhetoric and oracy

Traditionally, rhetoric studies the effect of a text, written or spoken, on its audience. Classical rhetoric starts from a belief that audiences are open to persuasion. It holds also that ways of presenting arguments can be taught, and that the validity of these arguments can be analysed. There is therefore much debate on questions such as whether eloquence or style of presentation of an argument can compensate for its faulty logic. The systematic study of rhetoric and the structure of discourse was founded by scholars such as Aristotle in his work on narrative and tragedy. Scholars such as the first century Roman orator Quintillian wrote textbooks on the art of speaking, discussing the choice of subject matter and the style of delivery appropriate to different speakers such as politicians, attorneys and preachers. It is perhaps not too much of an exaggeration to say that little progress was made between such work and the twentieth century. Indeed, Corbett (1965) uses the categories of traditional rhetoric to analyse famous public speeches. As well as work on narrative structure already mentioned, however, several scholars have recently pointed out ways of developing the traditional concerns of rhetoric in linguistically interesting ways, which draw on contemporary work in discourse, semantics and pragmatics. For example, different approaches are represented by Nystrand (ed., 1983) which has particular reference to written discourse; Widdowson (1979) which has particular reference to EFL and EST; and papers by Sperber and Wilson (e.g. 1983) which have particular reference to semantic and pragmatic theory.

Rhetoric traditionally has to do also with formal spoken language. Work by Sophists, two thousand years ago, on the successful pleading of legal cases is applied discourse analysis of great social relevance. Teaching of spoken language in the mother tongue often means hints on speech making, or training in interactional skills such as interviewing. However, formal spoken language is influenced by written style: spoken legal language provides an obvious example. Many types are in fact mixed: partly spontaneous spoken language but supported by written notes, such as much lecturing and public speaking. The general topic of the relationship between spoken and written language is too large to discuss fully here, but the following points are particularly relevant. Both written and spoken language show stylistic variation according to the formality of the context of utterance. However, spoken language varies more in form, between casual and formal, than written language does. Furthermore, the more formal spoken English becomes, the closer it moves towards written lexis and syntax. These generalizations are valid for educated standard English, although not always for non-standard varieties of spoken English, nor for other languages. It follows that extending students' functional command of spoken English, by giving them access to a wider variety of styles, means extending their competence in the direction of the standard written language.

As linguists have often pointed out, there are paradoxes involved in correcting or teaching informal language. They would argue that everyone has competence in the informal conversational varieties of their native language: this is simply what is meant by being a native speaker of a language. And I have already mentioned some arguments against teaching foreign learners productive competence in informal spoken varieties of language. Much of this section may therefore seem rather negative or to shade into something else, namely teaching written language. However, some of the confusions involved are rife in much educational research, and current work in the forms and functions of written and spoken discourse can make explicit some of these confusions.

Within the education systems in Britain and the USA, spoken language has in any case been largely undervalued until recently. Education has usually been based predominantly on written language: indeed education has often been equated with literacy. These assertions are inevitably broad and rather crude, but the general point should be clear enough. It is relatively recently that educationalists such as Barnes and Todd (1977) have argued for the value of informal small group talk amongst pupils with no teacher present. Such work usefully draws into question the taken-for-granted equation between education and formal written language. However, it may lack both a systematic formal description of the spontaneous spoken discourse in such teaching situations, and also lack a very convincing educational rationale. It is plausible that small group discussions help children to formulate their ideas, for example, but this is a commonsense observation, rather than a firmly demonstrated point about the relation of language and thought.

The term *oracy* is used to mean the ability in spoken language, either spoken production or listening comprehension. If we are thinking of teaching or assessing oral production, then this could involve, for example, getting pupils to tell stories, give explanations or short lectures to the class, criticise and challenge arguments put forward by other speakers, take part in or chair small group discussions, and so on. Such language would then be judged according to its appropriateness to the situation, whether this involves talking in a group of other pupils, or talking to single adult, teacher or examiner. The term "oracy" is particularly associated with the work of Wilkinson, which began to appear in 1965, with an influential book (Wilkinson *et al.*, 1965). (Many other books and articles by Wilkinson and his colleagues have since appeared: *see* Stubbs, 1981, for a more detailed review of part of this work.) The concern with assessing spoken English is, however, wider than this. In Britain, CSE (Certificate of Secondary Education) boards are obliged to set an oral component in their examinations, and such examinations characteristically attempt to assess such abilities as fluency, clarity, audibility, liveliness, intelligibility, developing an argument or sustaining an interesting discussion. Work on oracy is at present influential amongst British teachers, although it is not entirely satisfactory. The implication of the term appears to be that oracy is parallel to literacy, but has been neglected because no term happens to have been available in English. However, this implied parallelism is very dubious for reasons I have already discussed. The most general logical problem is that spontaneous behaviour is not intended to be assessed. In fact, the question arises as to whether such aspects of a pupil's life should be open to assessment at all: it is in practice impossible to separate a pupil's personality (e.g. his confidence in the test situation) from such language ability. There is a consequent danger that it is the examiner's competence (to elicit effective language) which is assessed, rather than the pupil's competence (to produce it). There is in any case no consensus about what constitutes effective speech appropriate to different purposes. This is because such speech can create and define social situations, as well as defining an individual's membership of social groups. Further, we know very little about language development after the age of about five years, and therefore have very little idea of the conversational competence to expect of ten- and eleven-year-olds.

At the very least, such attempts to assess children's spoken language would have to draw on what we do know about children's discourse and on work on the semantics and pragmatics of natural language. Recent work on child language has moved away from the "sentence centrism" which characterized Chomskyan work, and studies the acquisition of communicative competence in social contexts. Bates (1976), Ervin-Tripp and Mitchell-Kernan, eds (1977) and McTear (1981) are representative of what is now a very extensive literature, although it is largely concerned with the language of young children of up to about six or seven years. In turn, such approaches to child discourse have clear implications for educational research into the differences between linguistic interaction in the home and in school (e.g. Wells, 1981). In addition, any proposals to test children's oracy would have to come to terms with problems such as: the distinction between sentences, utterances, propositions and speech acts; overt and covert meanings, including concepts such as presupposition, entailment and implicature. The ability to make such distinctions is precisely what is being tested in the pupils (in tests proposed, for example, by Wilkinson *et al.*, 1974) and it is only fair that the testers should be able to make explicit just what distinctions the pupils are supposed to be able to make.

In summary, there are both educational research studies and also teaching and assessing techniques which ignore the organization of classroom talk as sequential discourse (*see* Stubbs, 1981).

Teaching about discourse

As part of the content of a syllabus, it is possible to teach directly about different kinds of discourse, such as casual conversation, formal meetings, diaries, songs, legal contracts, and so on: clearly a very long list of such discourse types is imaginable. The aim here would be to give a systematic understanding of discourse organization and structure, the great variety of discourse types in spoken and written language, and the relation between discourse types and social contexts. Such teaching may have different emphases. It may aim to develop students' own communicative competence by increasing the functional range of their language, productive or receptive. Or it may aim to teach linguistic theory directly (cf. p. 221). With younger pupils an intuitive approach would be appropriate, moving towards more explicit and theoretical approaches with older students. (cf. Stubbs, 1980, for discussion of how such textual analysis could fit into a more general English language syllabus; and Tinkel, 1979, for discussion of teaching linguistics in schools.)

There is one aspect of such teaching that I have so far only briefly mentioned, however (p. 224). This is the use of such analysis to open up ideological questions. Recent linguistics has largely ignored the rhetorical, social and public uses of language which are of central concern to educators, for example: the language of politics, law and religion; journalism and the media; technical language; translating and interpreting; and in general the kinds of socially weighted language used to establish and maintain control in school classrooms, courtrooms, doctors' surgeries, mental hospitals, or by "experts" and "science". There are, of course, isolated exceptions to this neglect (e.g. Bolinger, 1980a, 1980b). However, these areas have largely been the province of sociologists, literary critics and others. This is unfortunate, since linguists could offer a great deal to such topics. As Milroy argues (this volume), if socially responsible linguists do not do such analyses, then they will be done, but less well, by others.

A major principle, well studied by linguists, is that people have a very strong tendency to make sense out of nonsense. This is one way in which hearers or readers exploit the redundancy of discourse: they assume that utterances make sense and make predictions about what they think was meant. This applies at all levels, from typographical errors and slips of the tongue to the interpretation of political rhetoric, advertising or whatever. Linguistics has also developed powerful ways of analysing the syntax and semantics of deceptive language. There are different ways of deceiving through language, by smuggling in propositions without explicitly stating them, and this has been a major topic of the current linguistic interest in semantics, pragmatics and discourse presuppositions. There is very considerable theoretical debate in this area but significant progress has been made in studying the differences between propositions which are asserted, or presupposed or entailed by other propositions, or implicated but not stated in so many words. The theoretical debate centres not so much on the surface description of such facts, but on how precisely they should be accounted for within linguistic theory, for example within semantics or in a pragmatic component. (Kempson, 1977, provides a clear summary of the basic issues.)

Much of this work therefore gives detailed definitions of what speakers are committed to in discourse and what they can deny without logical contradiction. Such analyses are directly applicable to the ways, for example, in which news is presented in the media. To cite one very brief example, a recent BBC radio news programme announced:

Sir Geoffrey Howe explained that the budget measures were necessary, because

The use of the factive verb *explain* assumes the truth of the following proposition, in a way that a non-factive such as *claim* would not. Embedding propositions in this way can make them more difficult to identify, and more difficult to challenge. It would therefore be possible to study discussions between political commentators on radio and politicians or other public figures. One could study the propositions to which one or both speakers are committed at a given point in the discourse, whether such propositions have been asserted or are taken for granted, and which propositions are, conversely, under explicit questioning in some way. A detailed study of the syntax and semantics of factive verbs and related linguistic devices is a necessary prerequisite for such a study.[3]

Semantics has not characteristically been applied to practical issues, although it is clear that there are many problems in, for example, the interpretation of legal documents, which are essentially semantic. Linguistics is, however, beginning to provide the tools which would allow such applications in a principled way, and which would therefore answer this complaint from Enoch Powell (1980):

> To sit down to write about 'the English of politics now' is to be appalled by the difficulty of finding any objective instruments which would prevent description from being mere whimsy or subjective guesswork.

See Lerman (1980) for one such extended attempt.

A more adequate account of such features of language in use would demand a detailed discussion of work such as Foucault's (e.g. 1972) attempts to define the discourses which constitute such fields as medicine or economics, and Habermas' (e.g. 1979) work on communicative competence and universal pragmatics. Such a discussion is well beyond the scope of this chapter.

However, it should already be clear that recent work in pragmatics has therefore contributed many concepts which can help to analyse such rhetorical strategies. People have many everyday ways of talking about language, but they do not normally have available ways of talking precisely about such aspects of meaning. Again, I have had room here only for the briefest examples of a type which might be developed by a teacher in the classroom. The basic argument is that language is used for social control, but that the mechanisms of such control are describable and understandable, and that some escape is possible. As Bolinger (1980a, p. 387) argues:

. . . people . . . are bright enough to learn the language of language – with a bit of
help from linguists who have acquired a sense of their social responsibilities.

Conclusions

There is no well established body of work that represents the applications of
discourse analysis. Since discourse analysis is itself not a well defined field,
this is hardly surprising. What I have tried to illustrate in this chapter is the
re-emergent interest amongst both linguists and educators in analysing
connected discourse in socially important contexts. And I have argued that
linguistic approaches to discourse are beginning to provide explicit ways of
discussing aspects of language which are very relevant to the educational
process. I have no doubt that current work in discourse is a very rich source
of ideas for educational theory and practice, if it is well selected and
interpreted. Good teachers may justifiably feel that it provides only a
different slant on what they already do. A general problem with much
applied social research is that it tells practitioners, in different words, what
they know already, if only unconsciously. However, making explicit the
principles of good teaching practice is precisely one important aim of applied
discourse analysis. The systematic study of language in use provides many
ideas for teaching, from lesson plans to whole syllabuses. And just as
importantly, it provides a principled and explicit basis for work that is done,
by relating it to a coherent theory. This is what is meant by applied linguistics:
theory which suggests and illuminates good practice.

Notes

1. This course was taught in summer 1980 at the Peking Language Institute (Beijing
   Yuyan Xueyuan) under the auspices of the British Council. My colleagues on the
   course were Alan Cunningsworth and Cliff Garwood, and I am grateful to them
   for many valuable ideas. I have also used similar material in a much reduced
   version of the course taught at the University of Sana'a, Yemen Arab Republic, at
   Easter 1981. I am grateful to students on both courses for their ideas and reactions.

2. I should also make explicit what is otherwise not clear from my bibliographical
   references alone, that many of the studies discussed in this article derive from
   work originally done at the University of Birmingham, England, or are developments of ideas put forward in Sinclair and Coulthard (1975), although in several
   cases these studies have moved a long way from their origins. These studies are:
   Brazil et al., 1980; Burton, 1980; Carter, 1979; Harris, 1980; Malcolm, 1979;
   McTear, 1981; Montgomery, 1977; Roe, 1977; Stubbs, 1983b; Stubbs and
   Robinson, 1979; Tadros, 1980; Willes, 1978, 1981, 1983.

3. I am grateful to Andrew Gilling (personal communication) for discussion of such

analysis of argumentative discourse. My comments here summarize some aspects of his current work in progress.

Acknowledgements

For comments on a previous draft of this article, I am most grateful to Margaret Berry, Ron Carter and Mike McTear.

References

Adelman, C., ed., (1981). "Uttering, Muttering". Grant McIntyre, London.

Alatis, J. E., ed., (1968). Contrastive Linguistics and its Pedagogical Implications. Report of the 19th Round Table Meeting on Linguistics and Language Studies. University of Georgetown Press, Washington.

Alexander, R. (1980). A learning-to-learn perspective on reading in a foreign language. *System* **8**, **2**, 113–19.

Allen, J. P. B. and Widdowson, H. G. (1974). "English in Physical Science". English in Focus Series. Oxford University Press, London.

Allwright, R. (1979). Language learning through communication practice. *In* Brumfit and Johnson, eds, pp. 167–82.

Atkinson, P. (1981). Ethnomethodology and applied linguistics. *In* Eichheim and Maley, eds, pp. 64–89.

Barnes, D. and Todd, F. (1977). "Communication and Learning in Small Groups". Routledge and Kegan Paul, London.

Barnes, D., Britton, J. and Rosen, H. (1969). "Language, the Learner and the School". Penguin, Harmondsworth.

Bartlett, F. C. (1932). "Remembering". Cambridge University Press, London.

Bates, E. (1976). "Language and Context: the Acquisition of Pragmatics". Academic Press, New York.

Blum, S. and Levenston, E. A. (1978). Universals of lexical simplification. *Lang. Learn.* **28**, **2**, 399–415.

Bolinger, D. (1980a). Fire in a wooden stove: on being aware in language. *In* Michaels and Ricks, *eds*, pp. 379–88.

Bolinger, D. (1980b). "Language the Loaded Weapon". Longman, London.

Bradbury, M. (1965). "Stepping Westward". Secker and Warburg, London.

Bradbury, M. (1976). "Who Do You Think You Are?" Secker and Warburg, London.

Brazil, D., Coulthard, M. and Johns, K. (1980). "Discourse Intonation and Language Teaching". Longman, London.

Britton, J., Burgess, T., Martin, N., McLeod, A. and Rosen, H. (1975). "The Development of Writing Abilities (11–18)". Macmillan Education, London.

Brown, G. (1977). "Listening to Spoken English". Longman, London.

Brown, G. (1978). Understanding spoken language. *TESOL Quart.* **12**, **3**, 271–83.

Brumfit, C. J. and Johnson, K. eds (1979). "The Communicative Approach to Language Teaching". Oxford University Press, London.

Burton, D. (1980). "Dialogue and Discourse". Routledge and Kegan Paul, London.

Callow, K. (1974). "Discourse Considerations in Translating the Word of God". Zondervan, Grand Rapids, Michigan.

Candlin, C. N., Bruton, C. J., Leather, J. L. and Woods, E. (1977). "Doctor–Patient Communication Skills". Graves Medical Audiovisual Library, Chelmsford.

Carter, R. A. (1979). "Towards a Theory of Discourse Stylistics". Unpublished PhD Thesis, University of Birmingham.

Carter, R. A. (1980). Linguistics, the teacher and language development: a Review of Open University Course P232: 'Language Development'. *Educ. Rev.* **32**, 2, 223–28.

Carter, R. A. (1981). Back to basics: assessment, language and the English teacher. *Times Educational Supplement*, 20 February, 1981, 31.

Carter, R. A., ed. (1982). "Linguistics and the Teacher". Routledge and Kegan Paul, London.

Clarke, D. F. and Nation, I. S. P. (1980). Guessing the meaning of words from context: strategy and techniques. *System* **8**, 3, 211–20.

Cochrane, J. ed. (1969). "The Penguin Book of American Short Stories". Penguin, Harmondsworth.

Cole, P. and Morgan, J. L. eds (1975). "Syntax and Semantics", Vol. 3, "Speech Acts". Academic Press, New York.

Corbett, E. P. J. (1965). "Classical Rhetoric for the Modern Student". Oxford University Press, New York.

Crystal, D. and Davy, D. (1975). "Advanced Conversational English". Longman, London.

Czerniewska, P. (1981). The teacher, language development and linguistics: a response to Ronald Carter's Review of the Open University Course PE232, 'Language Development'. *Educ. Rev.* **31**, 1, 37–9.

Darian, S. (1979). The role of redundancy in language and language teaching. *System* **7**, 1, 47–59.

Davies, A. (1978). Textbook situations and idealised language. *Work in Progress* **11**, 120–33. Department of Linguistics, University of Edinburgh.

Dolley, C. ed. (1967). "The Penguin Book of English Short Stories". Penguin, Harmondsworth.

Dressler, W. V. ed. (1978). "Current Trends in Textlinguistics". De Gruyter, Berlin.

Eichheim, H. and Maley, A. eds (1981). "Fremdsprachenunterricht im Spannungsfeld zwischen Gesellschaft, Schule und Wissenschaften". Goethe Institut, Munich.

Enkvist, N. E. (1981). Some rhetorical aspects of text linguistics. *In* Eichheim and Maley, eds, pp. 172–206.

Ervin-Tripp, S. and Mitchell-Kernan, C. eds (1977). "Child Discourse". Academic Press, New York.

Feyerabend, P. (1978). "Science in a Free Society". NLB, London.

Flanders, N. (1970). "Analysing Teacher Behaviour". Addison Wesley, London.

Foucault, M. (1972). "The Archaeology of Knowledge". Tavistock, London.

Gannon, P. and Czerniewska, P. (1980). "Using Linguistics: an Educational Focus". Edward Arnold, London.

Genette, G. (1980). "Narrative Discourse". Blackwell, London.

Givón, T., ed. (1979). "Syntax and Semantics" vol. 12, "Discourse and Syntax". Academic Press, New York.

Gleason, H. A. (1968). Contrastive analysis in discourse structure. *In* Alatis, ed. pp. 39–63.

Godard, D. (1977). Same setting, different norms: phone call beginnings in France and the United States. *Lang. in Soc.* **6**, 209–19.

Gordon, J. C. B. (1980). A case-study in misinterpretation: a note on some disseminations of Bernstein by educationalists. *UEA Papers in Linguistics* (= University of East Anglia), **12**, 45–52

Gorman, T. ed. (1977). "Language and Literacy: Current Issues and Research". International Institute for Adult Literacy Methods, Tehran.

Grice, H. (1975). Logic and conversation. *In* Cole and Morgan, eds, 1975, pp. 41–48.

Gudschinsky, S. C. (1976). "Literacy: the Growing Influence of Linguistics". Mouton, The Hague.

Habermas, J. (1979). "Communication and the Evolution of Society". Heinemann, London.

Hall, E. T. (1959). "The Silent Language". Doubleday, New York.

Halliday, M. A. K. (1978). "Language as Social Semiotic". Edward Arnold, London.

Halliday, M. A. K. and Hasan, R. (1976). "Cohesion in English". Longman, London.

Hargie, O., Dickson, D. and Saunders, C. (1981). "Social Skills in Interpersonal Communication". Croom Helm, London.

Harris, S. (1980). "Language Interaction in Magistrates' Courts". Unpublished PhD Thesis, University of Nottingham.

Holmes, J. (1983). The structure of teachers' directives: a sociolinguistic analysis. *In* "Communicative Competence" (J. Richards and R. Schmidt, eds). London, London.

Hudson, R. A. (1980). "Sociolinguistics". Cambridge University Press, London.

Hutchins, W. J. (1977). On the structure of scientific texts. *UEA Papers in Linguistics* (= University of East Anglia) **5**, 106–28.

Kaplan, R. B. (1967). Contrastive rhetoric and the teaching of composition. *TESOL Quart.* **1**, **4**, 10–16.

Kaplan, R. B. ed. (1980). "On the Scope of Applied Linguistics". Newbury House, Rowley, Massachusetts.

Keen, J. (1978). "Teaching English: A Linguistic Approach". Methuen, London.

Kempson, R. M. (1977). "Semantic Theory". Cambridge University Press, London.

Labov, W. (1972a). "Language in the Inner City". University of Pennsylvania Press, Philadelphia.

Labov, W. (1972b). The transformation of experience in narrative syntax. *In* Labov, 1972a, pp. 354–96.

Labov, W. and Fanshel, D. (1977). "Therapeutic Discourse". Academic Press, New York.

Lerman, C. L. (1980). A Sociolinguistic Study of Political Discourse: The Nixon Whitehouse Conversations. Unpublished PhD Thesis, University of Cambridge.

Lester, M. ed. (1970). "Readings in Applied Transformational Grammar". Holt, Rinehart and Winston, New York.

Levine, A. ed. (1971). "Penguin English Reader". Penguin, Harmondsworth.

Lodge, D. (1975). "Changing Places". Secker and Warburg, London.

Longacre, R. E. (1977). Discourse analysis and literacy. *In* Gorman, ed. pp. 71–88.

Lunzer, E. and Gardner, K. eds (1978). "The Effective Use of Reading". Heinemann, London.

McTear, M. F. (1981). The Development of Conversation in Pre-School Children. Unpublished PhD Thesis, Ulster Polytechnic.

Malcolm, I. (1979). Classroom Communication and the Aboriginal Child: A Socio-linguistic Investigation in Western Australian Primary Schools. Unpublished PhD Thesis, University of Western Australia.

Maley, A. and Duff, A. eds (1976). "Words". Cambridge University Press, London.

Mandler, J. M. and Johnson, N. S. (1977). Remembrance of things parsed: story structure and recall. *Cognitive Psychology* 9, 111–51.

Michaels, L. and Ricks, C. eds, (1980). "The State of the Language". University of California Press, London.

Montgomery, M. (1977). "The Structure of Lectures". Unpublished MA Thesis, University of Birmingham.

Munby, J. (1978). "Communicative Syllabus Design". Cambridge University Press, London.

Nash, W. (1980). "Designs in Prose". Longman, London.

Nystrand, M. ed. (1983). "What Writers Know." Academic Press, New York.

Ochs Keenan, E. (1976). The universality of conversational postulates. *Lang. in Soc.* 5, 67–80.

Ochs, E. (1979). Planned and unplanned discourse. *In* Givón, ed., pp. 51–80.

Oller, J. W. Jr. (1979). "Language Tests at School". Longman, London.

Page, N. (1973). "Speech in the English Novel". Longman, London.

Pirsig, R. (1974). "Zen and the Art of Motorcycle Maintenance". Bodley Head, London.

Powell, J. E. (1980). The language of politics. *In* Michaels and Ricks, eds, pp. 432–39.

Pratt, M. L. (1977). "Toward a Speech Act Theory of Literary Discourse". Indiana University Press, Bloomington.

Price-Williams, D. and Sabsay, S. (1979). Communicative competence amongst severely retarded persons. *Semiotica* 26, 1/2, 35–63.

Propp, V. (1928). "Morphology of the Folktale". Trans. L. Scott. Indiana University Press, Bloomington.

Quirk, R., Greenbaum, S., Leech, G. and Svartvik, J. (1972). "A Grammar of Contemporary English". Longman, London.

Roe, P. (1977). "The Notion of Difficulty in Scientific Text". Unpublished PhD Thesis, University of Birmingham.

Rosen, H. (1978). Signing on. *The New Review*, Feb. 1978. Reprinted in *BAAL Newslett.* 7, June 1979, 4–13.

Roulet, E. (1981). L'analyse de conversations authentiques dans une pédagogie intégrée de la langue maternelle et des langues secondes. Paper presented to Colloque de Linguistique Appliquée de Berne, 1981.

Sampson, G. (1980). "Schools of Linguistics". Hutchinson, London.

Searle, J. R. (1975). The logical status of fictional discourse. *New Lit. Hist.* 6, 2.

Short, M. H. (1981). Discourse analysis and the analysis of drama. *Applied Linguistics* 2, 2, 180–202.

Sinclair, J. McH. ed. (1980). Applied Discourse Analysis. Thematic Issue of *Appl. Linguistics* 1, 3.

Sinclair, J. McH. (1981). Planes of discourse in literature. Mimeo, University of Birmingham.

Sinclair, J. McH. and Coulthard, R. M. (1975). "Towards an Analysis of Discourse". Oxford University Press, London.

Smith, F. (1973). "Psycholinguistics and Reading". Holt, Rinehard and Winston, London.

Sperber, D. and Wilson, D. (1983). Irony and the use-mention distinction. *In* "Radical Pragmatics" (P. Cole, ed.). Academic Press, New York.

Stein, N. L. and Glenn, C. G. (1979). An analysis of story comprehension in elementary school children. *In* "Discourse Processing (R. Freedle, ed.). Ablex, Norwood, New Jersey.

Strunk, W. Jr. and White, E. B. (1979). "The Element of Style", 3rd edition. Macmillan, New York.

Stubbs, M. (1980)."Language and Literacy". Routledge and Kegan Paul, London.

Stubbs, M. (1980). What is English? Modern English language in the curriculum. *English in Australia* **51**, 3–20. Reprinted in Carter, ed. 1982.

Stubbs, M. (1981). Oracy and educational lingusitics: the quality (of the theory) of listening. *First Lang.* **2**, 21–30.

Stubbs, M. (1983a). Stir until the plot thickens. *In* "Literary Text and Language Study" (R. A. Carter and D. Burton, eds), pp. 56–85. Edward Arnold, London.

Stubbs, M. (1983b). "Discourse Analysis: the Sociolinguistic Analysis of Natural Language". Blackwell, Oxford.

Stubbs, M. and Robinson, B. (1979). Analysing classroom lanugage. *In* "Observing Classroom Language (M. Stubbs, B. Robinson and S. Twite, eds), Block 5, PE232. Open University Press, Milton Keynes.

Tadros, A. (1980). Prediction in economics text. *ELR Journal* (= English Language Research) **1**, 42–59. Mimeo, University of Birmingham.

Tinkel, T. (1979). A proposal for the teaching of linguistics at the secondary school level, *MALS Journal* (= Midland Association for Linguistic Studies) **4**, Spring 1979, 79–100.

Todorov, T. (1969). "Grammaire du Décaméron". Mouton, The Hague.

Van Dijk, T. A. (1981). Discourse studies and education. *Appl. Linguistics* **2**, **1**, 1–26.

Van Dijk, T. A. and Kintsch, W. (1978). Cognitive psychology and discourse: recalling and summarising stories. *In* Dressler, ed., pp. 61–80.

Van Ek, J. A. (1975). "The Threshhold Level". Strasbourg, Council of Europe.

Von Faber, H. and Heid, M. eds (1981). "Lesen in der Fremdsprache". Goethe Institut, Munich.

Waters, H. S. (1980). 'Class news': A single-subject longitudinal study of prose production and schema formation during childhood. *J. Verbal Learning and Verbal Behaviour* **19**, 152–67.

Wells, G. (1981). Describing children's linguistic development at home and at school. *In* Adelman, ed., pp. 134–62.

Widowson, H. G. (1975a). "Stylistics and the Teaching of Literature". Longman, London.

Widdowson, H. G. (1975b). "An Applied Linguistic Approach to Discourse Analysis". Unpublished PhD Thesis, University of Edinburgh.

Widdowson, H. G. (1977). The partiality and relevance of linguistic descriptions. *In* Widdowson, 1979a, pp. 234–45

Widdowson, H. G. (1978). "Teaching Language as Communication". Oxford University Press, London.

Widdowson, H. G. (1979a). "Explorations in Applied Linguistics". Oxford University Press, London.

Widdowson, H. G. (1979b). Notional syllabuses. *In* Widdowson, 1979a, pp. 247–50.

Widdowson, H. G. (1980a). Applied linguistics: the pursuit of relevance. *In* Kaplan, ed., pp. 74–87.

Widdowson, H. G. (1980b). Models and fictions. *Appl. Linguistics* **1**, **2**, 165–70.

Wilkins, D. A. (1976). "Notional Syllabuses". Oxford University Press, London.

Wilkinson, A. M., Davies, A. and Atkinson, D. (1965). Spoken English. Educational Review Occasional Publications, 2, Supplement to 17, 2.

Wilkinson, A. M., Stratta, L. and Dudley, P. (1974). "The Quality of Listening". Schools Council Research Studies. Macmillan, London.

Willes, M. (1978). Early lessons learned too well. Supplementary reading to Language Development. PE232. Open University Press, Milton Keynes.

Willes, M. (1981). Learning to take part in classroom interaction. *In* "Adult–Child Conversation" (P. French and M. Maclure, eds). Croom Helm, London.

Willes, M. (1983). "Children into Pupils". Routledge and Kegan Paul, London.

9

Variation theory and language learning

Ralph W. Fasold

Introduction

In spite of the use of a special term, "variation theory" should not be thought of as a new linguistic model in competition with existing ones, but as an attempt to add a dimension to linguistic theory. It is self-evident that variation and change are pervasive throughout language. All one has to do is listen to the various geographical and social dialects of English (or any other language) or listen carefully to one's own language use in less and more formal styles to become aware of linguistic variation. And of course anyone who has tried to read Chaucer in the original or even the King James Version of the Bible is immediately made aware of language change over time. Variation theory is the attempt on the part of a number of linguists to develop linguistic theory in such a way that it can account for variation and change as an ongoing and observable phenomenon.

The very attempt to do this is somewhat controversial because it has been the usual practice in this century to think of language as a set of photographs taken with a still camera arranged on a page in an album (the various styles and dialect that exist at a given time). Historical linguistics has usually been thought of rather as a series of these pages arranged in (temporal) order. The kind of linguist I have just referred to would like to develop a theory that treats language more like a motion picture film. Most of the linguists working on variation theory, at least in the US, have used a version of transformational-generative syntax and phonology. This theoretical choice has been more a matter of convenience than conviction, and not all studies of linguistic variation have made that choice (cf. Trudgill, 1974).

The attempt to develop a "motion picture" theory of language has forced linguists to face two crucial issues that have a bearing on language learning. The first issue is the systematic nature of variation and change. The second, which in a way follows from the first, has to do with the nature of the linguistic knowledge or ability of people who know more than one language or dialect.

Variation and change

The serious investigation of linguistic variation and change that was begun by Labov (1966, 1969) revealed that the linguistic environment around an element undergoing variation systematically influenced the *frequency* with which each variant could be expected to appear. The term "linguistic environment" is being used here in a technical sense to mean the kinds of vowels, consonants and grammatical categories that occur close to the varying element. For example, it is a fact about English that the voiceless stops /p t k/ are always aspirated (i.e. pronounced [p^h], [t^h] and [k^h] when they occur at the beginning of a word, but are unaspirated (pronounced [p], [t] and [k] after /s/. The environment (no sound at all in the same word before the /p/ in *pill*, /s/ before the /p/ in *spill*) has a *categorical* effect on aspiration – categorical in the sense that there is *always* aspiration in word-initial position and *never* after /s/. The careful study of linguistic variation has revealed that the same kinds of environmental considerations regularly influence the frequency of one variant or the other. That is, linguistic environments have not only an always–never effect but an *often–seldom* effect as well.

To see how this might work, consider the rule of contraction in English. There is no doubt that the rule applies variably. A speaker can equally well say *He's a good man* or *He is a good man* without having violated the rule of English. The effect of contraction, of course, is to remove the first vowel (in some cases also the first consonant) in a particular class of words. The traditional way to express this in linguistic grammars is to invoke the concept of *optionality*. Contraction would be formally designated as an optional process and nothing more included in the theory about it. A grammar writer might point out in passing that contraction is rather more colloquial and the full form more formal, but this kind of information would not appear in theoretical statements.

The close study of contraction carried out by Labov (1969) revealed that, quite apart from stylistic considerations, particular aspects of the linguistic environment had a systematic influence. For example, if the word preceding a contractable word ends with a vowel, contraction is more likely. All else being equal, a speaker who says *Mary is going* is more likely to contract *is* that a speaker who says *Marion is going*. The grammatical category of the following construction also has a predictable effect. If a verb follows, contracton is most likely; if a noun phrase follows, contraction is less likely; and if the following construction is a locative expression or an adjective, contraction is least likely. If one had to bet, one would be well advised to bet that a speaker who said *The play is beginning* would contract rather than if they were to say *The play is a musical* or *The play is at the Folger Theatre*. And of the latter two sentences, the first is a better bet for contraction than the second.

It is not only possible to identify environmental influences that favour or disfavour contraction, but to determine that some of them have a greater effect than others. In the case of contraction, the various environments would be ordered as in Table 9.1. The percentages are from Labov's New York City study, but the *relative* ordering can be expected to be the same in any variety of English.

Table 9.1 Percent frequency of contraction by weighted environment (data from Labov, 1969)

Environment	Example	Percent deleted
Vowel precedes, verb follows	Mary is going	86
Vowel precedes, noun phrase follows	Mary is a girl	80
Vowel precedes, adjective or locative follows	Mary is at home	70
Consonant precedes, verb follows	Marion is going	65
Consonant precedes, noun phrase follows	Marion is a girl	37
Consonant precedes, adjective or locative follows	Marion is at home	25

A set of environments arranged in this way is ordered according to what Bailey (1973) calls *environment weight*. The environment that includes the most and strongest influencing elements is called the *heaviest* environment; the one with the fewest and weakest is the *lightest*. The contraction environments have been ordered from heaviest to lightest in Table 9.1. This arrangement makes it clear that the effect of the preceding sound is greater than the effect of the following construction. It also makes it clear what is meant by an "often–seldom" effect. Unlike the aspiration case, even the heaviest environment does not always produce contraction. In Labov's data, full forms were observed 14 per cent of the time in the environment most favourable to contraction. Similarly, the lightest environment did not prevent contraction, since speakers contracted once out of every four times in this environment. Except for the often–seldom rather than always–never nature of the case, the analysis of contraction parallels the analysis of stop aspiration. The environments are made up purely of linguistic elements in both cases. For this reason, a linguistic theory that takes variation into account will account for both.

The view of language variation I have just presented is related to a theory of language change through time (Bailey, 1973). Basically, this theory suggests changes begin in heavy environments and proceed through inter-mediate environments to the lightest ones. As this process continues, the newer forms become more frequent in the heavier and earlier environments until they may exclude the older form entirely. The replacement of the older forms by newer ones continues until it reaches the lightest environment, at which time the change is said to have gone to completion. Of course, not all variable rules in languages are on their way to completion. There is no reason to believe that contraction, for example, will go to completion, and the word *is* will disappear from the English language! Rules that are variable but are not on their way to completion are called *stagnant rules*.

Some of the more recent research on second language acquisition indi-cates that the same process may be at work when an individual learns another language. In an excellently conceived and executed study of bi-lingualism, Gatbonton-Segalowitz (1976) found evidence that a second language learner acquires features in the same way that new features move into a language over time. Gatbonton-Segalowitz examined the acquisition of English by native French speakers in Quebec. She studied in greatest detail the pronunciation of English /ð/ and /θ/ and word-intial /h/. Canadian French speakers are inclined to substitute [d] for [ð], [t] for [θ] and to drop initial /h/. For each of these pronunciations, Gatbonton-Segalowitz found that the English pronunciation would be mastered in some environments more readily than in others. She was able to arrange five environments from heavy to light, and discovered that the speakers who were learning English fell into a pattern similar in principle to the one for English contraction in Table 9·1. The results appear in Table 9·2. The differences between the two tables are, firstly, that Table 9·1 is a summary of the treatment of contraction by an entire sample of speakers, whereas Table 9·2 displays the results for each speaker individually. Secondly, Table 9·1 gives percentages of contraction in each environment, whereas Table 9·2 includes only three levels of variation; (1) indicates the exclusive use of [ð], (2) indicates the exclusive use of [d], and (1,2) indicates variation between [ð] and [d]. Thirdly (and trivially), weighted environments from a column in Table 9·1 and a row in Table 9·2.

A statistically significant majority of the subjects fit the above pattern. It would appear that the speakers towards the top of Table 9·2 have learned the pronunciation of English [ð] better than those towards the bottom of the table. Gatbonton-Segalowitz obtained independent evidence that this is the case. A group of native speakers of English were asked to rate the same subjects subjectively on their ability to speak English well. There was a statistically significant positive correlation of the rank order of their judgments and the rank order of the speakers as determined by Table 9·2.

Table 9.2 Variation between [ð] and [d] in the speech of Quebec French speakers learning English (from Gatbonton-Segalowitz, 1976)

Speakers	Heaviest		Environments		Lightest
	1	*2*	*3*	*4*	*5*
1	1	1	1	1	1
2	1	1	1	1	12
3	1	1	1	12	12
4	1	1	12	12	12
5	1	12	12	12	12
6	12	12	12	12	12
7	12	12	12	12	2
8	12	12	12	2	2
9	12	12	2	2	2
10	12	2	2	2	2
11	2	2	2	2	2

The Quebec French speakers are not the only ones who acquire foreign language pronunciations by the same mechanism that is found in language variation by native speakers. In a study of Japanese speakers learning English, Dickerson (1975), and Dickerson and Dickerson (1977), found the same patterns. One of the English consonants that is difficult for Japanese speakers is /z/. Dickerson found that the difficulty in pronouncing an English [z] depends very much on the phonological environment in which it occurred. The lightest environment for the production of an acceptable [z] (i.e the most difficult one) was immediately preceding /θ/, /ð/, /t/, /d/, /č/ and /ǰ/. Slightly less difficult were instances in which the target /z/ occurred immediately before silence. The next heavier (easier) environment was when /z/ preceded any consonant except the ones that define the lightest environment, and the heaviest was when /z/ occurred directly before a vowel. The percentage of acceptable pronunciation for a typical speaker when reading dialogues appears as Fig. 1. In the figure, "V" symbolizes vowels, "T", the

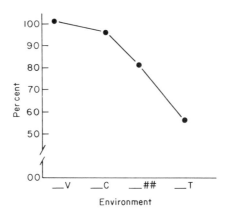

Fig. 1. Percentage acceptable pronunciation of English /z/ in four environments by a Japanese speaker. (Adapted from Dickerson, 1975, p. 403.)

consonants that make up the lightest environment, "C", all other consonants and "♯ ♯", silence.

The English /r/ is difficult for learners from many language backgrounds, including Japanese speakers. Dickerson and Dickerson (1977) present data that demonstrates that some environment inhibit the English pronunciation of /r/ more than others, as in the case of /z/. In particular, for prevocalic /r/, the Dickersons found that following low vowels were the heaviest environment, mid vowels next and high vowels the lightest. The data for one typical speaker appear as Fig. 2.

Gabonton-Segalowitz' work suggests that French speakers acquire more

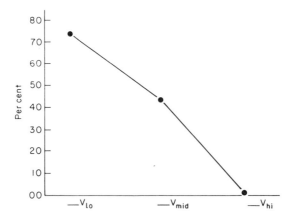

Fig. 2. Percentage of acceptable pronunciations of /r/ in three environments by a Japanese speaker. (Adapted from Dickerson and Dickerson, 1977, p. 20.)

English-like pronunciations in order by environment in the same manner as sound change through time. In other words, it seems quite natural to assume that Table 9·2 could have been produced with data from one speaker over time as well as with data from several speakers of varying proficiency levels at one time. The Dickersons were able to provide evidence of this through longitudinal study of their subjects. Data from the Japanese speakers learning English were collected three times over nine months. The pattern of progress was clear: by and large speakers increased the proportions of English pronunciations of /z/ and /r/ as time went on. At all three test times, the proportions of acceptable pronunciations was greatest in the heavier environments and less in the lighter environments.

All of this suggests the possibility of a higher level of sophistication in teaching the pronunciations of a second language than is usual in language classrooms. If it is generally the case, as it seems to be, that the difficult sounds of a second language are easier to pronounce in some phonological contexts than they are in others, it should be possible to structure the language teaching programme so that a difficult new sound is introduced and practised at first in the heaviest environments only. When the learners have gained proficiency in these contexts, the next harder environments could be drilled and so on. In the long run, the phenomena discovered by Gatbonton-Segalowitz and the Dickersons might well lead to really elegant tests of the mastery of pronunciation proficiency. The learners' speech could be tape-recorded and key target language sounds tabulated in various phonological environments. The score would be derived from the frequency of high quality pronunciations of the sound relative to environment weight. While a test of this sort is conceivable at present, it would no doubt be impratical to score such a test as long as a human evaluator has to listen to each sound in each environment for each speaker. Future advances in automatic speech recognition technology, however, may evenutally make it possible to score a test like this using a computer.

The research on second language learning from the variation theory perspective leads to an emphasis on the *continuous* nature of language learning that contrasts with the discrete *stage* approach often used in this kind of research. There is a continuous increase in the use of acceptable pronunciations across environments. The longitudinal studies reported by the Dickersons shows that there is another continuum in which learners produce ever higher proportions of target language pronunciations as time passes. A second look at Fig. 2 shows that there is yet another continuum, in the environments themselves. Figure 2 suggests, a bit misleadingly, that acceptable English /r/ is produced by Japanese learners least often before high vowels, somewhat more frequently before mid vowels and most often before low vowels, as if these were three distinct environments. Apparently the real generality is that /r/ is increasingly easy to pronounce the lower the tongue height of the following vowel. Some reflection on the articulatory facts of this suggested generality will show how plausible it is.

But there is more. Not only does the frequency of quality pronunciations increase along an environment continuum (where the environments themselves may be continuous in nature) and also through time, but there is a *style* continuum as well (Dickerson and Dickerson, 1977, p. 21, cf. Beebe, 1980). As the style becomes more formal, acceptable pronunciations of the target language sound increase, even when environment is controlled. Perhaps most surprisingly, it is not only the *quantity* of acceptable pronunciations that systematically varies, but the *quality* as well. So far, by simply presenting percentages of acceptable pronunciations, we have given the impression that either a learner can pronounce a target language sound, or not. But as the Dickersons point out, there is a *range* of increasingly close approximations of the target language sound. For example, a Japanese speaker may use any of the following sound segments as an approximation for English /z/: [ẓ] (a shortened [z]), [dz], [s] or nothing at all (L. Dickerson, 1975, p. 401). In learning /r/, Japanese speakers use [r], [ř], [l], [ḷ] and [ð] (Dickerson and Dickerson, 1977, p. 19). In each case, the variants that are observed can be understood as a more or less successful attempt by the speaker to master the foreign sound.

The examples we have used so far all have to do with pronunciation. Does the same apply to syntax? In an attempt to answer this question, Adamson (1980) reviewed quantitative data on second language acquisition and conducted his own experiment on the acquisition of English main verb negation by native speakers of Spanish. He concluded that the acquisition of this structure involves the variation between a series of less English-like and more English-like approximations of main verb negation, as the Dickersons found in phonology. However, learning syntactic rules was less likely to be influenced by environmental factors than learning phonology. While there was some evidence of environmental influence, much of the variation was better accounted for by combinations of grammar rules, some of them neither English nor Spanish, to which probabilities could be assigned. These probabilities were associated with the rule as a whole and not determined by the linguistic environment. Furthermore, as learning progresses, use of the more English-like rules increased in likelihood at the expense of the less English-like rules. Adamson found that much of what he observed was best analysed using the model developed by the Heidelberg Forschungsprojekt "Pidgin-Deutsch" (1978), a study of the acquisition of German by "guest-workers" in Germany from other countries.

According to Dickerson (1975, p. 406–407), all of this implies a new outlook on the part of language teachers.

The language teacher should not despair when he encounters variability; rather, he should adopt a point of view which *expects variability*. . . . The teacher is urged to look at degrees of attainment, not just at a right/wrong dichotomy of English versus non-English. Even if the student never reaches the target sound, credit should be given when, over time, he modifies his pronunciation from 'very wrong' to 'not so wrong' or from 'not so wrong' to 'almost right'. In addition, even though the student may not reach the target 100 per cent of the time, credit should be given when, over time, he increases the use of variants closer to the target.

Code-switching

Once linguists decided to construct theories of language that included change and variation, they were forced to revise the prevalent notion of what it meant to speak a certain dialect or style. The prevalent notion was that the object of study in linguistics was ultimately a single style of an individual speaker. This entity, called an *idiolect*, could then be collected with a set of sufficently similar idiolects to make up a dialect. A language would then be made up of a set of dialects. Strictly speaking, a separate technical grammar would have to be constructed for each individual idiolect, which meant that a language would be made up of hundreds of thousands, perhaps millions of grammars. This was not seen as a very great problem, since these myriads of grammars would be very similar to each other, differing in the occasional minor detail. Nonetheless, sometimes a linguist would become uncomfortable with this view of language and attempt to modify linguistic theory accordingly. None of these attempts was very successful.

The implications of the one grammar for each style and dialect view of language became particularly clear with the study of Vernacular Black English (VBE) in the United States. Early studies of VBE assumed a separate grammar with code-switching (e.g. Dillard, 1970). When a speaker of VBE was observed using the more exotic features of his dialect, such as the absence of the present tense forms of *to be*, he was assumed to be using the grammar of VBE. If he sometimes used the *to be* forms as called for by the grammar of standard English, it was assumed either than he had switched to his standard English grammar or was experiencing interference from one dialect while using the grammar of the other. The inadequacy of such a model becomes quite clear in passages such as the following one, spoken by a preadolescent black youngster in Detroit (Wolfram, 1969, p. 170):

Raymond, I thing he __ thirteen. Oh, and I got another one, he live back over that way -- his name *is* Robert. I think he __ eleven. And I'm eleven and Lonnie Joe, he __ twelve and Little Man *is* fourteen and Richard *is* twelve.

The speaker switches between constructions in which *is* is absent and those in which it is present rapidly in the same discourse. It would be difficult to discover a credible motivation for the claim that he has switched between standard English and VBE within this discourse. Furthermore, closer inspection would reveal that copula absence and presence is governed by the environmental conditions discussed earlier. In particular, the copula is absent whenever the subject is a pronoun and it is present whenever the subject is a noun phrase. Although the presence of a pronoun *versus* a full noun phrase *determines* treatment of the copula in this short passage, investigations of larger amounts of data show that subject type is really an often–seldom effect, not an always–never one. Similar variable constraints can readily be found for other features of this dialect and others. The discovery of variable constraints makes it clear that separate grammars with code-switching is not the correct way to account for this kind of variation.

Further evidence leading to the same conclusion was presented by Berdan (1975), who showed that the alternation between non-standard and standard features of English did not always co-occur in narratives by speakers of VBE. If speakers are assumed to switch dialects by switching from one grammar to another like a bilingual speaker switching from English to French would, it is reasonable to expect that *all* the features of VBE would be dropped in favour of the corresponding features of standard English at about the same time. Berdan's tabulations revealed that this was not the case; speakers would adopt some features of standard English while maintaining VBE for others. These latter features would alternate with standard English features later in the narrative, but some of the earlier standard features would have been replaced by VBE. There was very little evidence indeed for a cohesive "code".

Even if there is doubt about how appropriate the separate grammar approach is for explaining dialects and styles, it would seem to work much better as a model for what a bilingual speaker knows. When bilinguals use one language rather than another, they are assumed to switch from one grammar to another. When they speak a second language with a foreign accent, it is generally assumed that they are using grammar and pronunciation rules from the grammar of their first language while speaking the second (interference). A few scholars who have studied bilingualism have suspected that the notion of separate grammars for separate languages might be too simple even in some cases of bilingualism. Discussing this issue, Haugen (1972, p. 317) comes to the following conclusion:

> In the world of the bilingual anything is possible, from virtual separation of the two codes to their virtual coalescence. The reasons for this are clearly rooted in the possibilities for *variable competence* in the human brain.

Haugen sees quite clearly that it is not necessary to assume that every bilingual has two separate and distinct grammars. This is one possibility, but it is also possible that they have a single grammar which contains elements of two languages, but which is different from the grammars of each that a monolingual speaker would have. Degrees of distinctness and coalescence between these two extremes are also possible.

One scholar who agrees with Haugen is Poplack (1980). Poplack has studied switching between English and Spanish by people of Puerto Rican ancestry in New York City. A great deal of the code-switching she observed consisted of switches back and forth between English more than once in the same sentence (Poplack, 1980, p. 589):

> Why make Carol *sentarse atras pa' que* (sit in the back so) everybody has to move *pa' que se salga* (for her to get out)?

Her study led her to hypothesize that "bilingual speakers might have expanding grammars of the type depicted in Fig. 9.3." (Poplack, 1980, p. 615). I have reproduced her figure in slightly modified form as in Fig. 3. The shaded areas represent the relative amount of overlap as evidenced by code-switching.

Fig. 3. Representation of bilingual code-switching grammars. (From Poplack, 1980, p. 615.)

A dramatic example of just how extensively grammars of different languages can be merged is provided by Gumperz and Wilson (1971). They investigated the multilingual case of Kupwar, a village in the state of Maharashtra, India. The major linguistic and social groups are the two land-holding groups, the Jains, speakers of Kannada, and the Moslems, speakers of Urdu; and the landless labourers who speak Marathi. The three languages have been in contact for hundreds of years without any of them replacing any of the others. There are cultural and social reasons for such stable multilingualism. Not only do the three languages exist in the village, but almost all the local men use two or all three of them. Therefore, not only the village, but the individual villagers are multilingual. The duration and intensity of the contact among the three languages have had a profound effect on their grammars.

The three languages are not particularly closely related historically. Urdu and Marathi are both Indo-Aryan languages, but not especially closely related members of that family. The degree of relatedness might be compared to the relationship between French and Spanish. Kannada is a Dravidian language from an entirley different language family with strikingly different grammatical features. Over the centuries, the three languages as spoken in Kupwar have developed a converged grammar to the extent that they all share the same grammar differing only in lexicon and morpho-phonemics. As Gumperz and Wilson (1971, p. 155) put it: "We may say, therefore, that the codes used in code-switching situations in Kupwar have a *single syntactic surface structure*".

An example of how it works is to be found in the subordinate construction of indirect statements and questions. In Urdu and in Marathi, indirect quotations are introduced by the conjunction *ki* meaning "that", in the following manner:

S_1 ki s_2
He said   that   I'm going now.

In Kannada, the indirect quotation comes first and the conjunction is a form of the verb meaning "say", as follows:

S_2 conj S_1
I'm going now   so saying   he said

In Kupwar, all three languages use the construction found in standard Urdu and Marathi. The examples below compare standard Urdu (U), Kupwar Urdu (KuU), Kupwar Marathi (KuM), and Kupwar Kannada (KuK).

U	bol-o	ki kəhā	gəy-a	tha	kəl
KuU	bol-o	ki khā	gəe	te	kəl
KuM	sang-a	ki kutt	gelə	hota	kal
KuK	kel ri	ki yəlli	hog	idni	ninni
	tell	*that where*	*went*		*yesterday*

The sentence means "Tell (me) where you went yesterday." Kupwar Kannada, although it retains Kannada words, has altered the syntax radically to fit the coalesced local grammar. The case of Kupwar bilingualism seems strong evidence that Haugen is right and that even whole language bilingualism need not entail a separate grammar for each language a bilingual knows.

It may appear that Haugen's insight has simply turned up a new horror for language teachers. Not only do language teachers have to get across new syntactic patterns, pronunciations and vocabulary but, it would seem, have to do their best to prevent students from acquiring a merged grammar that does not conform to the standard of either the old language or the new one. There are two reasons why this is not something to worry about. First of all, it seems that merged grammars are most likely to develop in communities where two languages are used in everyday life, such as among Puerto Ricans in New York or the residents of Kupwar. Secondly, and more important, it is not clear that merged grammars are always and everywhere to be avoided. Poplack concluded that the most intimate "intra-sentential" switching represented both the highest degree of merger and the *greatest degree of bilingual acquisition*. To see why this is so, it is necessary to understand the two constraints Poplack found on code-switching: (1) the free morpheme constraint and (2) the equivalence constraint.

The *free morpheme constraint* predicts that a switch from one language to another cannot occur if the last item spoken in one language or the first in the other is a bound morpheme. For example *-iendo* is the approximate Spanish equivalent of English *-ing*. The free morpheme constraint predicts that a switch producing an utterance like "eat*iendo*" will not occur. In fact, Poplack knows of no attestations of such a switch unless one of the morphemes has been phonologically integrated into the language of the other (Poplack, 1980, p. 586). The *equivalence constraint* means that a switch will not occur within a constituent that does not map onto the structure of the other language in a straightforward manner. For example, consider the following sentence in the two languages:

English:	He	: would bring it	: fast
Spanish:	(él)	: la trajera	: ligero
	he	*it would bring*	*fast*

By the equivalence constraint, switches can only occur at the points marked by colons. It is not possible to switch within the phrase meaning "would bring it" because the mapping between the two languages is not direct. In English, the pronominal object follows the main verb, in Spanish it precedes it. The verbal semantics that English handles with the modal auxiliary "would" are handled in Spanish in the verb morphology. As a result, while it is possible, for example, for a bilingual to say:

He would bring it *ligero*

it would *not* be possible to say either:

*He it *trajera ligero*

or

*He would bring *la ligero*

Given the equivalence constraint, Poplack's hypothesis is quite credible. A speaker who is insecure with the syntax of one language or the other will "play it safe" and switch between sentences most of the time to avoid the risk of an equivalence constraint violation. At the sentence level, the speaker is dealing with a constituent large enough so that direct mapping is usually or always possible. A very skilled bilingual speaker, who is familiar with the morphology and syntax of both languages, is free to switch within sentences since his high level of competence in the syntax of both languages will prevent him from running foul of the equivalence constraint.

Poplack was able to support her hypothesis with quantitative empirical data. The Puerto Rican subjects whose language use was observed were all residents of a neighbourhood in New York City. In addition to and in conjunction with the gathering of tape recorded speech samples, the community was studied by means of the anthropologist's technique of participant-observation, much of it by Pedro Pedraza, himself a community member. Furthermore, the people whose language samples were analysed were asked to complete a language-attitude questionnaire. One of the questions on the questionnaire required respondents to self-report themselves as "mainly Spanish speakers, English speakers, or bilingual." Over half said they were "mainly Spanish speakers"; the rest claimed to be bilingual. No one claimed to be mainly an English speaker. Participant observation led the investigators to conclude that the self-reports were accurate in the main.

Of the 1293 instances of switching by those who reported themselves to be bilingual, 53 per cent were intrasentential. Of the 542 switches by Spanish-dominant speakers, only 31 per cent were intrasentential. This different was significant by a Chi-square test at the .001 level of confidence (Poplack, 1980, p. 609). This result is the more impressive when we examine the sort of switching the speakers engaged in that was *not* intrasentential. The Spanish-dominant speakers used mostly tag-type switches, including inter-jections, fillers, tags and idiomatic expressions. This kind of switch demands, if anything, even less proficiency in the second language than inter-sentential switching, since these elements have a great deal of freedom of occurrence in the sentence. The bilingual speakers, when their switches were not of the intra-sentential type, usually switched between sentences.

A danger in an analysis of this sort, where the switch type of Spanish-dominant speakers versus bilingual speakers is tabulated, is that some other variable that correlates with language ability might be the real reason for the results. For example, if the Spanish-dominant speakers were also those who made frequent trips to Puerto Rico, or had less education than bilinguals, then it might be these factors that account for the distribution of switch types and not the language factor directly. A multi-variate statistical technique could be used to control for this kind of interaction. The usual statistical test used in such an application would be analysis of variance, but due to the uneven distribution of switches among groups of speakers representing various putative independent variables, analysis of variance would have been unreliable. Instead, Poplack used an adaption of the *VARBRUL 2* analytic procedure developed by David Sankoff and others (e.g. Rousseau and Sankoff, 1978). This procedure has the capability of providing meaningful results even with poorly distributed data. The result showed that reported language ability not only was statistically significant in its association with switch type independently of other possible factors, but that it was the most important single factor influencing switch types (Poplack, 1980, pp. 612–613).

We are left with a different impression of code-switching than the usual one. Rather than being evidence of poor language learning, it may be an indication of very thorough learning. Does this mean that students in language classes should be taught to switch continually between their native language and the one they are learning? The answer is no doubt "no", largely because rapid and frequent switching is a natural development in bilingual communities where two languages are used for everday tasks. It is probably usually the case that students learning a second language in school are learning it not so much so that they can join in a bilingual community, but for personal enrichment, to learn to read in a second language, or to aid them in joining a more or less monolingual community they have immigrated to. If they do find themselves in a bilingual community where switching is used, they will acquire the ability soon enough in that context and would not need to be taught it. On the other hand, it now appears that the ability to switch frequently and rapidly deserves rather more respect than contempt.

Conclusion

It no longer seems wise to view the variation and interaction of a learner's old and new languages as a tangled wasteland to be crossed as soon as possible. On the contrary, on close inspection this kind of variation is found to be rather orderly, and holds the potential for more accurate, fine-grained language instruction and testing than we now have. Even frequent switching between languages within the same discourse by functioning bilinguals now seems more a measure of success in second linguistic acquisition than of failure, and, in any case, seems to be *required* for normal interaction in some bilingual communities. Basically, language teachers and students of second language acquisition must learn not to be embarrassed by inter-language variation, but to approach it with respect and the expectation that the early and intermediate stages of language learning have their own order and system. As Bickerton (1981, p. 205) describes a language learner's progress:

. . . as that knowledge [of the target language] increases, he will progressively reorganize that imperfect system, and the meanings that he attaches to the morphemes (and, consequently, the ways in which he uses them) will change accordingly. But those meanings can only be determined within the system he has at any given time. They cannot be determined from the system of the target language. Only the acquisition analyst, with his target-oriented dichotomy between "acquired" and "not acquired", and its artificial, totally arbitrary criterion points, can make that kind of mistake.

References

Adamson, H. (1980). A Study of Variable Syntactic Rules the Interlanguage of Spanish-speaking Adults Acquiring English as a Second Language. Unpublished doctoral dissertation, Georgetown University Press, Washington DC.

Bailey, C.-J. (1973). "Variation and Linguistic Theory". Center for Applied Linguistics, Washington DC.

Beebe L. (1980). Sociolinguistic variation and style shifting in second-language acquisition. *Language Learning* 30, 2, 433–447.

Berdan, R. (1975). The necessity of variable rules. *In* "Analysing Variation in Language" (R. Fasold and R. Shuy, eds), pp. 11–26. Georgetown University Press, Washington DC.

Bickerton, (1981). Discussion in "New Dimensions in Second Language Acquisition Research" (R. Anderson, ed.), pp. 202–206. Newbury House, Rowley, Massachusetts.

Dickerson, L. (1975). The learner's interlanguage as a system of variable rules. *TESOL Quart.* 9, 401–407.

Dickerson, L. and Dickerson, W. (1977). Interlanguage phonology: Current research and future directions. *In* "Interlanguages and Pidgins and Their Relation to Second Language Pedagogy" (S. P. Corder and E. Ronlet, eds), pp. 18–29. Librairie Droz, Neufchâtel: Faculté des Lettres and Genève.

Dillard, J. L. (1972). "Black and English: Its History and Usage in the United States". Randon House, New York.

Gatbonton-Segalowitz, E. (1976). Systematic Variations in Second Language Speech: A Sociolinguistic Study. Unpublished doctoral dissertation, McGill University.

Gumperz, J. and Wilson, R. (1971). Convergence and creolization: A case from the Indo-Aryan/Dravidian border. *In* "Pidginization and Creolization of Language" (Dell Hymes, ed.), pp. 151–168. Cambridge University Press, Cambridge, UK.

Haugen, (1972). "The Ecology of Language". Stanford University Press, Stanford.

Heidelberg Forschungsprojekt "Pidgin-Deutsch" (1978). The acquisition of German syntax by foreign migrant workers. "Linguistic Variation Models and Methods" (D. Sankoff, ed.), pp. 1–22. Acadmic Press, New York.

Labov, W. (1966). The Social Stratification of English in New York City. Center for Applied Linguistics, Washington DC.

Labov, W. (1969). Contraction, deletion and inherent variability of the English copula. *Language* 45 (4), 715–752.

Poplack, S. (1980). Sometimes I'll start a sentence in Spanish *y termino en español*: Toward a typology of code-switching. *Linguistics* 18 (7/8), 581–618.

Rousseau, P. and Sankoff, D. (1978) Advances in variable rule rule methodology. "Linguistic Variation: Models and Methods" (D. Sankoff, ed.), pp. 57–69. Academic Press, New York.
Trudgill, P. (1974). The Social Differentiation of English in Norwich. Cambridge University Press, Cambridge.
Wolfram, W. (1969). A Sociolinguistic Study of Detroit Negro Speech. Center for Applied Linguistics, Washington DC.

Index